HOUSE DECORATION IN NUBIA

ART AND SOCIETY SERIES
General editor: Peter J. Ucko

HOUSE DECORATION IN NUBIA

Marian Wenzel

First published in 1972 by
Gerald Duckworth & Company Limited,
3, Henrietta Street, London W.C.2.

ISBN 0 7156 0532 1

Printed in Great Britain
by Jarrold & Sons Ltd, Norwich

CONTENTS

LIST OF PLATES

LIST OF FIGURES

ix

LIST OF COLOUR PLATES

xi

Plate 1
Gemai E., Murshid, detail of Pl. 78. Poem by house-owner on leaving his house in 1964. The crocodile was made by the decorator Muhammad Suleiman in 1942. *Photo* T. Higel

Preface

I am grateful to numerous individuals and institutions who have helped me in this work. They include the last District Commissioner of the Halfa region, Hassan Dafalla; the Wadi Halfa Resettlement Commission, which provided transportation; the Sudan Antiquities Service; and the University of Khartoum, Sudan Research Unit, which sponsored the survey and whose students Ahmad Muhammad Ali al-Hakim and Mustafa Ibrahim Taha took part in the field work.[1] Peter and Margaret Shinnie provided valuable material from Debeira West, and Herman Bell advised about the spelling and identification of place-names. I am particularly grateful to Thomas Higel of the Colorado Expedition, Joel Shiner of the Southern Methodist University, Texas, and Milorad Medić of the Yugoslav Society for the Protection of Historical Monuments, who have provided photographs. Kazimierz Michalowski, of the Polish National Museum, Warsaw, has kindly permitted reproduction of medieval paintings from Faras. Abdulla Sabbar, Khartoum, Hasan Zaroug, University of London, and Nabil Shehabi, of the London School of Economics, have given invaluable assistance and advice concerning Arabic translation.

Above all, I offer thanks to the Nubian people, in whose sorrow I share at the loss of their traditional homes. This sorrow was expressed by someone on the outside of an abandoned house in Gemai East, Murshid (Pls 1, 78):

> Departed from the fatherland whose breeze I love,
> The smells of homeland are those of gardens.
> I left it with tears pouring from the eyes;
> I left my heart, and I have no more than one.
> I forsook it not by my own will,
> But by the decision of Destiny;
> And what a miserable Destiny is mine.
> *Fare Well*

MARIAN WENZEL

I

Introduction

This book describes the character and evolution of certain house decorations in northern Sudanese Nubia which largely disappeared under the flooding of the Aswan Dam in 1964. The decorations were sculpted in mud relief, or sculpture on stone, they cannot be retrieved even if the waters recede, and the best of them are lost for ever. Those artists who are alive are men of late middle age, who have turned to other professions, and who are offered no incentive to revive the art. In regions south of the flood area where the technique is still found, it is practised in a rudimentary way. This book summarises the results of the only survey made of this work before it was destroyed.

Some house decorations were on outer doorways facing the river and were visible to passengers of river boats moving along the Nile. The patterns stood out from the dark mud of the houses because the designs were often given a contrasting surface of white lime. A layer of fresh mud was added to the façade so as to cover the area designated for decoration, and this new mud was either mixed with lime or painted with an additional layer of white. The design was then cut through to the dark mud below or, in some cases, punched out with a triangular or circular metal cutter. The circle, which could also be produced by drawing round a bowl or biscuit tin, was a principal design element, so that most compositions could be seen as a patterned background for rows of circles. These rows were usually, but not always, inset with objects such as saucers, dinner-plates or even automobile headlights, which gleamed like pearls against the dark ground (Col. pls 2, 3).

There were other basic design elements employed as a background for circles. These were a pointed or rounded arch outlined over the door-lintel, which the artists referred to as a 'dome', two hooks or flags put at the outer edges of the dome, and inscribed columns which flanked the door. The more elaborate composi-tions were created by multiplying these basic design elements. Three or more domes were piled over the door-lintel, hooks were added to the side columns as well as to the domes, and the number of columns was increased to as many as three or four at each side of the door, while domes were superimposed on the columns, and so on. Decorated columns were added to the corners of the house.

Figurative elements were also used: long-legged birds faced each other each side of a central dome; lions, their eyes set with red glass, brandished swords at one or both sides of the door; crocodiles were threatened by a man with a gun. More rarely, the man with gun threatened the lion with sword. These figurative elements were multiplied or were changed in place, or stood upon elegant ground lines with punched-out triangles replacing grass.

Although the façades were the most notable feature for casual tourists, it was not only the exteriors of the houses that were decorated. A similar ornamental technique was used inside, and while façade decorations were seldom coloured, interior decorations sometimes were. Around the large town of Wadi Halfa, one artist, Hasan Arabi, made a sharp aesthetic distinction about where colour should be used and where it should not. For outside he felt that the simple contrast between white lime and dark mud was better, and he produced coloured exteriors only under strong demand. Inside the house he favoured colour, particularly in one special room called the *diwan* (Fig. 3e), which was designed for the use of male wedding guests and left empty at other times, unless it was used as a store-room for crockery and clothes (Col. pl. 14). In this room lively conversation and dancing took place, and Hasan Arabi felt that colour encouraged the gay mood.

Interior house decoration in the Wadi Halfa region was principally confined to two areas of the house: to the central courtyard or *hosh*, where doorways were decorated in a modest way, and to a smaller, subsidiary courtyard next to the *hosh* and the two rooms opening on to it. These were the *diwan* and another room, the *diwanin hasil* (said to mean the 'room of the *diwan*') which was designed for the use of the bride and her female guests. The *diwan*, which was always open to the north to admit a cool breeze, was the biggest room in the house, much bigger than the *diwanin hasil* (Fig. 3e). It was given the most elaborate interior decoration, often in colour. Round three walls passed a band, or hori-zontal geometric design. At the southern end, one or more domes were set

4

upon it, surmounted by crescents and surrounded by birds, flags or pots of flowers. Under these domes, superimposed upon the horizontal band, was a row of circles, sometimes composed of orange and lavender lustre saucers, imported from Japan.

When we began investigating this Nubian house decoration, we expected to find that it derived from an ancient tradition. Yet on examining the Wadi Halfa district, it became clear to us that the striking mud relief decoration originated only in the mid 1920s. The technique was said to have been invented by one man. He was Ahmad Batoul, a Nubian from Wadi el-Arab or Bal-lana in Upper Egypt. When he began working, he held an insignificant job. He was a builder's assistant, who smoothed the surface of the newly built house, putting on a layer of fine mud to conceal the underlying rough-mud building structure, called *jalus*. He thought up the decoration as a special finishing touch to enhance the plates that the women were putting up over the doors. Initially people laughed at him for doing women's work, but as more and more people wanted him to do this decoration, others copied him, and finally he was able to employ as his assistant the builder for whom he first worked.

After we had analysed numerous accounts, not only from the local inhabi-tants who lived in the houses but also from the artists themselves, the sequence of events emerged as more complicated. Two other decorators, the Arab Sayyid Ahmad Hogla from South Halfa, and Jabir Abdulla Bab al-Kheir, a Negro of southern slave origin from Debeira, both claimed that they had been first to do relief, in the 1920s, and denied that they had been influenced by Ahmad Batoul. In fact their contribution was considerable. Moreover, certain house-builders, both in Egyptian Nubia and also much further south along the Nile than the Wadi Halfa region where Batoul worked, and so outside his sphere of influence, were acquainted with the technique of mud relief and employed it in a modest way. But whatever the true course of events, it is certain that most people between Wadi Halfa and the Egyptian border believed that it was Ahmad Batoul who had invented mud relief, and he gained great prestige as its originator. What decoration there had been before his time, the people could only with difficulty recall.

The later personal history of Ahmad Batoul was a tragic one, consisting of a conflict between him and certain other decorators who attempted to undermine his standing. In the years after Batoul began to work, house decoration ceased to be a trivial job in the hands of an unimportant menial who worked for the builder; it became a grand art in the hands of masters, who were patronised by their admirers, and whoever fell out of favour lost. Ahmad Batoul lost. He ended up simply preparing the mud ground for decoration in houses where the actual decoration was done by his chief rival, a man who entered the field much later and whose best work dates from after 1940. This was Hasan Arabi, a local Nubian from Argin, just north of Halfa. Hasan Arabi was related in some way to most of the people who hired him, and his designs were copied from European tin boxes. He was highly talented. By 1956 Ahmad Batoul was dead. It is curious that Ahmad Batoul retained his prestige even though he fell out of fashion, a fact that was never properly explained to us. The very people who put Batoul out of work by hiring other artists were those who most strongly praised his contribution. His output was remarkable. Between 1927 and 1946 he decorated more houses than any other artist, not counting the many examples of his work which were destroyed in the Nile flood of 1946. He seems to have been a man of considerable charm. On entering a dwelling in Faras East, we were told that the decoration was by Ahmad Batoul.

'You mean,' we said, 'the man who is now dead.'

'Dead?' exclaimed the housewife, at once uttering loud cries, 'He was like my son.'

Most of the decorations discussed in this book were made before 1960. Shortly before 1964, new designs were added to the façades. These were huge concentric circles or arrows which signified that the house was doomed. They meant that a Government team, to which this mark belonged, had assessed the value of the condemned property and arranged for money to be reimbursed and the families to be moved away. The families, consisting of about 35,000 Nubians, were to be taken by train to the site of Khashm el-Girba, near the Ethiopian border (Fig. 1), where palm trees did not grow, and where much rain fell. Different diseases were there to strike the children and old people, and there would be little immediate incentive to decorate the new houses of corrugated metal and cement (Pl. 2).[1] Even those people who understood what was in store for them and refused to leave the flood-endangered Wadi Halfa, or who went to places other than Khashm el-Girba, would be slow to reintroduce the decoration of their homes.

In our work in spring 1964, we examined most of the villages during the last few days before the removal of their inhabitants to Khashm el-Girba. Others we did not reach till the people were already gone and their houses left a desolate shell. Roof beams, windows, and doors had been sold by the Sudanese Government to a local contractor who removed them himself. As a result, roofs had collapsed and a great deal of decoration had been damaged well before it was destroyed by the rising Nile. Information about the extremely rich area near the Egyptian border was gathered in some haste.

Further south, below the Second Cataract, the people were being removed more slowly and the waters of the first flooding in the summer of 1964 had not affected the villages. We were, therefore, able to examine these houses with

6

greater care. By the time we reached the southernmost point of research, few people intended to move, and most of them regarded the flooding as a distant threat. They had not interrupted their normal practices of house-building and land cultivation. Thus we examined the southern part of the region concerned under nearly normal conditions. What was lost in precious data about elaborate works of art round Wadi Halfa was compensated in the South by evidence of uninterrupted ritual practices and folk-customs. These folk-customs, long since abandoned in town-influenced regions, nevertheless gave important clues to the origin of the decoration round Wadi Halfa.

Plate 2
Kashm el-Girba, resettlement site for the Sudanese Nubian population, photographed by W. J. Kidd in 1964

CHAPTER ONE

The Nubian People, their Homeland and Homes

The Nubians are a non-Arab population, who are partly Negro[1] and who speak an indigenous tongue.[2] The land in which they live, which forms the geographical region known as Nubia, lies half in Upper Egypt, from Aswan to the Egyptian border slightly south of Abu Simbel, and half in the Republic of the Sudan (Fig. 1). In the Sudan it extends southwards for several hundred miles from the northern border village of Faras, past the town of Dongola to where the Nile makes a bend to the north-east. Faras and Dongola were at one time capitals of a medieval Nubian Christian kingdom, and of the provinces of Nobadia and Makuria, respectively.[3] Of the two, only Faras lies within the scope of the present book, which treats solely of the area of Sudanese Nubia affected by the Aswan High Dam flood, from the Egyptian border to a point almost 150 miles to the south (Fig. 2).

The entire Republic of the Sudan, of which Nubia is but a part, consists of a vast plain, bounded on its north side by a desert. Through this the Nile forms a passageway, depositing a limited degree of arable land along its banks. In Nubia, the land is mainly rocky at or near the surface and covered by thin, poor soil. The landscape is broken by low, flat-topped sandstone hills, inter-sected by steep-sided gullies. The territory on the east bank of the Nile presents wide stretches of gravel with occasional dunes, while the west bank is laden with sand which perpetually blows from the Sahara. Thus there are few roads along the west bank. Even donkey and camel transport prefer to pass along the

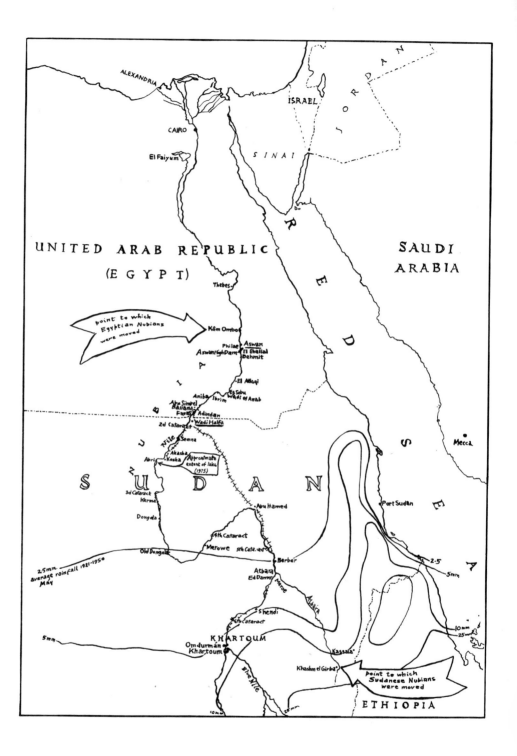

east Nile bank, where the railway also leads to the sizeable border town of Halfa, or New Halfa, as the settlement which still remains after the initial flood is called.

Nubia begins north of latitude 19°, in a region where there is virtually no rain. Dry, northerly winds blow throughout the year, and in the winter these increase to bring sandstorms. All agriculture depends on irrigation, much of which is effected by the ancient method of the water-wheel. The inhabitants of Nubia form riverain communities, clustered in villages along the Nile banks. They live by cultivating date palms and a form of millet called *dura* from which most of their food is made. Nubians love their land, but life is hard, and they need to supplement their income from outside sources. In ancient times, they profited from the Nile trade routes carrying gold, ivory, and slaves to Egypt. In the twentieth century, many of their able men have found employment elsewhere, in Cairo or Khartoum, where they are cooks, drivers, house-boys or police. Numbers of them work in the railway-yards at Atbara. These men send home money to support their wives and relatives and many only come back themselves once in a few years. Thus most of the actual cultivation is done by women, children, and old men.

Nubians are Muslim, and women have a position in society clearly subservient to the men. Women do not discipline the children. Children are disciplined by men or boys just past the age of puberty. In the absence of men, these boys also discipline the women. Even so, the same absence of men has allowed Nubian women a greater freedom to move about and greet strangers than is apparent in other Muslim communities where the men are home all the time. In the Halfa region the women were not veiled and had their own local dress, which consisted of a long flowing robe of black gauze, called the *jerjar*, worn over a short cotton frock.[4] The *jerjar* had an immense train (the word *jerjar* means 'long') so that the devil could not see their footprints, and they wore it with much gold. The *jerjar*, with tucks and ruffled sleeves, was clearly based on European garb of the late nineteenth century. It replaced the semi-nudity prevalent before then.[5]

The River Nile, south of Aswan, is broken by five stony passages of islands and large boulders known as 'cataracts'. The first is at Aswan itself, the second six miles south of Wadi Halfa,[6] and the third near Kerma, outside the region dealt with in this book. The Second Cataract, eight and a half miles of impassable rapids and granite rocks, introduces a region known as the *Batn al-Hajar*, or 'Belly of Rocks',[7] which extends south to Dal (Fig. 2), where the Nile becomes less turbulent. The Second Cataract is of importance here because it has acted as a partial cultural barrier between the Wadi Halfa district and those parts of Nubia to the south. In the villages surrounding Wadi Halfa, there

11

Figure 1
General map

had been considerable influence of urban life. This influence had modified some factors of village life which yet persisted unchanged south of the Second Cataract. Certain aspects of this cultural change, in particular the quick adop¬ tion and abandonment of new fashions which both developed out of and broke away from recently assimilated practices, were responsible for a good deal of wall decoration. Yet the west bank, because of its lack of roads, was artistically more conservative, except in villages such as Argin and Faras where there were good ferry services to the east bank, and access to the regular *suq* lorry (market bus) to Wadi Halfa.

The policy of the central government in Khartoum, both under British rule and after Sudan independence in 1956, has been to tolerate and even encourage a certain degree of tribal government in Nubia, by which some judgements were made according to tribal rules[8] and children were educated in Quranic schools supervised by the local sheikhs. These tribal authorities also helped to collect taxes and control local building. Their tribal structure dictated the names of places.

Four ethno¬linguistic groups have been distinguished among the Nubian¬ speaking tribes in Egypt and the Sudan. The one that is relevant here is the Mahas, who extended southwards from Korosko in Egyptian Nubia to Kerma, north of Dongola.[9] Kerma was the linguistic frontier of another group, called the Danaqla, which was concentrated round Dongola and is well out of the flood¬threatened area, as well as south of the area concerned in this book.[10] The Fadicca linguistic group, variously spelled as Fadaykiyya or Fadidja, is a title sometimes applied to the northern part of the Mahas, who are mostly in Egypt. Authorities differ so widely about the location and distinguishing characteristics of the Fadicca group, that for the purposes of this book they will be regarded as one unit with the Mahas.[11] The Kenuzi group were named after the Banu Kanz Arabs who converted Aswan Nubians to the Muslim faith and intermingled with them from the eleventh to the fourteenth century, at a time when other Nubians were still Christian.[12] They are centred even today round Aswan. But after former Aswan Dam floodings earlier in this century, certain of the Kenuzi moved south to Debeira in the Wadi Halfa district.[13] Another colony on the Nile bank opposite Wadi Halfa lived by working on the river boats. As they were newcomers in the Halfa district, they fell under the jurisdiction of the Halfa region tribal authorities, who were Mahas.

The Halfa region Nubians were ruled by a tribal leader called a *nazir*. His combined legislative and judicial power was controlled only by the central government. The *nazir* Saleh Isa Abdu lived in Debeira on the east Nile bank, and this book owes much to his kindness and co¬operation. He was the most

Figure 2
Map of the area under survey in this book

12

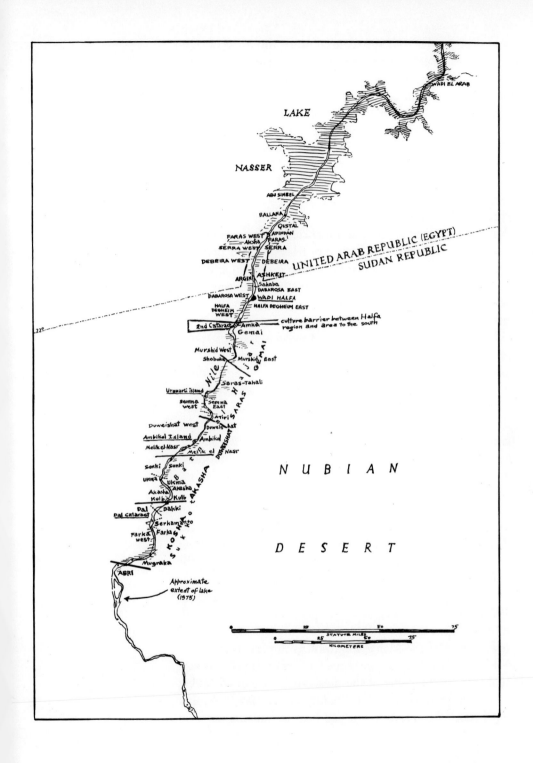

LAKE

NASSER

WADI EL ARAB

ABU SIMBEL

BALLANA

QUSTAL

FARAS WEST APINDAN
Aksha   FARAS
SERRA WEST   SERRA

UNITED ARAB REPUBLIC (EGYPT)

DEBEIRA WEST   DEBEIRA

SUDAN REPUBLIC

ARGIN   ASHKEIT
Sahaba
DABAROSA WEST   DABAROSA EAST
HALFA   WADI HALFA
DEGHEIM   HALFA DEGHEIM EAST
WEST

22°

2nd Cataract   Amka
Gemai   culture barrier between Halfa
region and area to the south

Murshid West
Shoboka   Murshid East

Nile

Saras-Tahali

Urawarti Island

Semna   Semna
West   East
Atiri
Duweishat West   Duweis East
Ambikol Island   Ambikol
Melik el Nasr
Melik el Nasr

NUBIAN

Sonki   Sonki
Ukma   Ukma
Akasha   Akasha
Kulb   Kulb

Dal   Dakki
Dal Cataract
Serkamatto
Farka   Farka
West

DESERT

Mugraka

ABRI

Approximate
extent of lake
(1975)

STATUTE MILES
0   25   50   75

KILOMETERS
0   25   50   75

important native authority in the endangered area, since the *nazir* of Abri lived south of the flood area. Saleh Isa received guests in chairs, placed on a large Egyptian carpet on the sands, shaded by a palm-frond fence. Behind was his ample house, with more chairs inside for meetings and spacious quarters for members of his immediate family. After the visit of Princess Margarethe of Denmark to Wadi Halfa in 1962, the *nazir* was made a Knight of the Danish Order of the Dannebrog.[14] We were with him when members of his tribe trotted up on donkeys to announce that the first people of Debeira had been removed to their new home at Khashm el-Girba. The army had gone alongside to prevent anyone leaping out of the train. He said that it was hard for these people to leave the graves of their ancestors.

Place-names within the threatened territory of Sudanese Nubia are confusing without reference to the land divisions to which they related. Land divisions depended on divisions of authority within the tribe, which decreased in impor-tance after the *nazir*. The chiefs of sections, directly below the *nazir*, were called *omdas*,[15] and the land which each controlled was an *omodiya*. Within each *omodiya* were smaller divisions called *sheikhships*, each governed by a tribal sheikh. These can be likened to villages, and the *omodiya* to groups of villages. Each *sheikhship* was in turn divided into small hamlets, called *hillets*. Thus every geographical site in Sudanese Nubia had three names, those of its *omodiya*, its *sheikhship* and its *hillet*. For instance, the Kenuzi settlement in Debeira West was rightfully called *omodiya* Debeira, *sheikhship* Hassa, *hillet* Nag el-Kenuz.[16] Most authors have preferred, with lack of precision, to cite only one of these names. In this work, where one name is given, it is the *omodiya*; where two, the *omodiya* and the *sheikhship*; where three, the *omodiya*, *sheikhship* and *hillet*. Occasionally this order cannot be followed. If only the names of the *omodiya* and *hillet* are known, the specific term *hillet* will be used.

Between the Egyptian border and Wadi Halfa, where most relief decoration occurs, there were six *omodiyas*, some on one and others on both sides of the Nile. These were Faras, Serra, Debeira, Argin, Ashkeit and Dabarosa, listed from north to south. Faras, Serra, Debeira and Dabarosa extended to both sides of the Nile. Ashkeit was only on the east bank, and Argin only on the west bank. Where an *omodiya* lay on both banks of the Nile, its name was frequently accom-panied by 'East' or 'West' to indicate which of the two parts was being discussed, and this practice will be continued here.

The special Nubian dialect of the Mahas linguistic group has been called Mahai, Mahasi or Marisi.[17] Maris, the Coptic name for Upper Egypt, was also used, along with Nobadia, as the name of the northern kingdom of Nubia from the time of the Nubian conversion to Christianity in A.D. 543,[18] At that time its capital was at Faras,[19] but previously it had been at Ballana, just over the Egyptian border, where a vast treasure was found buried with slaughtered attendants and horses, in spectacular fifth-century royal graves.[20] Although the origins of these pre-Christian Nubians have puzzled scholars, it is now felt that there was considerable cultural continuity between them and the Nubians of Pharaonic times. Yet the Mahas tongue seems to have little in common with Meroitic, the language spoken by the powerful negroid group to the south of Nubia whose Napatan ancestors conquered Egypt to become the 25th dynasty (725 B.C.). The Napatans, when pushed out of Egypt by the Persians, settled at Meroe and ruled the Nile south of Egypt until about the fourth century A.D.[21]

Nubia was Christianised in the sixth century, and after that time church and mortuary inscriptions were written in Greek, Coptic or Nubian but not in Meroitic.[22] Recent archaeological work has shown that one reason may be that much of Nubia, including the Mahas area, which was occupied in Pharaonic times until about 800 B.C., was virtually uninhabited during much of the Meroitic period. This may have been due to a fall in the level of the Nile which prevented cultivation. With the introduction of the water-wheel in late Meroitic times, in the first or second century A.D., habitation was again possible, and certain Nubians, along with other Nomads from elsewhere, seem to have returned and resettled their hereditary land.[23] The time of resettlement up to the adoption of Christianity included the so-called 'X-Group' period. At that time, Meroitic culture was weak, and may not have greatly affected the new settlers.

Nubia has been Christian longer than it has been Muslim. Nubians were Christians for roughly 800 years, and Muslims for little over half that time. Yet it is thought that Nubians never participated so actively in Christianity as they do in Islam. The Nubian Church was a branch of the Coptic Monophysite Church centred in Cairo. It gained only occasional support from this parent Church after North Africa was conquered by the Arabs in A.D. 700 and in the last centuries of its existence, till shortly after 1500, seems to have had small contact with any Christian centres elsewhere.[24] Nubian Christianity probably dissolved into superstition in its final years, and the remarkable paintings recently rescued from its churches show many individual traits. The frescoes of the church at Faras, discovered and removed by the Polish expedition, demonstrate that doorway decoration in the Middle Ages strikingly resembled some decoration of today (Fig. 50a, t; Pls 82, 87, 88).[25] The circumstances under which this continuity existed is a problem which we shall presently discuss.

The history of Nubian house decoration is, of course, closely allied to the history of the Nubian house. The Nubian house is made of mud *jalus* construction, in which horizontal courses of lumpy mud mixed with small stones and dung are covered with a smooth surface layer of mud (Pl. 3); the walls are about eighteen inches thick and help keep the rooms cool in hot weather. In the stony

Batn al-Hajar region, some stone is used in building. At present, most Nubian houses consist of ample rooms grouped around a large central courtyard (Pl. 4; fig. 3e, f), but this was not always the case. Archaeologists excavating medieval villages in Dabarosa and Debeira West discovered that in the Middle Ages houses were maze-like warrens of rooms with virtually no courts (Fig. 3a).[26] A similar complex, consisting of small rooms without courts, was inhabited as late as 1911, according to a wall inscription, and could be seen in a ruined state near the Nile bank in Debeira East (Fig. 3b). Yet the nineteenth century travellers Burckhardt and Ensor state that Nubian houses were small huts of mud or stone, with few rooms.[27] The mud huts, which were often too low to allow comfortable standing, were roofed over with dura stalks and palm leaves. The stone huts were also low and were placed on the declivity of the hills. They consisted of two round rooms, each with its own entrance, one for women and one for men. The travellers do not mention decoration in these huts.

Plate 3
Gemai E., Murshid, detail of a house wall built in mud *jalus* construction. Layers of lumpy mud are covered with a smooth surface of fine mud mixed with sand. *Photo* T. Higel

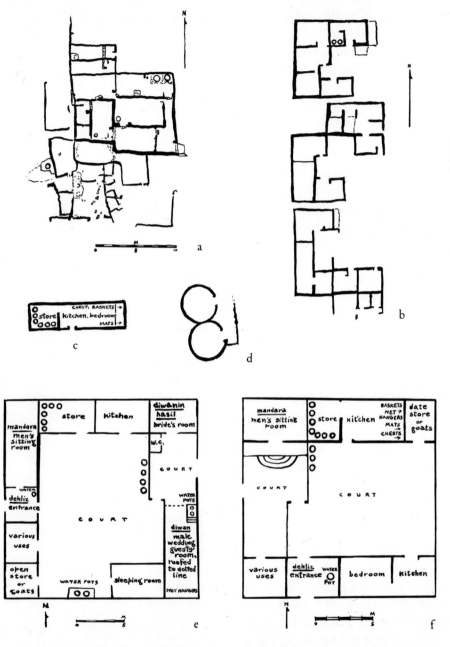

Figure 3
Sudanese Nubian house-plans, medieval to modern

a *West Wadi Halfa, Dabarosa Island*, Christian Nubian houses, after Hewes. Circles are storage pots
b *Debeira East*, ruined house complex near the Nile. Inhabited in 1911 according to a wall inscription
c *Saras, Duweishat and Kosha*, typical two-room house unit with baskets and mats hung on an end wall, nineteenth century and modern
d *Saras, Duweishat*, round houses with stone foundations, old, of unknown date, all abandoned, ruins found on hill slopes. Door-ways face uphill
e *Wadi Halfa region*, house-plan, typical from Egyptian border south through Gemai, for houses built after 1925
f *Saras through Kosha*, typical recent house-plan for houses larger than two-room units of type c

Remains of old houses, particularly common in the Batn al-Hajar region, support the unflattering accounts of early travellers. Those on the declivity of the hills had been made of mud over a round stone core, their ruins forming small enclosures, often no more than eight feet across, which were still used as pens for goats but not as modern living quarters (Fig. 3d). The old huts on flat ground consisted of modest, rectangular two-room units, part for sleeping and part for storing dried food in tall mud jars (Fig. 3c). Some had recently been incorporated into newer, larger structures, in which a central court had been added and enclosed by other, larger rooms (Fig. 3f), and their pattern was copied and enlarged for the new rooms. Other small, low-roofed rectangular house units, in their original state without courtyards, were still being lived in throughout the *omodiyas* of Duweishat and Kosha, south of the Second Cataract. Most were in Duweishat, the southernmost portion of the Batn al-Hajar, where living was generally poor and where this type of house was still being built. In Kosha, a richer region, they were always the oldest houses near the Nile and were usually inhabited by dissatisfied child brides. The head of the family had built a new house on higher ground, and the old houses were given to newly married sons. Old houses north of the Second Cataract, on low ground near the Nile, were either destroyed in the 1946 flood or abandoned at early dates, so that only remnants survived. Yet these remnants, such as the house-complex of Debeira East (Fig. 3b), showed that house-plans of the Halfa region and those south of the Second Cataract, where no such complexes existed, differed in early times. For instance, we saw no remains of round house units around Wadi Halfa, such as were common in the Batn al-Hajar. In spite of this, old houses both north and south of the Second Cataract were alike in having small rooms and few or no traces of painting or relief.

It would be useful to establish when Nubian houses gained their present ample proportions, allowing decoration to expand, and in particular, when they acquired courtyards. Burckhardt, writing in 1813 and Henry Light, writing in 1818, noticed some houses with courtyards in Egyptian Nubia, at Ibrim and Derr, as well as in a few other unspecified villages, and also south of Nubia, around Berber and Damer.[28] There the houses consisted of a large yard divided into an inner and outer court, not unlike Mahas Nubian houses today (Pl. 4; Fig. 3e, f). The women and animals stayed in rooms off the inner court, while the men of the house and male guests slept in the outer court on *angarib* beds[29] or on the floor. Ensor, travelling in 1872 and 1875, was impressed with Dongola, which he said was the first place on the banks of the Nile deserving the name of a town, albeit a shabby one.[30] He described a house which he said was one of the biggest in the town. It consisted of one room on the ground floor with enclosures at the back for wife and family and a courtyard for the goats and fowls.[31] He did not mention seeing any courtyards to the north. Gleichen, who visited Nubia in the 1880s, said that Wadi Halfa consisted of ten or twelve mud hovels, and that one house in Dongola was better constructed

18

Plate 4
Saras, Saras-Tahali,
Agremasho, house plan
laid out with an inner
and outer court. The view
from Kitchener's fort
looks towards the rest-
house once used by
English officials

than the mud huts elsewhere, having three rooms.[32] Later, from material gathered between 1899 and 1905, he wrote that in general, the houses of Dongola Province had good courtyards.[33] It is clear from these writers that houses of Mahas Nubians were still small until after the 1880s, while larger houses could be found to the north and south.

Walled houses with courtyards in North Africa are often due to conversion to Islam and to the Muslim habit of keeping women from strangers' eyes.[34] Egyptian Nubia, Dongola and Berber, where courtyards were noticed in the nineteenth century, were nearer regions of strong Islamic power than was Nubia of the Mahas, Egyptian Nubia being nearer Cairo, while Dongola and Berber were nearer the pilgrim route from Mecca which passed through Berber and continued eastwards to the Red Sea.[35] The men and women of Halfa and the Second Cataract region not only lived in houses lacking courtyards but also went naked except for loin-cloths and amulets, which was certainly in conflict with Islamic views, while people of Egyptian Nubia clothed themselves.[36] Furthermore, according to recent views, it was not until the eighteenth century that the Mahas Nubians began to return to the Nile, having lived as desert nomads since the troubled period of Islamic influx about 1500.[37] This history would have kept their way of life free from Islamic influence for some time, just as it seems to have kept the Mahas dialect purer from Arabic taint than other Nubian dialects to the north and south.

Throughout the eighteenth and nineteenth centuries the standard of living round Wadi Halfa and the Second Cataract remained very low owing to constant invasions by a warlike Sudanese tribe called the Shaiqiyya, who were centred south of Dongola around Merowe.[38] Shaiqiyya power was not broken until the Mamluk Turks arrived in Dongola on their flight from Cairo in 1811 and suppressed this tribe to ensure their own safety.[39] The Mamluks themselves were conquered in 1819 by Muhammad Ali of Egypt, who then established Egyptian rule in Nubia. But by that time the Nubians were in a depressed economic state which did not markedly improve until the British arrived in the Sudan in 1885 to reconquer it for Egypt from insurgent Mahdist forces. The British who continued to rule the Sudan in agreement with the Egyptians until 1956, virtually created the town of Wadi Halfa as a governmental and railway centre.[40]

Curiously enough, the Shaiqiyya, after British occupation, returned to the Wadi Halfa district in some force, in the new rôle of house-builders. They took advantage of Government encouragement offered to Nubians in the 1920s to build new houses away from the fertile land near the Nile, which was needed for cultivation. Those Nubians who, because of town employment, could well afford better housing, either did not know how to build themselves, or were not home to do so. Men employed in Cairo or Khartoum sent back their wives with the house-plan and money to pay the builder. Although local builders existed south of the Second Cataract, along with house-owners who knew how to build, the Shaiqiyya also performed some building there, while certain Second Cataract builders came north to work around Wadi Halfa. Often it was not apparent whether a builder had been a Shaiqiyya or a Nubian from the Second Cataract region; north of Halfa he would be known as 'a builder from the South'. There were two main periods when builders from the South came north to work: in the mid twenties and early thirties of this century, and after the disastrous Nile flood of 1946. In the first period, most such builders were in fact Shaiqiyya from Abu Hamed or Manasir, and in the second period most of them were Nubians from the Batn al-Hajar, from around Saras. Between 1935 and 1945 few new houses were built and much decoration was done so embellish houses built previously, sometimes when it was felt that the façade needed new plastering in fresh mud. By this time the job of plastering was no longer necessarily allied with building or builders, but had become associated with decoration, and was a kind of commercial art.

It is not clear whether southern builders had any influence on the peculiar house-plan used recently around Wadi Halfa (Fig. 3e), which differed from that common south of the Second Cataract (Fig. 3f) and also from that in Kenuzi settlements in the Sudan. Shaiqiyya houses in their own territory are different again, consisting of a central house unit which is surrounded by a walled courtyard rather than of rooms which are placed up against a wall to surround the courtyard, in the modern Nubian way (Fig. 3e). The Wadi Halfa house-plan resembled that south of the Second Cataract in that both were formed of units surrounding a courtyard space. This space was divided into two parts, a large area for women and men of the household, and a smaller courtyard for men and for receiving guests. The room for guests was made particularly spacious and large. The difference between Halfa region plans and those south of the Second Cataract lay in the character of the rooms opening on to the smaller courtyard and the nature of the guests for whose reception they were intended. The difference was apparently related to a difference in social custom. North of the Second Cataract, and to some extent in the *omodiya* of Gemai which includes the Cataract itself, the rooms were designed to receive wedding guests, and south of the Second Cataract they were not.

In every Sudanese Nubian house, the rooms in which the wedding took place were those given the most elaborate decoration, and naturally, whether these rooms were large or small, to some degree determined whether decoration would be extensive or insignificant. Around Wadi Halfa weddings took place in the men's room adjoining the subsidiary courtyard, the *diwan* (Fig. 3e).

Although one side was completely open to the north, the three remaining sides gave ample room for decoration, including a patterned surround placed around the cement stand which supported water-jars. No sense of indelicacy was felt in the fact that the *diwan* faced the *diwanin hasil*, the enclosed room in which sat the bride and her female guests. Yet such a confrontation of women with possibly strange men was thought intolerable south of the Batn al-Hajar and was regarded as 'old-fashioned' in Saras. In these southern regions (Fig. 3f), the weddings took place in smaller, interior rooms of the house, which offered less scope for decoration.

When men of the Halfa region entertained their friends during the course of a normal day, they did not use the *diwan*. Halfa region men boasted two sitting-rooms, the *diwan* for weddings, and for everyday use, the *mandara*, which was an enclosed room with windows facing the front of the house (Fig. 3e). The *mandara* was entered by a doorway to the right or left of the main entrance antechamber, or *dehliz*. The *mandara* was not decorated, although the window exteriors and the doorway leading into it from the *dehliz*, often were. While passing through the *dehliz*, it was possible for male guests entering the *mandara* to glance into the central courtyard and possibly to glimpse some women of the house. Such an occurrence would have been thought intolerable to men south of the Batn al-Hajar, who entertained their guests in a *mandara* built on to the subsidiary courtyard, in place of the *diwan*, which did not exist (Fig. 3f). The doorway to the central court which led from this courtyard was placed at right angles to the courtyard entrance from outside, so that casual visitors could not see through to the area inhabited by women. The *mandara* in these southern areas was fully enclosed, unlike the *diwan*, and often raised above the rest of the house and entered by steps. It had windows on three sides, looking out of the house and on to the smaller court, unlike rooms in the women's quarters which were not given windows (Pl. 5). If the *mandara* walls were ever decorated, which was rare, they were painted by the house-owner, his son or a hired artist in a manner quite different from wedding decoration (Fig. 18).

The arrival of Shaiqiyya builders in Sudanese Nubia, which marked the commencement of better and more elaborate housing, happened to coincide with a crucial event which did much to encourage the building of larger rooms. This was the break-up of the old Saras-line railway, begun under the Egyptians in 1875 and extended as far south as Kerma by the British during Kitchener's River War. It was made obsolete by a newer desert railway begun in 1897 and was officially abandoned in 1905.[41] The local inhabitants were happy to receive the iron rails, which they everywhere used as roof beams (Pl. 6). The rails had great advantages over the log beams in use before. In the first place, they were not susceptible to the white ant, which rapacious termites, once in a

Plate 5
Kosha, Farka, Osirmat, a house built of mud *jalus* and in the foreground a stone hut used for animals. The room with windows to the outside is the *mandara*, or men's sitting-room. Windowless walls enclose the women's quarters

Plate 6
Akasha, Ukma, Eresab, men laying railway lines for use as roof beams

roof beam, could pass into walls. There they lived on the plant materials mixed with the mud *jalus*, and could easily cause destruction of the entire house. Secondly, the rails were straighter and longer than the acacia wood branches available to Nubians for carpentry and spared the cutting of palm trees, which could be put to better uses in their live state, providing dates, or palm branches used in weaving mats, baskets and fencing. With railway lines as beams, rooms became larger, and the new, increased wall space stimulated the develop-ment of wall decoration.

CHAPTER TWO

House Decoration: Sources of Design

The system of house decoration described in this book was practised for only forty years. Mud relief ornament came into general use about 1927 and was largely destroyed as an art, along with its resulting monuments, by the Aswan Dam flood in 1964. A kind of house decoration had existed before the twenties, but this consisted mainly of actual objects hung up on the walls in ornamental patterns. In the Halfa region, relief decoration replaced these hanging objects. Some walls were painted as well.

Although hanging objects were ultimately superseded by surface ornament, they continued to influence the appearance of house decoration. Fortunately, south of the Second Cataract, decoration by objects was still practised;[1] so it was possible to compare the pictorial forms with their concrete precursors and to trace the evolution of a school of primitive art from its formal origin to its premature end.

Objects suspended on walls were functional rather than purely decorative, and their suspension fulfilled one of five principal functions:

(1) They were objects used in the wedding ceremony, and arranged after-wards on the inner walls to remain throughout the married life of the individuals involved.
(2) They were hung up to keep termites from eating them.
(3) They were hung up to keep out devils, or to deflect the evil eye.
(4) They were special decoration for the men's sitting-room.
(5) They were special decoration for doors.

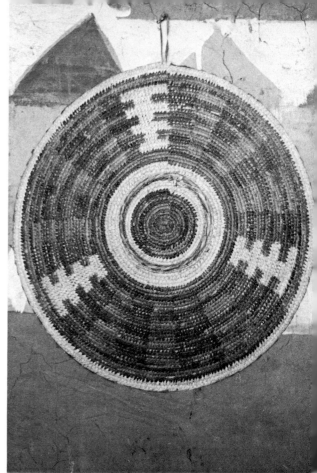

The wedding ceremony was not only one of the most important rites in the life of the Nubian villager, but also the key to much decoration. Its details varied slightly from place to place and occasionally incorporated some Christian reminiscence, such as a mud cross made on the forehead of the bride (at Ashkeit). The objects used in the wedding ceremony, afterwards hung on the house walls, were part of a group of ritual objects which, once brought into the house, could not be removed from it for seven days unless protected by cautionary, ritual acts.

First in importance were the mats sat upon by bride, bridegroom and guests. These mats were put down by the women on the first day of the wedding, and remained there until the fortieth day (at Duweishat East, Melik el-Nasr, Tur-mukke). The bridegroom and bride both had a reserved place for sitting, which was marked by a special mat, either on an *angarib* bed, or on the floor. The number of mats put down for the bride, bridegroom and guests together had to be an

Plate 7
Gemai E., Murshid, typical mat woven of *dom* palm fibre. *Photo* T. Higel

Plate 8
Gemai E., Murshid, basket lid hung on a frieze of painted decoration.
Photo T. Higel

even number. At the end of forty days they were rolled up and placed on wooden pegs near the ceiling to form a decorative row (Pl. 9; fig. 4). The mats were made from bands of woven *dom* palm fibre, dyed different colours and sewn together to a size of about four by six feet (Pl. 7). They were usually edged with a zigzag pattern of prominent stitching. In some cases (Kosha, Mugraka, Saras, Atiri, and Duweishat, Ambikol), the mats were larger in size than the mats used elsewhere, and attached horizontally along the wall itself. In such cases they were of plain neutral tone or wide coloured bands, and the zigzag formed a horizontal pattern along the wall (Fig. 5).

Another decorative feature relating to wedding ritual consisted of circular, shallow basket lids (Pls 8, 9), hung to make a frieze of circles above, or below, the frieze of matting (Figs 4, 5; Pl. 1). This kind of basket lid, called *tabag* or *tabaqa* in Arabic, is used throughout Egyptian Nubia and the Sudan, particularly in Kordofan.[2] Yet such basket lids were used more widely throughout the Sudan as covers for food than as wall decoration. In Egyptian Nubia (Pl. 9), particularly among the Kenuzi,[3] and in Sudanese Nubia from Saras, Semna,

Figure 4
Kosha, Farka, Farkenkonj, large and small basket lids arranged on the wall to make a pattern under a row of rolled mats, suspended on pegs. Bowls are hung in string hangers

27

south to Dongola, they were used to decorate walls. In regions where the decorative use of the *tabag* was particularly refined, two sizes were hung in alternate rows (Fig. 4; Pl. 9). These consisted of a large size, about one and a half feet in diameter, and a smaller size which was about half as big. In the Wadi Halfa district, Gemai and parts of Saras, the use of basket lids as wall decoration had died out and been replaced by paintings which featured large circles, imitating the lids (Pls 27, 35; Col. pl. 19). In some cases, larger and smaller circles were used in the painted designs (Pl. 27), duplicating the two sizes of basket lids (Fig. 4).

The *tabag* lids used to be employed both as lids and as trays to carry food, but in recent years metal trays were preferred, and the basketry survived mainly as lids.[4] However, wedding ceremony tried to follow old traditions, and although the food was now served on metal trays, covered by *tabag* lids, the gifts to the bride and groom were placed alongside them on *tabag* trays, as in earlier times. In Saras, Atiri, the lids themselves formed a gift to the groom who paid a visit to every house in the village and was given a *tabag* from each.

Basket lids were coilwoven by the housewife in vibrant patterns of many colours for which dye was bought in the *suq* market. One pattern woven on them at Akasha was a cross. Throughout Sudanese Nubia, the cross was the motif most commonly used to mark lids of any food container, particularly the

Plate 9
Aniba, Egyptian Nubia, house interior and wall decoration of rolled mats, saucers and two sizes of basket lids. *Photo Violet Macdermot*

28

Figure 5
Saras, Atiri Duweishat;
Duweishat, average interior
with *angarib* bed,
suspended mats, baskets,
basket lids, fly-whisk fans,
coloured whisk brooms,
photograph, square mirror
and saucer inserted into
the mud wall

tall mud storage-pots (*gusseiba*) used for preserving grain and dates (Fig. 6a–k, o).
In Ashkeit, two crossed sticks could be substituted temporarily for any lid over
food. This cross, though traditional, was recognised as a survival of Christian
custom,[5] and caused some embarrassment to the men, who were more devoutly

Figure 6
a–m storage-pot lids with
cross markings, made by
indented finger prints or
incised lines
a *Duweishat, Ambikol*
    Akasha, Ukma
    Kosha, Serkamatto and
    Kosha, Dal
b *Duweishat, Ambikol*
    Kosha, Serkamatto
c *Akasha, sheikhships*
    Akasha and *Ukma*
    Kosha, Serkamatto and
    Kosha, Farka
d *Duweishat, Ambikol*
    Akasha, Akasha
    Kosha, Serkamatto and
    Kosha, Dal
e *Kosha, Serkamatto*
f *Akasha, Ukma*
    Kosha, Dal and
    Kosha, Serkamatto
g *Kosha, Serkamatto*
h *Kosha, Serkamatto*
i *Kosha, Dal*
j *Kosha, Serkamatto*
k *Kosha, Serkamatto*
l *Kosha, Mugraka*, lid by
    professional potter
    Khalil Saleh
m *Kosha, Farka*, lid by
    Khalil Saleh
n *Akasha, Akasha,*
    Shergiya, basket lid
    with woven cross
o *Akasha, Akasha,*
    Shergiya, basket lid
p *Duweishat, Ambikol,*
    storage pot with cross
    lid

Muslim than the women. In Kosha, Mugraka, some storage-pots were made by a male professional potter instead of by housewives.[6] Because he was a devout Muslim, the potter did not want to use the cross in his designs. Yet since the women who bought his pots kept asking for a cross on the lids, he tried to produce something like a cross design without actually making two lines cross (Fig. 6l, m).

The food served under *tabag* lids, like the lids themselves, was not just native to Nubia. The food was *kisra*, an unleavened millet-bread pancake, cooked on a metal plate called a *sadj*.[7] After cooking, the *kisra* was folded and rolled, and served with various kinds of egg, yoghurt or bean dips. *Kisra* is widely known among Bedouin Arabs, and is mentioned as the staple food of the Christian kingdom of Alwa, south of Nubia, in the Middle Ages.[8] Equipment for making *kisra*, like the metal or gourd scoop used for pouring the batter on to the *sadj*, was a traditional gift to the bride and was included among the gifts placed in the basketry containers alongside the bride and groom.

As well as mats used for sitting upon and baskets used for covering food, certain other, smaller items relating to the actual wedding festivities appeared

a

b

c

d

e

f

g

h

i

j

k

l

m

n

p

o

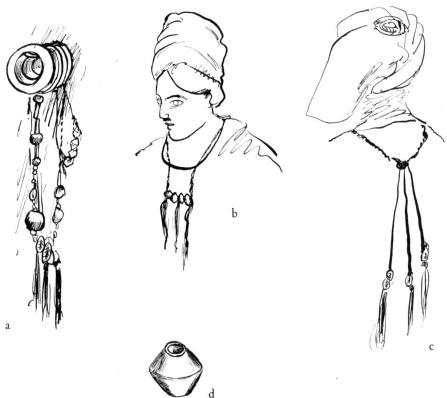

later as decoration on house walls. These included raffia hand-brooms or whisks in green, purple-red and orange (Fig. 5), which were used ceremonially to sweep the mud floors of the wedding chambers, as well as little square woven flags attached to a stiff handle (Fig. 5; Pl. 10), which served as fans or fly-whisks for the guests. In Ashkeit it was said that, in former times, ostrich eggs and feathers had played some part in the wedding ritual and were suspended from the ceiling and walls. Margaret Shinnie saw ostrich eggs set on top of mud posts at Debeira West, *hillet* Nag el Kenuz, and Burckhardt cited elevation of ostrich eggs as a custom in Danier, further south along the Nile.[9] The ritual function of these objects was not specified.

Wall space was given to objects which had been worn or held by members of the wedding party. The groom carried a sword, a knife and a stick which his companions took care that he should seldom put down during the wedding, and which he in fact retained until the next new moon (Pl. 11).

The bride's and groom's ritual beads and the bracelets of the bride were hung on a single nail (Fig. 7a).[10] Beads were most evident in Duweishat, a

stony mountainous region with gold-mines worked by ancient Egyptians and, recently, by Italians. The groom had a special necklace called *gurit*, with four silver beads, cowrie shells, and red and green tassels (Pl. 11; Fig. 7b, c, d). The four silver beads hung in front, with a tassel each side of the group. They were strung on a leather thong and were weighted at the back by a bunch of cowrie shells and more tassels. The cowrie shells were brought into the region by itinerant Nigerian tribespeople, Fallata or Takarir.[11] It was also possible to buy cowries in Egypt. The bride's necklace was less standardised than the groom's. It was made of large round beads alternating with smaller tubular ones (Fig. 7a). The beads were of amber, agate and coloured glass and were seldom obtained in one place. Her bracelets were of ivory, lathe-turned (Fig. 7a). They were of a type not unique to Nubia and available in Omdurman. Yet the Nubians thought that this type was very old and that it was worn by women before the gold ornaments could be obtained which women wore recently. Thus ivory bracelets were the preferred adornment for weddings, because to use them was to follow the old ways.

We have now listed certain items which functioned during the course of a Nubian wedding and which were later attached to walls to form a permanent decoration. If they were employed further during the course of home-making, they were replaced. If they wore out, as happened to basket lids and mats, they were renewed. But there were other things put on walls during the actual wedding which were later removed and thrown away. For example, a pot of green foliage, often palm branches, was attached to the wall of the room in which the bridegroom sat. On the morning of the second day of the wedding the bridegroom went with his attendants to the river to gather it. He renewed it every morning for seven days. On one of these days, the bride went with him to the river to wash her face.[12] The bridegroom had to chase her back and if he caught her he whipped her, but not hard. The green foliage is important because, just as in some areas images of baskets and mats adorned the walls, rather than the objects themselves, so, too, palm branches could be painted on the walls (Fig. 21p; Fig. 22e, i, k, t, u).

Objects hung high up to keep termites from eating them[13] were slung from the ceiling rather than attached to the walls, but they hung in front of the walls and added to the visual complex. The objects were, principally, clothes, food and household treasures. The clothes were piled over a wooden log suspended horizontally between two ropes. Food and treasured items were placed in bowls or in baskets woven deeper than the *kisra* lids, which were hung in individual nets or hangers of braided black wool, with tassels at the bottom (Figs 4, 5). Most nets for hanging were imported from Dongola[14] but, according to an older tradition, they were home-made, in which case they were constructed of palm straps. The housewife sometimes added her own, fancier, tassels to store-bought hangers, or decorated the existing ones with silver foil. The silver foil was not merely for decoration. Like saucers, mirrors and tin-can lids, it diverted the evil eye.

Although the nets for suspending food were principally functional rather than decorative, around Wadi Halfa they were not normally used, as town-bought cupboards had replaced them for food storage and the nets were only filled with special containers for the duration of a wedding. At this time they were filled with good china and regarded as wedding decoration (at Ashkeit). Otherwise, the nets were left empty (Pl. 43). South of the Second Cataract, the hangers were in daily use. Tradition dictated which kind of suspended container was used for what. Grain and dried beans were kept in baskets, while meat was kept in a wooden bowl.

Of the suspended food containers, wooden bowls (Fig. 8b) and gourds (Fig. 9a–i) were given decoration which formed an important aspect of Nubian native art. The bowls, called *dabkar* in Arabic, were made by special carpenters, while the gourds were made by housewives. The carpenters making bowls were not always local; one who had worked recently in Duweishat, in 1953, came from Sukkot, which is the local name for the *omodiya* of Kosha to the south of Duweishat. Some wooden bowls were imported from Omdurman and as far away as Darfur Province.[15] However, bowls were being made by local carpenters in Duweishat, on Ambikol Island, as recently as 1954. They were given the local name of *tayin*. The wood used for them was acacia of two varieties, *haraz* and *sunt*.[16] The carpenter brought a piece of wood as big as a round coffee-table surface (Pl. 11), and cut a core from it. Afterwards he shaped the outside with an axe, and applied the decoration with smaller tools. The women who made decorated gourds were always local women, or women of Dongola. They engraved the decoration on to the gourd with a heated piece of metal.

Wooden bowls, like the *tabag*, were made according to a standard pattern throughout the Sudan, and there was little difference between those made in Nubia and those made elsewhere. Stock patterns of decoration were based on the X between parallel bars and triangles in rows. The pattern fitted between two incised grooves running round the inside and outside of the rim (Fig. 8b). Yet, in spite of the standard character of these designs, they were very like patterns carved on Nubian wood locks[17] (Fig. 8c, d), on wood or stone house lintels (Fig. 8a), and on some mud relief work south of the Second Cataract (Fig. 8e), where the decorators were builders who frequently had some knowledge of carpentry. It would seem that the X between parallel lines was a motif which could be applied to a number of media, but which was most popular for wood-working.

35

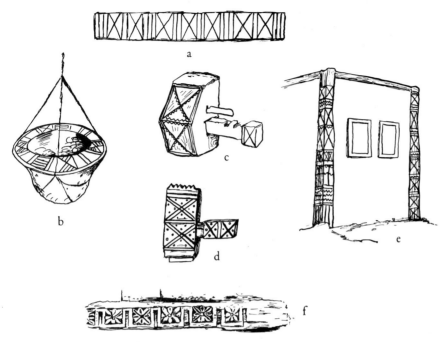

Patterns used in decorating gourds were more particular to Nubia than those of wooden bowls. The main pattern was a zigzag band between two or three parallel lines drawn to each side of it (Fig. 9a–h). On some gourds, every other angle formed by the zigzag was filled up with parallel, slanted lines, forming a row of triangles (Fig. 9b, f). A unique feature was that below this zigzag there was quite frequently a vertical line, made into an arrow pointing to the rim band (Fig. 9b–g). There was also another kind of embellishment extending down from the rim band into the space below, which often took the form of a triangle (Fig. 9b, d, g, h). It is interesting that archaeological excavations have revealed that a particularly fine type of pottery was being used in Nubia in the Middle Ages, often buff or orange, the usual colour of gourds.[18] Certain of the shapes markedly resembled those of modern gourd vessels (Fig. 9i).[19] The decoration was both geometric and figural, showing birds,[20] fish,[21] scorpions[22] or horned antelopes,[23] but most decoration had one particular characteristic: a horizontal, decorative band round the upper portion of the vessel (Fig. 9j, k). A vertical decorative element extended down from the rim band and was placed at regular intervals round the pot. Among these were triangles, as on the gourds, which contained a cross or branch (Fig. 9j, k).[24] The cross or branch replaced the arrow motif of the gourds (Fig. 9b–g), whose design may reflect a debased medieval tradition.

Colour Plate 1
Saras, Saras-Tahali,
Arusa, crocodile skull
surmounting doorway
painted in earth colours
by Osman Kheiri
(pp. 39–40, 181)

Colour Plate 2
Akasha, Ukma, Arau, old woman seated by a courtyard doorway over which there is one plate (p. 40)

Colour Plate 3
Detail of the plate in (2), which must be one of the earliest introduced into the region

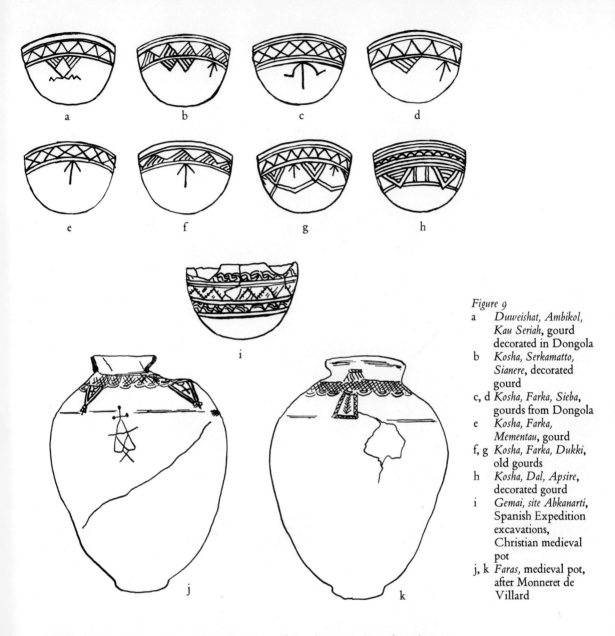

Figure 9
a   *Duweishat, Ambikol, Kau Seriah*, gourd decorated in Dongola
b   *Kosha, Serkamatto, Sianere*, decorated gourd
c, d *Kosha, Farka, Sieba*, gourds from Dongola
e   *Kosha, Farka, Mementau*, gourd
f, g *Kosha, Farka, Dukki*, old gourds
h   *Kosha, Dal, Apsire*, decorated gourd
i   *Gemai, site Abkanarti*, Spanish Expedition excavations, Christian medieval pot
j, k *Faras*, medieval pot, after Monneret de Villard

Objects put up against the evil eye were possibly of pagan origin but their use did not transgress the tenets of Islam, since the evil eye is an acknowledged danger in Islamic teaching. Devils and djinns are feared throughout the Islamic world, and precautions are taken against them.[25] Nubian men are more active in the communal framework of Islam,[26] and would freely admit that certain

Plate 12
Debeira E., horns hung
above the door to
protect against the evil eye

household decoration was to that end. The women, on the other hand, might say that something had been put up to prolong life, and this would be denied by the men since, according to Islam, one's days are numbered and life cannot be prolonged.

The evil eye could be projected on to something by intention or by accident. Around Abri, as each village had its carpenter so each village had someone with the evil eye. He could be hired for pay and taken, with his eyes covered, to some place upon which he cast evil. But possessing the evil eye was not always an

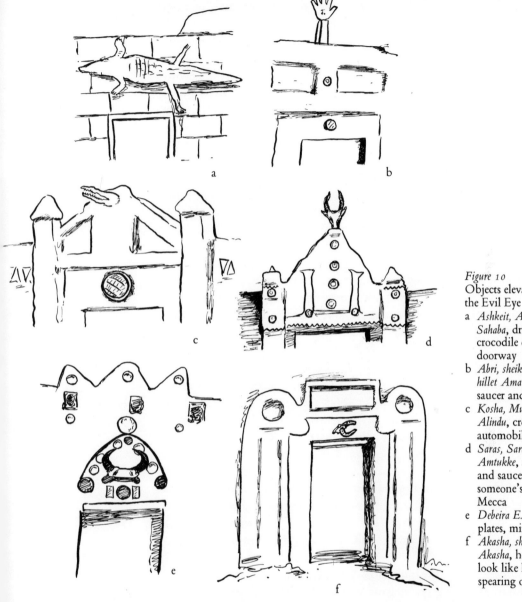

Figure 10
Objects elevated to divert
the Evil Eye
a *Ashkeit, Ashkeit South,
   Sahaba,* dried
   crocodile over a
   doorway
b *Abri, sheikhship Abri,
   hillet Amarok,* tin hand,
   saucer and mirror
c *Kosha, Mugraka, Sheikh
   Alindu,* crocodile skull,
   automobile headlight
d *Saras, Saras-Tahali,
   Amtukke,* antelope head
   and saucers, put up for
   someone's return from
   Mecca
e *Debeira E.,* horns, saucers,
   plates, mirrors
f *Akasha, sheikhship
   Akasha,* horseshoe set to
   look like horns,
   spearing outwards

advantage. One man killed his own daughter. It was known that whenever he made a verbal simile, something dreadful would occur. Once he came home with male guests and his daughter, a fine-formed teenager, did not go to join the women. He said, 'Look at her romping around like an Arab mare', and the girl

39

dropped dead. If someone with the evil eye wanted to have his power removed from him, he had to visit a sheikh.[27]

The technique of deflecting the evil eye from something one wished to protect was simple enough. That which was in danger, such as a new house or a new child, was embellished with some extraneous object of a bright or startling nature, so that the evil eye was diverted. Favourite items used for this were mirrors (Fig. 10e), automobile headlights (Fig. 10c), and tin cut-outs, either crescents or, as in Abri, hands (Fig. 10b). Dried crocodiles (Fig. 10a)[28] and crocodile skulls were equally effective because they frightened evil away. Horns 'speared the evil' (Pl. 12; Fig. 10d, e),[29] although horns belonged to a special category and might be put up for other reasons, such as fulfilling a vow made to a holy man. A horseshoe could be attached to the wall in such a way that the ends protruded outwards, like horns (Fig. 10f). But this might also be to catch luck, since a horseshoe found on the ground with the open side towards you is lucky, and should be put on the wall (at Ashkeit). South of the Second Cataract, the gate or flat roof of a mud building was sometimes enlivened by a peaked contour over the entrance. At the uppermost point various items, such as pots, crocodile skulls (Fig. 10c; Col. pl. 1) or the heads of antelopes (Fig. 10d), were set to form a silhouette against the sky. This was said to be done to attract the people', or 'for a shout', but behind such statements lay the intent to attract glances away from the main body of the house, and so to protect it.

The most obvious feature of Nubian house decoration was the use of inset saucers and dinner-plates (Col. pls 2, 3). Much curiosity has been shown about these plates since their initial appearance at about the turn of the century.[30] A report heard in Egyptian Nubia before 1910 attested that the plates were put up over the door to ensure a plentiful supply of bread in the house; yet it was observed that bread was never served on china, but always in baskets, which were not put up over doors.[31] It was elsewhere remarked that plates were put up to deflect the evil eye.[32] Although earlier authors reported that pebbles were used in the older houses in the same way,[33] our investigations suggested that shells were used in older houses in the same way (Pl. 13; Fig. 11). Saucers seem to have replaced the shells, being whiter, shinier and more striking. This transition was confirmed by local accounts.[34]

Two kinds of shells were inset into walls. These were, first, the small, uniform Nile shells seldom exceeding an inch in length (Pl. 13), and secondly, large shells of different species brought by the gipsies, or *halebs*, from the Red Sea, and sold as charms.[35] North of Wadi Halfa, the large shells were placed over outer doors, sometimes surrounded by saucers (Fig. 11d). In recent years they had not been using the small shells on walls, but only on mud storage-pots, sometimes alternating with chips of broken porcelain, or surrounding an inset

Plate 13
Saras, Semna, Sukkator,
doorway decoration with
shell insets, made by a
woman in 1939

mirror (Fig. 11b, c). However, on the older, abandoned houses of Debeira East (Fig. 3b), near the river's edge and ruined by flood, there was considerable evidence that the little local shells had previously been in wider use. They were set in patterns along walls of interior rooms, either as friezes in combination with saucers, or outlining some familiar image, like a crocodile or a bird. In one early piece of mud relief in the same building complex (Fig. 11a), stylistic-ally dating to the 1920s, the shells were placed into the relief much as saucers were set into reliefs of a later time. In the same way, in an early relief by Ahmad Batoul dated 1927, also found at Debeira East at another site, small Nile shells were arranged around the central pictorial image of birds (Fig. 32c). It was clear that most pattern-making with the Nile shells had been abandoned around Wadi Halfa by the thirties and forties and only the exotic Red Sea shells (Fig. 11d) retained in use. Even the storage-pots decorated with Nile shells, although sometimes still used, were dated by householders to before 1935.

South of Wadi Halfa, shell decoration for the first time appeared in houses where people still lived. In Gemaj, *hillet* Diffinog, the shells were set into relief work as in Debeira, but more frequently they formed a wall frieze in a branch

pattern reminiscent of painting by women (Fig. 11e). Even here, the shell patterning was in the oldest section of the house. In one case, it was remembered to have been already old in 1930. The practice of shell decoration was most alive in the stony region of the Batn al-Hajar where men still built and lived in the simple huts described by Burckhardt. In Saras East, Semna, in the *hillets* of

Plate 14
Gemai E., Murshid, wall decoration of pin⁄ups from candy⁄box lids.
Photo T. Higel

Sukkator, Sindas and Agri, shell decoration on storage⁄pots and walls was being made as recently as 1961. Shells were used in geometric patterns over outer doorways (Pl. 13; Fig. 11i, k, l), on storage⁄pots (Fig. 11j), and accompanying baskets, mats, coloured whisks and lime⁄white handprints to make a frieze on interior walls. Saucers were thought desirable, but were rare, and spots of white lime were substituted. In Saras, Atiri, the shells outlined oval forms which in one case proved to be a scorpion, an image noted for its powers of deflecting evil (Fig. 11m). But other groups of ovals in the same frieze were enigmatic. They most closely resembled the fruits of the *dom* palm,[36] which were hung up in clusters to keep out djinns, as were bags of earth from a holy man's tomb.

Special decoration for the men's sitting⁄room, like decoration for rooms where weddings were held, could be replaced by paintings made directly on the walls. For instance, one thing frequently hung up in sitting⁄rooms was a drawing made by a schoolboy son (Col. pl. 4), and sometimes schoolboys were

43

Figure 12
Kosha, Farka, Gjinengurka,
motifs from a popular
broadsheet illustrating the
holy man Sayyid Ahmad
Rufai

allowed to paint on the walls. Their childish sketches, on paper scraps, shared pride of place with pin-up girls, black, white and Chinese, taken from calendars and candy boxes (Col. pl. 4; Pl. 14). *Playboy* pin-up girls were censored from copies arriving in Egypt, but they were sometimes accessible in Khartoum and a few filtered into Nubia. As was the case with other pictures of white women (Pl. 22) the cheeks were usually pencilled with tribal marks. Further decorations were pictures of holy men (Col. pl. 4), and a curious class of broadsheet printed with saintly iconography, such as lions carrying swords, representing heroic Islamic notables, and a singular image of the holy man Sayyid Ahmad Rufai (Fig. 12), to whom there was a small cult flourishing at Wadi Halfa. The saint himself, who protects from snakebite, was represented enwrapped with snakes. Picture-postcards of desirable objects, such as automobiles, aeroplanes and the army on manœuvres, were often arranged to make a kind of frieze suggestive of the frieze of mats and baskets in the marriage rooms. The pictures of automobiles and aeroplanes also belonged to a distinct

Plate 15
Serra East, sandstone
lintel made by Salim Ali
in 1935. *Photo* J. Shiner

class of painted decoration, that which greeted the householder on his return from Mecca (Fig. 14). Means of transportation were shown as well as the holy sites.

Special decoration for doors consisted of embellishment put on functional parts of the door, including the carved wooden lock[37] (Figs 8c, d, 13b; Pl. 17), the lintel (Pl. 15; Fig. 8a), and the fabric of the door itself, as well as cut-work panels of wood or tin which were sometimes inset over the top of the door (Fig. 25c; Fig. 26a). The most typical design used on locks and lintels was the X between parallel bars, which was also common on wooden bowls. However, lintels were not always of wood; sometimes they were made from stone. Lintel-making was in fact the only stone-carving performed by modern Nubians, and for this they used native Nubian sandstone (Pl. 15). Although the formula of an X between parallel bars is simple in the extreme – so simple that its origin cannot really be defined – it is suggestive of some crude borders made on Nubian lintels of the Christian period, when stone-carving was more common (Fig. 8f).[38]

Plate 16
Ashkeit, lockmaker
Abdulla Kheir al-Sid,
working on the last lock
to be made in the Wadi
Halfa district before the
move to Khashm
el-Girba. The lock was
commissioned by the
Sudan Research Unit,
University of Khartoum,
in March 1964, and was
decorated with circular
designs. *Photo* J. Shiner

a

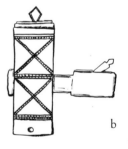

b

Decorated locks north of Wadi Halfa (Pl. 16) occasionally departed from this formula into more intricate designs based upon the circle.[39] The people said that these designs were taken from Egyptian chests (Fig. 35a), or from the patterns used on women's jewellery. Further, a form of lock was popular which was given a protrusion at the top (Fig. 13b). Although no such origin was suggested, the outline resembled that of the wooden tablets or alphabet boards upon which were inscribed phrases of the Quran in the Quranic schools[40] (Fig. 13a). All these forms, the X between parallel bars, circle variants and anthropomorphic shapes, found their way into the technique of mud relief. Yet, in one way or another, they all reflect much older aspects of household decoration.

Figure 13
a *Faras West*, painting,
  black outline on pink,
  representing a board
  with verses from the
  Quran such as are used
  in Quran schools. The
  birds depicted on it are
  pigeons. Made 1964
b *Ashkeit, Ashkeit South,
  Sahaba*, lock by
  Farajalla Amber

46

CHAPTER THREE

Art of the Nubian Family

In Egyptian Nubia most house decoration was done by builders or by women, while male professional artists for this work were found mainly in Sudanese Nubia towards the Egyptian border.[1] The technique of relief sculpture in mud practised by these men is known elsewhere in Africa, as in Ghana[2] and Northern Nigeria.[3] But in Upper Egypt, Egyptian Nubia, it was seldom seen except towards the Sudanese border, where much of it was said to have been made by Nubians from the Sudan, as at Ballana (Pls 32, 77). The Egyptian Nubian's art was mainly painting and not relief. This does not mean that professional decorators in the Sudan did not know how to paint. In the thirties there was great enthusiasm for unpainted relief, or relief cut into a white-lime surface laid over a dark mud ground; but when this popularity waned, most decorators turned to painting or to painting their relief, particularly indoors. These professional decorators had started as workers in mud; but once they became artists, independent of the house-plastering trade where mud was the obvious medium, it was natural that they should experiment with paint.

The environment which allowed menial craftsmen to develop into professional artists required a predisposition of the local inhabitants towards art, which would lead them to hire professionals. The Nubian householder had a developed aesthetic taste which was not shared by other Sudanese, even in the capital of Khartoum and its adjoining native city of Omdurman. The crude mud dwellings of Omdurman, stretching far into the distance either side of

47

Figure 14
Debeira East, Hassa, Hayya,
painting made to celebrate
the return of a pilgrim
from Mecca in 1963. Blue
paint on a white ground

brilliantly lit roads, lack decoration, and are bewailed by Nubians who must live in them. As Nubian artists of the flood area have moved south, there is new interest in decoration around Dongola. But here, too, a certain appreciation of art, in the form of house decoration with baskets and mats, already existed. Such an appreciation was lacking elsewhere in the Sudan. When artists left Nubia and went to live in Atbara or Khartoum, they turned to other jobs.

The members of Sudanese Nubian households who encouraged the hiring of professional artists to decorate their homes were frequently artists themselves. Alongside the art made by professional decorators there also existed an art made by members of the Nubian family which was not unlike some of the women's painting in Egyptian Nubia. Women, men – who were either house-owners, grown sons, or bridegrooms marrying into the family – and boys, all had their own kinds of wall painting. Anyone in the family might do an additional painting, designed to be seen by persons returning from the pilgrimage to Mecca, or *Hajj* (Fig. 14). The woman who made wall paintings was either the house-wife, who did so because she felt it ought to be done, or the daughter about to be married, who prepared the rooms in which the bridegroom was to be received. Most Nubian girls married very young, so that there was no particular group of girls' painting. Both brides and women used limited patterns traditional to their own village. Of the art made by men, the bridegroom's art was more like the art of women than was the art of a householder enlivening his sitting-room. The

bridegroom tried to follow that type of design traditional for weddings, which was the women's art. But he often added extra features, such as automobiles or mosques, which made it clear that his was not really the art of women (Fig. 15).

Each of the three family groups, women, men and boys, employed a limited imagery in their art which was consistent within their group. Exceptions, of course, could always be found, and we shall discuss later the enigmatic area of Gemai, Murshid, where it was impossible to distinguish the artist. The traditional village formulas of the women were often based on arrangements of objects employed before. Men painted flags, belonging to certain *sufi* dervish groups,[4] or the Sudanese flag. They painted crescents, stars, automobiles, boats and pin-up girls. Boys painted domestic animals such as camels, donkeys and dogs, which no one else depicted, and also scenes of everyday life in which *suq* lorries carried people to market while onlookers relaxed under palm trees (Pl. 17;

Figure 15
Kosha, Farka, Sherif Irki, painting by bridegroom and house-owner's son, Abdu Hasan Fadl, for his wedding in 1964. Turquoise, purple, magenta on a white ground

Plate 17
Kosha, Dal, Deffatte, a wall decorated by schoolboys in typical imagery including a *suq* lorry. The wooden lock has a hole for the hand to pass through from outside to insert the key, here shown in the lock

a

b

Figure 16
a *Saras, Atiri, Atiri*, schoolboy drawing made 1964, lavender and blue-green paint on an unpainted mud ground
b *Kosha, Mugraka, Fard*, schoolboy drawing in white lime on mud

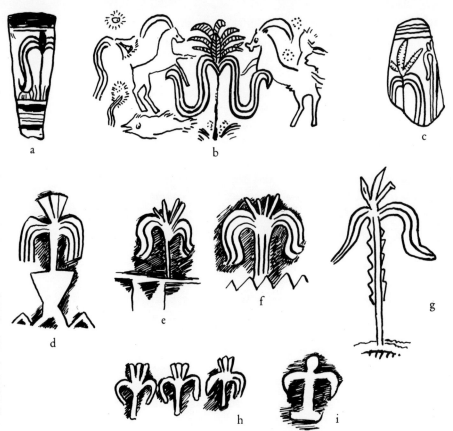

Figure 17

a   *Medinet Gourob, Fayum, Egypt*, pottery fragment, recent Mycenaean (after Hélène Danthine)

b   *Ligortyno, Crete*, recent Minoan pottery

c   *Mycenae, Greece*, recent Mycenaean pottery

d   *Saras, Saras-Tahali, Mugufil East*, painting by a bride, 1964

e, f *Saras, Saras-Tahali, Mugufil East*, females' painting

g   *Saras, Atiri, Farki*, schoolboy drawing, 1964

h   *Duweishat, Ambikol, Angasa*, females' painting

i   *Duweishat, Ambikol, Angasa*, females' painting

Fig. 16). Women never painted scenes of everyday life, and men did so rarely.

Both men and women painted wild animals of an apotropaic and mythical character, such as crocodiles, scorpions and lions with swords. Boys, who had the widest repertoire of images, sometimes painted these too. Women alone painted fish, although a few fish were made by male professional artists. 'Fish mean nothing', we were told, 'unless they have been painted by a woman' (Faras). The reason for this was not given. Everyone painted flowers and birds. Like palm branches, they entered the repertoire of traditional female design. South of the Second Cataract, in Duweishat, Ambakol, and Saras, Saras-Tahali, Mugufil, the women represented the palm tree as a fleur-de-lis (Fig. 17d, e, f, h, i), in the manner of some ancient pot decoration (Fig. 17a–c).[5] Some boys copied this (Fig. 17g), but men never did since they preferred more naturalistic representation (Fig. 18a).

Each group within the family employed not only special imagery, but also

51

special materials. Men, who controlled money, bought colours in the market, while women and boys usually painted with earth colours and lime which they had themselves dug out of the hills. Each villager knew what colours might be found nearest his village, and how far one must go to locate others. Colour was discovered where earth had eroded. It was collected in sacks, carried back by camel or donkey, and purified by a washing process. Round Saras, Saras-Tahali, doorways were painted in a vivid sienna earth colour which was highly prized and difficult to obtain (Col. pl. 1). In this case it had been bought in the market by the householder, or he had paid someone to go to the hills and fetch it. The earth colours dug out and used by women and boys were often of inferior quality, sometimes just a local clay, of only a slightly different colour from the mud initially employed in house-building. Blue was available to some women because it was the blueing necessary for whitening clothes. They used it more in the Halfa region than in the Batn al-Hajar, where it was too expensive or too rare and was used mainly by men or by male professionals who received their colours from the men who had hired them. Those schoolboys who did not paint with earth colours, drew with chalk. In Faras, chalk was used by both women and boys. We found sticks of chalk in deserted houses in Faras West kept in pottery jars, sorted by colour. The sticks would have been pounded by mortar and pestle, mixed with water and treated as powder paint. The chalk must have been market-bought, and forms an exception to the general rule that women used only home-made colours. South of Faras, on the west bank of the Nile, the more conservative women of Debeira West painted with a local, buff-orange earth colour which in Argin, however, had only recently been discovered. The Argin women made their paintings with white lime and household blueing, like decorators commemorating the *Hajj*.

Art produced by the three family groups did not occur in the same pro-portions in each place. Where there was painting by women, pictures made by schoolboys were rare, and vice versa. For instance, Saras was a region for women's art, as was Debeira West. Boys did not paint there, but they did paint in Duweishat, where women's art was uncommon. Moreover, the painting of both women and boys tended to die out in regions where male professional art had taken a strong hold. This was less so south of the Second Cataract than in the Wadi Halfa district. South of the Second Cataract women decorated rooms where the wedding was held and professional artists decorated other rooms, principally the men's sitting-room (Fig. 19), while around Halfa professional artists were called in to decorate the wedding chambers and the women were left to decorate the main courtyard or *hosh*. The *hosh* was unrelated to ritual observances and the women, therefore, had less interest in decorating it. Decoration by householders was sporadic, and could occur anywhere, inde-

Colour Plate 4
Saras, Semna West,
Sayegnambi, wall of a
men's sitting-room
decorated with pin-up
girls, the picture of a
holy man, saucers and
schoolboy drawings
(pp. 43–4)

*Colour Plate 5
Ashkeit, hillet
Hakmanerki,
house-owner Abdu
Saber and his diwan
decoration, 1960
(p. 53)*

Colour Plate 6
Ashkeit, Ashkeit South,
Sahaba, horned mud
sculpture made by a
house-owner
(p. 54)

Colour Plate 7
Serra East, hillet Artinoka, females' painting type
B, in earth colour on mud
(pp. 69–74)

Colour Plate 8
Gemai E., Murshid, painting by Melik Muhammad
Hasan, showing patterns of mats, hanging baskets,
fly-whisk flags and a yellow circle, possibly the
bride's bracelet, over a crescent
(pp. 30–4, 88)

pendently of other art near by. It was found when the house-owner was exceptionally original or exceptionally house-proud.

House-owners who embellished their property almost always did so by painting. Their paintings sometimes possessed even more vivid colour than the work of the professional artists, since what the man had saved in not hiring an artist, he could afford to spend in the Wadi Halfa market buying brilliant powder colours. An example was the decoration in Ashkeit, *hillet* Hakmanerki, by Abdu Saber, a twenty-five-year-old *farrash* or servant at the local school (Col. pl. 5). He decided to decorate his house because he felt like doing so, and because he enjoyed colour and wanted to have it around. He obtained his paint from the market along with much beer, and threw everybody out of the house until he was done. He painted the *diwan*, using principally bird and flower forms and brightly coloured circles. It so happened that Abdu Saber lived in an area where there were many works by professional artists, and his images may have been copied from some of these. However, he avoided the usual custom practised by women and professionals of having a single pattern band round three sides of the room, with isolated motifs placed above or below. Instead, he created vast squares of colour extending to the top of the walls, painted in orange, yellow, black and blue. His plants and flying birds were superimposed upon them.

The coloured backgrounds of Abdu Saber's paintings were extremely unusual: normally house-owners painted on a whitewashed wall and their designs were set out in blue silhouette. The whitewashed wall was a device borrowed from *Hajj* art, where it was thought to be essential. When women whitewashed the wall on which they painted they whitewashed only one band, several feet wide, running horizontally, and never the whole wall (Fig. 21d). An example of painting on a full white ground was made in the Batn al-Hajar by Muhammad Idris of Duweishat, Melik el-Nasr, Nerri, who worked in a region where painting was little known. He decorated his sitting-room with blue silhouettes of reindeer, boats and men climbing a palm tree to pick dates (Fig. 18). The reindeer, which is an unusual image in this art form, may have resulted from the influence of an Egyptian commercial artist, Sabri, who worked north and south of Duweishat and who painted reindeer (Pl. 23) and one elk (Fig. 19a). Although the blue and white colours were borrowed from the style of painting made in honour of the Mecca pilgrimage, a reindeer could hardly be further removed from Islamic imagery.

House-owners only seldom practised the medium of mud relief. In Ashkeit, hillet Ari, a man and his sons made crescents in relief over all the doors, and in Gemai, Amka Sharg, Nobenok, in a house on a rocky prominence to the right of the road going South, the owner cut a large relief on his house front in 1959.

a

b

c

Figure 18
Duweishat, Melik el-Nasr, Nerri, sitting-room decoration by house-owner Muhammad Idris Ahmad Medani in 1958, blue silhouette on a whitewashed surface

53

It showed a man shooting a crocodile. The house-owner, Muhammad Osman Fadl, said that he had never looked at any other reliefs of crocodiles and men, but had seen real men shooting crocodiles and had taken his idea from this.[6] He had in fact almost certainly seen other crocodile-hunt reliefs, since they abounded in Gemai and Halfa Degheim, only a few miles to the south and north. But it was clear that he was proud of his work and did not hesitate to place his own decoration near the professional work of Sabri and Dawud Osman, in the same house-complex (Pls 20–23). When, by the autumn of 1964, this house was deserted and its owner had moved away, there was left a piece of paper with a crayoned message in English attached to the façade. It said, 'This is a very nice and good house.'

There was only one three-dimensional work in the whole of Sudanese Nubia. This was found in Ashkeit, *hillet* Sahaba, north of Wadi Halfa. A tall, white-washed pillar had been given a black painted face, and was surmounted by horns (Pl. 18; Col. pl. 6). It adjoined a small hut in poor condition (Pl. 18). The façade had been remodelled, given round windows and painted with birds, flowers and the name of God in the usual blue and white. The artist had been living in Egypt and had inherited this hovel from his father. When news reached him of the Aswan High Dam and impending destruction of his property, he hurried back quickly to beautify the house in order to earn more compensation money from the Government. We were not informed if this ploy had been successful, nor why he had wanted to make sculpture.

The nature of the blue and white painting adjoining the mud sculpture, in particular its use of flowers and holy words, showed familiarity with the usual technique of painting which is designed to be seen by people returning from the *Hajj* pilgrimage to Mecca.[7] Trips to Mecca were a lifelong ambition for many people and the return from such a trip was a cause for celebration. It was thought propitious for the returning pilgrim to gaze on the colours of blue and white, representing purity, as he re-entered his house, and its doorway surround was prepared for his arrival by being painted in these tones (Fig. 14). The background was always white while blue paint was used to write some Quranic phrases, sanctifying the pilgrim's entrance, over the door. It was also thought desirable to remind him of his journey by painting pictures of what he had seen on his trip, such as the Kaaba shrine and Muhammad's tomb, as well as the different means of transportation he had employed, such as trains, aeroplanes and boats. Ritual objects used for purification and prayer were there, too, such as prayer-mats, basins and ewers for cleansing before prayer (Pl. 19), along with flowers and foliage. Although *Hajj* painting might be done by any member of the family, it had more influence on the personal art of men who were householders than on the art of women, boys or even professionals.

Plate 18
Ashkeit, Ashkeit South, Sahaba, ruined house, with façade painting and sculptural decoration added recently in order to obtain government compensation money

Plate 19
West Degheim, Degheim North, Kenuz, painting made on the east façade, facing the Nile, to celebrate the owner's return from Mecca

Despite the religious character of *Hajj* painting, associated with a faith noted for taboos against figural representation, *Hajj* art easily led to depiction of the human form. In 1961 the entire male population of the Kenuzi village in West Degheim went to Mecca, and upon return were rewarded with *Hajj* painting on whitewashed façades, consisting of multi-coloured pictures of boats, boatmen and the house-owner at prayer (Pl. 19). These Egyptian Kenuzi had their own artists, who elaborated Meccan imagery more than did the Sudanese Mahas who excluded the human figure and limited colour to blue and white. The temptation to depict the human form in *Hajj* painting was a source of concern in Saras, where the people had decided that *Hajj* painting should be dropped 'because it was against religion'. Yet from all accounts it was flourishing in Dongola, and was being exploited by the Egyptian commercial artist, Sabri. It appeared that *Hajj* painting might have been instrumental in accustoming some Nubian men to a wider range of representational art than was traditional. *Hajj* painting was by definition a result of contact with outside. The contact was both with Islam itself, which provided some images used, and with large cities such as Cairo, where the Western influence of advertising, films and newspaper illustration had accustomed Muslims to pictures of the human form.

The Egyptian commercial artist, Sabri, now in Dongola, has had a great effect on the art made by Nubian house-owners in recent years. He was a Copt, who in 1959 hid for political reasons in the Second Cataract area, on Kokki Island (Appendix A, no. 23). His work was rooted in advertising art, yet fell within all the subject groupings previously familiar in men's sitting-rooms and in *Hajj* painting. These were: Mecca scenes, Quranic writings, automobiles (Fig. 19b), aeroplanes (Pls 20, 21), pin-up girls and the army on manœuvres (Fig. 19d), as well as birds and wild animals (Pls 21, 23; Fig. 19a, e). Comments concerning him reveal his character:

'He came from his homeland in 1959 to the Kokki Island. He stayed for a month. He did the drawings during the month that he stayed there. He takes 270 piastres[8] for decorating the *diwan*. He decorated more than five *diwans* for this price' (at Gemai East, Amka Sharg).

'The artist Sabri first fled to the Sudan in 1956, when the Sudan became independent. Nobody knows what he did wrong in Egypt; he said he got bored. In Farka there is somebody called Jafar who knows a lot about him. Jafar made these tribal marks on Sabri's face like Hasan Beshir,[9] like the Shaiqiyya tribe. The police were after him and he had been thrown out of the Sudan a couple of times and came back. Jafar suggested that if he really wanted to be Sudanese he should make these marks on his face. But seven days later the police caught him. They said that if he were really Sudanese

Plate 20
Gemai, Amka Sharg, Nobenok, painting by Sabri, *c.* 1959, on a south wall. The aeroplane is the one which takes people to Mecca

these marks would have been made when he was a little boy, not when he was forty' (from Saras, Saras Tahali, Mugufil).

'First he came to Abri, and then he was thrown out to Aswan. He went to Egypt about three times, and came back about three times. At Farka he made this friend Jafar and told Jafar he left his family there and couldn't live there. So together they got this solution. But the Sudanese police said these marks

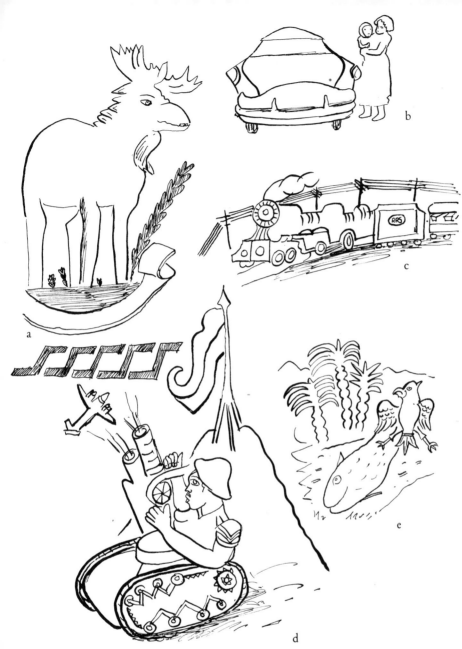

meant nothing. They took him to Egypt, but then he came back. So out of kindness they gave him Sudanese citizenship. Before that he spent six months in Halfa and then he went to Abri. From Abri he wanted to go to Dongola to hide there. The first time he went back from Abri was 1957.

The police were after him because you cannot live here unless you are Suda‑
nese or have Sudanese nationality. When he came back to Egypt they turned
him back on the next steamer to the Sudan. They said Egyptians don't have
these marks on their face. So he could find no home. When he came to the
Sudan he was only a week when the Sudanese police made him take the
steamer again to Egypt. So all his being driven back and forth so many
times took only a few weeks' (fronr Saras, Saras Tahali, Mugufil).

'Sabri, the Egyptian artist, is now at Dongola. He decorates houses, or any‑
thing where people ask. They began to decorate their houses in Dongola
recently. Sabri is a Copt and about forty. He married a woman here at
Farka. Then he divorced her and went to Dongola and married there. If as
well as an automobile or an aeroplane you want a guest taking cups off the
table you tell Sabri and he makes it. He graduated from a school [see below].
In Dongola they have paintings made when people come back from the

Plate 21
Gemai, Amka Sharg,
Nobenok, painting by
Sabri in an exterior
alcove facing north.
Photo J. Shiner

Plate 22
Gemai, Amka Sharg,
Nobenok, portrait of
Queen Elizabeth painted
by Sabri in the men's
sitting-room, east wall,
c. 1959 inscribed, 'This a
job painting by Sabry'.
Tribal marks have been
added to her face by
another hand. *Photo*
T. Higel

Hajj. For this he draws, as well as aeroplanes, inscriptions from the Quran, pictures of an Islamic sword and pictures of someone welcoming the man back from the *Hajj.* He is a professional artist and has no other job, and people demand him very much. He is a good handwriter also for the fronts of houses, and in addition to decoration he writes the name of the owner of the house or shop very beautifully. People from Khartoum bring him things to write. He draws antelopes, cars, all sorts of things. He charges three pounds for a small sign' (from Saras, Semna West, Bishangi).

'Sabri is now rich. He didn't make his own house. He married recently and is still in the bride's house. He doesn't keep his money because he drinks too much and spends it haphazardly. He was a Copt, but then he was converted to Islam and married this woman' (from Saras, Semna West, Bishangi).

Those Nubians who had known Sabri were unable to specify the character of the art school which he had attended. When Mustafa Ibrahim Taha encountered the artist in 1965, he was told by him that the school had been an Italian one, in Italy. Mustafa entertained some doubts about the truth of this remark. However, Italian artists in both Cairo and Alexandria have produced house decoration which resembles the work of Sabri, and it is believed in Alexandria that some Egyptian commercial artists do study in Rome.[10]

Plate 23
Gemai, Amka Sharg, Nobenok, deer and crocodile painted by Sabri on the west wall of the men's sitting-room, *c.* 1959. *Photo* T. Higel

One might have expected the art of Nubian men to show a greater concern with Islamic motifs than the art of Nubian women, since men bear more responsibility in carrying out Islamic ritual and laws.[11] Except for their painting of Quranic phrases and ritual flags on walls, this is not the case, for reasons more deep-seated than the recent attractions of figural representation. When Islamic culture was introduced into Nubia, as into the Sudan generally, it was legal rather than artistic values which were received.[12] There was nothing to replace the strong Christian tradition of image-making already there. The resultant poverty in Islamic art is apparent to any visitor to Khartoum. In an intermediate centre such as Wadi Halfa there was even less evidence, other than *Hajj* painting, of what might be called Islamic art. As had been said, Islamic taboos against representational art were little observed. Quranic writing was used magically, in amulets and to protect house entrances, but seldom in the decorative sense common to Islamic art elsewhere. Apart from the Mecca scenes in *Hajj* paintings, religious building such as mosques were seldom depicted, except by Quranic teachers who happened to become bridegrooms. Nor were there many mosques which possessed minarets or differed markedly from other flat mud buildings.[13] Yet there was one kind of religious structure which was constantly repeated in paintings around Wadi Halfa. This was the domed tomb of a holy man or Muslim saint (Pl. 24). It was most frequently depicted by women, not men.

The most important category of Nubian household art is the art of women, which will now be considered in detail. First of all it is necessary to differentiate between two kinds of painting which were made by women. The first kind consisted of simple marks made in liquid on a given surface with the peculiarity that these marks had a magical function and not a decorative or imitative one (Fig. 20). The second kind was both decorative and imitative, and only occasionally magical in function (Figs 21–3). The marks of the first kind of painting took the form of splashes of blood thrown against both sides of a door following the sacrifice of an animal (Fig. 20a), handprints made in blood or white lime (Pl. 25; Fig. 20c–f, q, s), and magical figures designed in mud over doors and on storage-pots at the Festival of Ashura, which were wiped off and renewed each year.[14] Some of these last seemed to be based on the cross (Fig. 20j, k, l, o, t), while others were a row or composition made of a number (preferably odd) of magical marks (Fig. 20f–h, n, o, p). In the cases when these marks were put together to form compositions of rectangles, they began to resemble some female's painting of the second group (Fig, 21f–i, k), where a band of rectangles in white lime or earth colour was painted around the room, or as a door surround.

Plate 24
West Degheim, Degheim N, Kenuz, imitation of a holy man's tomb made by schoolboys, who set it up in the village as a good deed. To one side are sticks for flags, and on the top is a light bulb. Photographed after the village was deserted

Plate 25
Duweishat, Ambikol,
Angasa, lime handprints
on an exterior wall, near
the entrance, made by the
girl photographed
with them

But this latter painting differed essentially from the Ashura marks both in material, which was paint rather than brown mud, and in function, which was not to give magical protection to the house but to imitate and replace a row of hanging mats.

In areas where women made magical marks on doorways and storage-pots they did not paint the interiors of their houses, being content with decorative

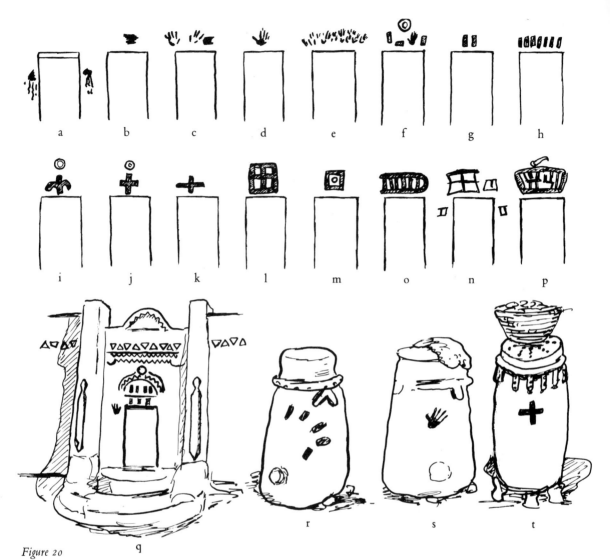

Figure 20

Ritual and protective marks made in blood and mud

a *Kosha, Mugraka, Filin*, blood splashes made at the Id, house entrance

b, c *Kosha, Farka, Abu Sarieda*, handprints and spots of blood made in 1963 at the Id, when a goat was killed, courtyard doors

d *Kosha, Dal, Jedid*, bloody handprint made after slaughtering a sheep. In two-room house, over entrance into the store-room

e *Kosha, Farka, Kalumar*, eleven handprints in blood made at the Id by a schoolboy, over the doorway leading from the main courtyard into the men's sitting-room complex

f *Kosha, Serkamatto, Baash*, handprint in blood accompanied by a saucer and mud marks made for Ashura, on a courtyard doorway

g *Kosha, Farka, Sabinsum*, Ashura marks in mud over a courtyard doorway

h *Akasha, Akasha, hillet Akasha*, Ashura marks which had to be an odd, not even number, placed over a courtyard door
i *Kosha, Serkamatto, Sianere*, outside entrance, Ashura mark like a fleur-de-lis, under a glass jar lid set in the wall
j *Kosha, Serkamatto, Sianere*, Ashura mark in shape of a cross over all four courtyard doors of the same house as 'i'. Made by the wife's mother before 1961
k *Kosha, Dal, Farket Island*, cross-form Ashura mark, exterior doorway, of which the people were ashamed, first saying it was by children, then trying to scrape it off
l *Akasha, Akasha, Shergiya*, Ashura mark over an outer doorway, made by a woman
m *Akasha, Akasha, Shergiya*, Ashura mark over courtyard doorway
n *Akasha, Akasha, hillet Akasha*, courtyard doorway, Ashura mark
o *Akasha, Akasha, Shergiya*, Ashura mark over a courtyard door
p *Akasha, Akasha, Abushuna*, Ashura marks made in 1963, horn put up in 1959, over interior doorway leading into the store-room
q *Kosha, Mugraka, Filin*, outer doorway by Osman Kheiri, with added Ashura marks and handprint in blood made later than the house building in 1959
r *Kosha, Mugraka, Filin*, Ashura marks on a storage pot in the same house as 'q'.
s *Kosha, Farka, Masongur*, handprint in mud on a storage pot, for Ashura
t *Kosha, Serkamatto, Sianere*, cross-form Ashura mark on storage pot in same house as 'i' and 'j'

arrangements of baskets and mats; where wall painting began to replace the mats the use of magical marks was dropped. A progression from magical marks made by women to simple but more extensive wall painting, and then to elaborate wall painting which in turn was replaced with wall painting by men, developed from South to North. Magical marks were most prevalent in Kosha, and less so in Akasha, north of it. Simple painting began in Duweishat, in the Batn al-Hajar, where Ashura marks were not made, and white-lime handprints (Fig. 21b, c, i, j, l–n; Pl. 25) replaced the handprints of blood found further south (Fig. 20c, d, f). The northern, lime handprints were thought to be purely decorative, and used as a filler for wall friezes (Fig. 21a–c), while the blood handprints over doors further south were stated by women to prolong life. The only example of lime handprints used as a wall frieze as far south as Kosha (at Kosha, Serkamatto, Taruwe) occurred in a store-room where the handprints also covered the storage-pots in the manner of Ashura marks. No one stated that in this case they possessed a magical, protective function, but it is possible, since the Ashura marks and cross lids put on storage-pots in the same region were thought to protect the contents of the pot. This use of handprints on storage-pots was not encountered anywhere north of Kosha. The most southern women's painting, in Duweishat, remained highly stylised and geo-metric, consisting of squares and zigzags reminiscent of the zigzag edging to mats (Fig. 5; Fig. 21e–i). North of Duweishat, in Saras, women's painting began to acquire more obvious representational features ranging from palm branches to scorpions, which continued to be characteristic of such painting until the Egyptian border (Fig. 21p–w; Figs 22, 23).

Figure 21
Females' painting type A
a *Duweishat, Melik el-Nasr, Nerri*, frieze of white-lime handprints and circles along with tin-can lids, made 1963. House interior
b *Duweishat, Ambikol, Farhana*, frieze of lime handprints, and white dots which replace shells that the women used some time ago. House interior
c *Duweishat, Melik el-Nasr, Nerri* band and handprints in white lime made 1963, with hanging-basket lids. House interior
d *Kosha, Dal, Jedid*, white band painted as background for basket lids. Interior, 1955
e *Duweishat, Melik el-Nasr, Turmukke*, darker mud ground with lighter mud painted on top. Interior
f *Duweishat, Ambikol, Ambikol Island, hillet Gnjere*, paler mud painted on darker. Interior, painted 1951
g *Duweishat, Melik el-Nasr, Turmukke*, lighter mud on a darker mud ground. Interior
h *Duweishat, Melik el-Nasr, Hawate*, lighter on darker mud, 1957. House interior
i *Kosha, Serkamatto, Raselgeid*, white-lime framework and handprints painted on mud. Interior, store-room, 1963
j *Duweishat, Melik el-Nasr, Nerri*, white-lime decoration with one tin-can lid, made by women for the purpose of beauty in 1948. Courtyard
k *Duweishat, Ambikol, Ambikol Island, hillet Gnjere*, red-brown earth colour on brown mud. Outside entrance, painted 1961
l *Duweishat, Ambikol, Angasa*, decoration of handprints and white-lime rectangles by the housewife, who also made imitation prayer mats in white lime on the walls. The handprint custom began in this village in 1952. Crocodile in relief by a farmer, Abd al-Rahim Mukhtar, who did part-time wall smoothing. Interior room
m *Duweishat, Ambikol, Angasa*, white-lime handprints, fleur-de-lis, outside façade
n *Duweishat, Ambikol, Angasa*, outside entrance, white-lime handprints, fleurs-de-lis
o *Saras, Atiri, Mugufil-narti* (Mugufil Island), white-lime painting on mud, interior
p *Saras, Atiri, Mugufil-narti*, white-lime painting on mud, interior, same house as 'o'
q *Saras, Atiri, Mugufil-narti*, white lime on mud with touches of blue earth pigment found nearby. Interior, painted 1949; motif called the moon over date trees
r *Saras, Atiri, Mugufil-narti*, white lime on mud, interior, same house as 'q', painted 1949
s *Saras, Atiri, Mugufil-narti*, white-lime, blue, ochre painting, interior, by one girl in 1949
t *Saras, Atiri, Mugufil-narti*, same house, colours as 's', made 1949
u *Saras, Saras-Tahali, Mugufil East*, white lime on mud, lavender touches. Painting made in 1964 by girl two days before her marriage, interior room
v *Saras, Saras-Tahali, Mugufil East*, white-lime painting made by women for decoration, not for a wedding, interior room
w *Saras, Saras-Tahali, Mugufil East*, darker on lighter mud, decoration on inside and outside of house, made by women when renewing worn mud surface of wall

All women's painting made in the form of horizontal wall friezes fell into one of two variant groups (which I shall call 'type A' and 'type B'). Type A was initially a band painted round the wall which was thought to imitate a mat; baskets were sometimes hung on this band (Figs 21, 22; Pl. 1a). The band was retained longest when the custom of painting began to die out: 'As for the habit of putting baskets on these walls, it was once a habit in this village but they dropped it for this painting, and now they are dropping the painting, making just a yellow line in the bridegroom's room' (at Saras, Mugufil Island).

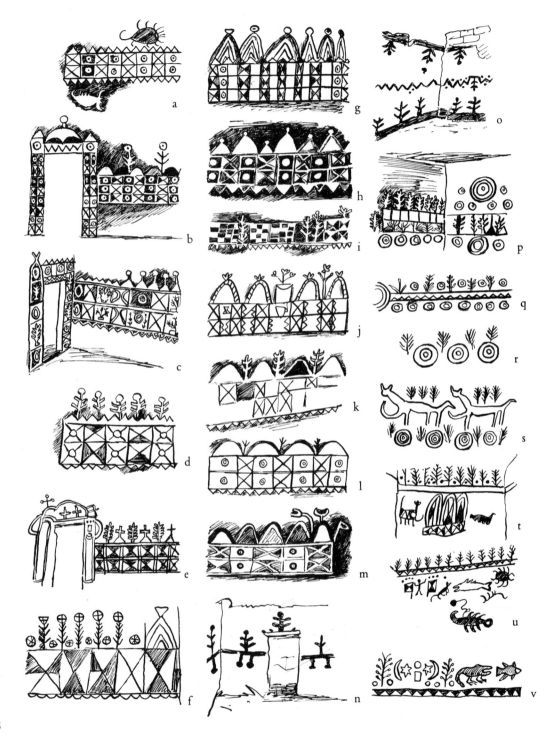

a
b
c
d
e
f
g
h
i
j
k
l
m
n
o
p
q
r
s
t
u
v

68

Colour Plate 9
Wadi Halfa, Museum of
New Mexico Expedition
house, 1964, Jabir Bab
al-Kheir working in
Nile mud and sand to
make the wall relief of a
crocodile
(pp. 117–20)

Colour Plate 10
Deheira E., hillet Shabka,
façade facing west
decorated in 1944 by
Jabir Bab al-Kheir,
with a water wheel
between two trees at the
top
(pp. 123–4)

Figure 22
Females' painting type A
a *Gemai E., Murshid Adurma*, painting in blue, ochre, rust-red, white, courtyard wall
b *Gemai E., Murshid, Gokkon-kode*, interior room, painting in blue and white
c *Gemai, Murshid*, painting in white and yellow on mud, with purple touches, made in 1934 for a wedding, interior room
d *Gemai, Murshid, Adurma*, blue and white painting, made in 1936 in *diwan*
e *Gemai, Gemai, Said, diwanin-hasil* entrance painted in orange, white and blue
f *Gemai, Gemai, hillet Artinassi Island, Sanb*, decoration in lavender, ochre and white, for a wedding in 1957, interior room
g *Gemai, Gemai, Artinassi Island, Sanb*, painting in red, blue and white, *diwanin hasil*, west wall
h *Gemai, Murshid West*, after T. Higel photo
i *Gemai, south Murshid East*, after T. Higel photo
j *Gemai, Gemai, Said*, lavender, red and white painting in the *diwanin hasil*
k *Gemai, Amka, Amka Alibek*, red, blue and white painting, decorated in 1943, for a wedding, house interior
l *Gemai, Gemai, Diffinog*, red, white and blue painting, interior room
m *Gemai, Gemai, Diffinog*, gold, blue, pink, white painting, *diwan*
n *Degheim West, Degheim N., Kenuz, dehliz* painted in rust colour on a mud ground
o *Degheim West, Degheim N., Kenuz*, interior room, terra-cotta on a white-washed ground
p, q *Faras West, hillet Kamgana*, earth-red, blue, white painting by women for the wedding of the house-owner's daughter in 1963, interior room. The *diwan* house-plan was not followed for this house built in 1938
r, s *Faras West, hillet Kamgana*, paintings in earth-red on mud, interior rooms
t, u *Faras West, hillet Kalsuj*, paintings in red, blue and white in *dehliz* and *mandara* of house with undecorated diwan
v *Faras West, hillet Kalsuj*, paintings in red, blue and white in the *diwan*

The mat-like band of type A was always given a geometric filling of X forms and circles, fitted into squares (Pl. 26). The circles were said to represent basket lids. Only rarely did naturalistic representations intrude inside the band (Pl. 27; Fig. 21u). If this happened, it was usually a sign that the frieze had been painted by men, not women (Pl. 35). The band was surmounted by combinations of scallops, zigzags and vertical palm branches, which might end in a circle or cross (Fig. 21q, r; Fig. 22b, d–f). The palm branches may have indicated that a particular kind of mat was being represented in which palm branches were allowed to extend from the border at regular intervals, making a kind of stiff fringe (Fig. 36b). But such mats were usually reserved for outdoor use, in particular for enclosure fencing. Individual palm branches were put up during the wedding ceremony, and also laid over graves.[15] A characteristic of type A painting was that the band was most enriched along that end of the room where the marriage chests (Fig. 35) were kept, and that the band continued from this wall on to the two adjoining walls, but was given an abrupt conclusion before it reached the end of these walls (Fig. 21 o, p, q, s; Fig. 22a, d, m, p). When mats were unrolled along the walls for decorative purposes they were similarly arranged.

Type B women's painting could have developed from type A. In type B

Plate 26
Gemai West, Murshid West, traditional female's painting. The circles on the frieze represent basket lids. *Photo* T. Higel

Plate 27
Gemai E., Murshid, wall painting derived from the traditional female's art. Naturalistic representations of basket lids (see Pl. 8) suggest that this was painted by a man. *Photo* T. Higel

painting the zigzags surmounting the geometric band of type A (Fig. 22g, h, j–m) became enlarged and ultimately developed into architecture: a repeat pattern of peaked or domed structures surmounted by crescents and flanked by hooks (Fig. 23). This repeat pattern was the distinguishing characteristic of type B painting. The shapes were sometimes said to represent tombs of Muslim saints, with flags at the sides (Fig. 24), but the female artists frequently claimed not to know what it was they were painting; these were the traditional shapes. Furthermore, although a stylistic progression from type A painting to type B could be discerned, the two kinds of painting were made in a completely different way. Type A was made by painting on to the mud wall with a sharpened palm leaf used as a brush, its end hammered flat with a stone. Type B was made by spreading a thick layer of earth colour over the area intended to be worked, marking the patterns on to this surface with a knife, and then scraping away the unwanted colour (Col. pl. 7).

Painting of type B had a curious distribution which seemed to be an intrusion into the area where painting of type A was found. Most women's painting made north of Wadi Halfa, towards the Egyptian border, was of type B. Yet an isolated pocket of type A painting, remarkably like that south of the Second Cataract at Saras, existed on the Egyptian border at Faras West (Fig. 22p–v). The only difference between this and more southern work was that the band with palm branches was sometimes combined with a more elaborate pictorial imagery than was known further south, displaying crocodiles, fish, human beings and lions carrying swords. Type A painting even seemed to have been known in Egypt; the immigrant Kenuzi tribeswomen west of Wadi Halfa made a kind of type A painting (Fig. 22n, o).

Those regions near Wadi Halfa which were least influenced by urban culture produced type B women's painting, while women in the regions most influenced by urban culture made painting which was not like type A or type B. Serra West and Debeira West were regions which had difficult access to Halfa and they were places which had virtually rejected male professional art to the extent that there were only two or three houses in those villages which were decorated in mud relief. Type B women's painting was everywhere, even on the house façades. In the immediate vicinity of Wadi Halfa, such as in South Halfa, Argin and Ashkeit, women's painting was rare and lacked the horizontal band common to both type A and type B painting. It consisted of isolated images of scorpions, plants and birds. All these town-influenced works, which revealed their origin by their fragmentation and their departure from the established pattern observed to both North and South, were painted with a brush and colours bought in the market. This was a technique quite different from that of scraping away earth colours which was used in women's painting of type B. It was closer, in fact, to the technique used in type A, except that a brush had replaced the sharpened palm leaf.

There was some evidence that type B painting was over one hundred years old. A curious variation, in earth tones combined with white-lime blobs

Figure 23
Females' painting type B

a *Debeira East*, ruined house complex near the Nile, interior room, tan and white on darker mud
b *Debeira East, hillet Fakkiriki*, backing for water-pot stand in *diwan*, cement relief, made by the housewife in 1938. Only relief by a woman in the Halfa region
c *Debeira East, hillet Fakkiriki*, red, blue painting on mud in room off the courtyard, made in 1938 for a girl's wedding by the same woman who made 'b'
d *Debeira West, dehliz* painting in rust earth colour
e *Serra West, hillet Sheikh Ouweis el Qurani*, dark coffee earth colour, after Margaret Shinni
f *Serra East, hillet Sinkat, diwan* painted in 1939 for a daughter's marriage, in red, yellow, blue and white
g *Serra East, hillet Sinkat*, painting made beside door of *diwanin hasil* in pink earth colour on brown mud
h *Serra East, hillet Sinkat*, painting made on east courtyard wall, around entrance to the *diwan* area where was 'g'
i *Serra East, Sinkat*, painting on east and south walls of the *diwan* in the same house as 'g' and 'h'
j *Serra East, hillet Abdinirki*, painting by women in the *diwan*, pale sand colour on brown mud
k *Serra East, hillet Abdinirki*, courtyard painting, south wall, painted in earth colour by women in a house where the *diwan* was decorated by Jabir Bab al-Kheir in 1929 (fig. 38a)
l *Serra East, hillet Abdinirki*, interior wall painting in earth colour with white blobs, said to date *c.* 1850
m *Serra East, hillet Abdinirki*, courtyard entrance into interior room, adjoining painting 'k'
n *Serra West, hillet Aksha*, east façade painted in sand tone on mud
o *Serra West, hillet Aksha*, east façade, sand tone on mud
p *Serra West, hillet Aksha*, south wall of courtyard, red-brown sand colour on brown mud, same house as 'r' and 's'
q *Serra West, hillet Aksha, dehliz* painting in light reddish sand on darker mud, on house deserted in 1946 or before
r *Serra West, hillet Aksha, dehliz* painting in blue, red and white in same house as 'p' and 's'
s *Serra West, hillet Aksha, diwan* painting in red, white, orange and grey, same house as 'r' and 'p'
t *Faras East, hillet Siwe*, painting made with the red clay which lies under grey sand; *diwanin hasil* entrance in house where the *diwan* was decorated by Ahmad Batoul. Painted for a marriage
u *Faras East*, east wall, *diwan*, decoration in earth colour for a marriage
v *Faras East*, south end wall of the *diwan* also shown in 'u'
w *Faras East, hillet Siwe*, decoration in earth colour above the water-pot stand in the *diwan*, adjoining painting 't'
x *Faras East*, painting in dark red, blue and white in the *diwan*, decoration for a wedding, made in the house of the bridegroom

(Fig. 23l) appeared in Serra East, *hillet* Abdinirki, in a ruined house of small dimensions thought to date about 1800. It had been the house of the grandfather of one Muhammad Nur Murran, who had himself died in 1937 at the reputed

Figure 24
Serra East, tomb of a holy man

age of 140 years, and everyone knew that the decoration of this house had been made well before the British reconquest of the Sudan in 1898. The technique of scratching away sandy earth colour applied to a mud surface to form the design was the same as that employed recently to make type B painting but, curiously, the peaked forms with flags looked even less like tombs of holy men than more modern examples. One characteristic shared with modern examples was that the flags branched out from the body of the central structure (Fig. 23d, g, i, j, l), rather than being planted in the ground alongside the tomb, as was usually seen in actuality (Fig. 24).

There are problems about the evolution of women's art which can now, after its destruction, never be solved. Throughout Saras and Gemai, type A painting was known to be relatively new, replacing arrangements of baskets and mats. In Saras, Mugufil Island, it was said: 'The women's decoration is not a new thing to women of thirty or forty. They inherited it from their grandmothers. But they remember that there were baskets before. The baskets are still made here, being important for covering *kisra*, but they now stack them up, not putting them on walls.' The same notion was held in Gemai, Amka Sharg: 'Women used to hang up baskets round the room for decoration; they dropped this habit and replaced it with painting. The decorative circles replace the baskets.' Yet type B painting, which seems formally to derive from type A, is older than any, one can remember.

CHAPTER FOUR

Professional Decorators South of Wadi Halfa

From Wadi Halfa south to Kosha those people who made mud relief decoration between the years 1920 and 1940 were house-builders. Between 1940 and
1964 the house-builders still made most decoration, but some was made by the
builders' assistants who were house-smoothers or plasterers, and a certain proportion was made by a new class of artisan, called 'decorators' or professional
artists (see Appendix A). Builders usually made simpler designs than plasterers,
since plasterers specialized in surface finishing which included decoration, and
builders did not. Professional artists made the most elaborate decoration of all.

In the Wadi Halfa district the transition from the builder as house-decorator
to the plasterer had happened at an earlier date and was complete by 1925. By
1940 most plasterers who had been noted as decorators in the 1930s had become
professional artists who were hired to decorate houses without plastering them
first, and at that time some artists had entered the field who did not perform the
job of plastering at all (see Appendix B, nos 6, 10, 14). When decoration became distinct from plastering, the technique of mud relief began to die out and be
replaced by the technique of painting. Most houses in the Wadi Halfa district
decorated after 1950 were decorated with painted designs.

South of Wadi Halfa in 1964, some information was still available about the
payments received by the builder-decorator whose class was nearly extinct to
the north of that town. If a builder decorated a house he had just made he did
not expect payment for his work but only some baksheesh when it was done

Figure 25
a *Kosha, Serkamatto, Deshna,* south entrance by Osman Ahmad Khalil, mud relief, saucers, square piece from an automobile headlight·
b *Kosha, Farka, Sabinsum,* east entrance doorway by Osman Ahmad Khalil in mud relief, painted terra-cotta and white
c *Kosha, Farka, Farkenkonj,* north entrance to men's sitting-room courtyard by Osman Ahmad Khalil around 1960, unpainted
d *Kosha, Farka, Gjinengurka,* west façade of his own house decorated by Ibrahim Osman Ahmad and painted in bright pink, green, gold and white. House built by Osman Kheiri

(Appendix A, nos 6, 7, 9). If a builder was asked to decorate some part of a house which was already complete, he would be offered a set sum (Appendix A, nos 4, 8, 9, 15, 18) or, if the house-owner wished him to replaster the area to be decorated, he would be paid per *diraa* (58 cm) of plastering, at a higher rate than the rate for plastering without decoration (Appendix A, no. 6). One builder-decorator south of Saras (Appendix A, no. 18) complained that decoration rarely brought him enough money to make it financially worth-while. Building was worth much more per *diraa* than plastering or decoration was ever worth, and often took less time. Building south of Wadi Halfa cost up to 17 piastres the *diraa* (there are 100 piastres in the pound). A house with a sizeable ground-plan (Fig. 3f) could bring a builder as much as £100. Plaster-ing with decoration was only 5 to $6\frac{1}{2}$ piastres the *diraa*. Therefore most builders preferred to leave decoration to professional plasterers since they lost money spending time that way.

The job of plasterer was less secure than that of builder; not all houses which were built by a professional were plastered by one. Often the women were still those who added the final layer of smooth mud to the rough surface left by the builder. A plasterer could be assured of work only if he were able to attach himself to a builder who was well established. In this case he was given a set sum for plastering including decoration, or a smaller sum for plastering without (Appendix A, no. 24). Otherwise, if he had not located a builder with whom to work regularly and was in search of patrons, he added decoration to his plastering without being asked to do so and he was paid nothing (Appendix A, nos 20, 21, 25). The decoration was only a kind of advertisement for his plastering work. If the people liked his decoration he might be asked to do more plaster work and, ultimately, he might receive extra payment for the decoration. In the Wadi Halfa district plasterers who had not been paid for decoration in the 1920s were being paid by 1931 (Appendix B, no. 3) but in the Batn al-Hajar there were some who were decorating without pay as recently as 1960 (Appendix A, no. 25).

Those builders south of Wadi Halfa who engaged in decoration were often versatile in a number of crafts of which building and decoration might be but two (Appendix A, nos 3, 4, 5, 8, 15). The patriarch Osman Ahmad Khalil (Fig. 25a–c), who worked in Saras and Kosha between 1924 and 1963, was a builder, decorator, lockmaker and carpenter, and also produced cut-work designs in tin, placed over the door as a kind of grille (Fig. 25c). His son, Ibrahim Osman (Fig. 25d, 26a), was a builder, decorator and carpenter. The form of decoration practised by these two men consisted largely of simple arches moulded in mud over the door, geometrical shapes hollowed deeply into the mud surround of the door (Fig. 25a, b) and gateway entrances with arched tops which had flanking subsidiary arches and projections over the apexes (Fig. 25b, c, d), such as is done even further south along the Nile.[1] They painted their work with flat colours. A builder Hasan Taffoul of Semna who died in 1939 (Appendix A, no. 15) had also been a carpenter, maker of artificial limbs and metal tools, boat-builder and house-decorator. He also knew how to construct water-wheels. His four sons were all builders who made some decoration (Appendix A, nos 15–18), but they avoided carpentry and metal-work.

Northwards from Kosha towards Wadi Halfa the number of operations of the housebuilder decreased; specialists performed those jobs which the builder no longer did. In Saras and Gemai most builders were decorators, but they were not carpenters. Accordingly carpentry, like decoration elsewhere, was left to specialists and became more elaborate. Carved wooden locks of a more modern form and with increased decoration came into use.[2] Yet these highly decorative locks did not have the metal keys found in simpler locks to the south, because

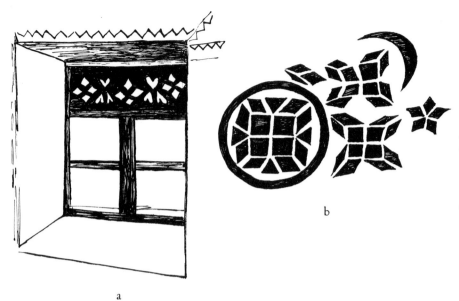

Figure 26
a *Kosha, Serkamatto, Deshna,* window inset of pierced tin by Ibrahim Osman Ahmad in 1964
b *Kosha, Serkamatto, Deshna,* stencil wall painting in green by the carpenter Ali Muhammad Abakr, 1960, men's sitting room, interior wall

carpenters were now so specialised that they did not work in metal as they had done further to the south (Appendix A, no. 12). Wooden keys were substituted which had nails for prongs.

Mud relief made by builders also became more complex as they practised fewer other crafts. Abdoun Muhammad Fadl (Appendix A, no. 7) and Mahmud Itnan (Appendix A, no. 9) of Saras, both active from the late thirties to the late fifties, worked out a geometric style which changed little over the years but which had greater surface elaboration than was common further south (Fig. 27; Fig. 28a, b). Their geometric style emphasised vertically repeated forms. As many as three domes were placed one above the other over the door, separated by bands of zigzags (Fig. 28a). At each side of the door were inscribed columns, marked vertically by X forms separated by zigzags or double lines (Fig. 28a, b), the same designs as were used locally for decorating locks (Fig. 8c, d). The whole composition was painted with vivid gold or sienna earth colour and inset with saucers and automobile headlights. There was very little figural decoration, but these two builders made nearly identical lions (Fig. 27a, b; Fig. 28a) and Abdoun created a crocodile which resembled the lion in that both had hatched coats, club-like legs and zigzag toes (Fig. 27b). The Saras style was borrowed by other builder-decorators who came to work in that region, such as Osman Ahmad Khalil (Fig. 28c), or by some who left the region to help in the massive rebuilding performed round Wadi Halfa after the destruction caused by the 1946 Nile flood (Fig. 28d, e).

78

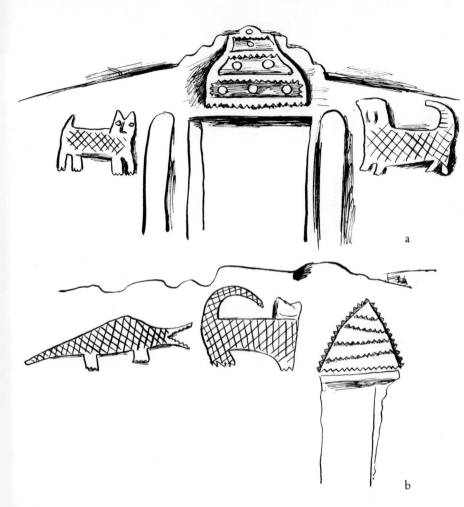

Figure 27
a *Saras, Saras-Tahali,*
  Kada, relief made by
  Mahmud Muhammad
  Osman Itnan in 1948,
  uncoloured mud, south
  entrance
b *Gemai, Gemai, Artinassi*
  Island, hillet Jaddi-gur,
  east façade by Abdoun
  Muhammad Fadl, 1954

   Although most builders south of Wadi Halfa only decorated houses which
they built, there were four who not only fulfilled numerous commissions just of
decoration but also developed original styles. All of them had connections with
Wadi Halfa. Sayyid Ahmad Hogla (Appendix A, no. 3) built and decorated
in South Halfa from 1930 to 1946, where his work was prominent along the
main road (Pl. 28). His decoration closely resembled that to the North, which
he claimed he had not seen, and he may be credited with the invention of a
string-course border, like a decorated cornice, running just under the roof (Pl.
28). He also worked part-time as a labourer on archaeological excavations, and
he may have noticed this detail on archaeological remains.[3] Sayyid Ahmad
did not ascribe much importance to house decoration, and he performed it
only until he could begin bricklaying in the town of Halfa itself. Dawud

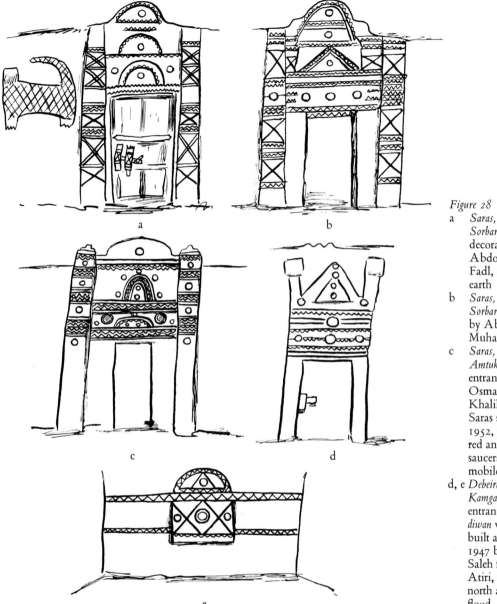

Figure 28

a   *Saras, Saras-Tahali, Sorbar*, south façade decoration by Abdoun Muhammad Fadl, coloured in red earth

b   *Saras, Saras-Tahali, Sorbar*, south entrance by Abdoun Muhammad Fadl

c   *Saras, Saras-Tahali, Amtukke*, west entrance decorated by Osman Ahmad Khalil from Farka, in Saras style, made 1952, painted earth-red and inset with saucers and automobile headlights

d, e *Debeira, Hassa, Kamgana*, south entrance and south *diwan* wall of a house built and decorated in 1947 by Muhammad Saleh from Saras, Atiri, who came north after the 1946 flood

Osman (Appendix A, no. 8) and Muhammad Suleiman (Appendix A, no. 14) were Second Cataract builders who journeyed north of Wadi Halfa during the decoration vogue of the early 1940s, turning to work of that sort. Muhammad Suleiman continued to build around Faras but Dawud Osman did no

building in the Halfa region. When working north of Halfa, Dawud was influenced by local designs (Pl. 71; Fig. 43c, e). Muhammad Suleiman, although less technically accomplished, remained more inventive (Pl. 84). They both returned to the Second Cataract in the late forties and fifties when decoration round Wadi Halfa ceased. The fourth builder was Saleh Hasan Taffoul (Appendix A, no. 18) who learned decoration from his three builder brothers (Appendix A, nos 15, 16, 17) and worked with them around Wadi Halfa before returning to his native Saras, Semna.[4] He took special orders to make *manwara* cupboards dug into the wall, with lacy relief surrounds (Fig. 29).[5] Doorway decorations were little fancied in Duweishat and Kosha where he practised.

In addition to builders engaged in decoration there were in Saras and Gemai some unique professional decorators who performed painting in direct imitation of women's art. Very little is known about them because most houses where they had worked were vacated before they could be examined in the autumn of

Plate 28
South Wadi Halfa, entrance facing south decorated in mud relief by Sayyid Ahmad Hogla, builder, *c.* 1935. *Photo* J. Shiner

Figure 29
Cupboards (*manwara*) by
Saleh Hasan Taffoul of
Saras, Semna

a *Kosha, Dal, Farket Island*, 1958, incised mud coated with white lime
b *Kosha, Serkamatto, Araser*, 1961, white lime with blue outlines, made in the house of the Sheikh of Serkamatto, Abdelrahim Abddai
c *Kosha, Dal, Dambo*, 1959, incised mud coated with white lime and painted pink, blue, orange and green

1964. However, because some of the paintings were signed, it was clear that the authors were men.[6] There was some slight evidence that professional artists and painters, not builders or workers in relief, existed south of Wadi Halfa. In Saras, Saras-Tahali, *hillet* Mugufil, a house was described as belonging to Muhammad Beshir, artist. A door on a house in a near-by *hillet*, Amtukke, made in 1954 by the carpenter Abdulla Ahmad Dijab, was painted by another individual who was a professional painter and who was paid separately. The wall decoration of only one painter of this kind was discovered in an area still under occupation. In Saras, Saras-Tahali, *hillet* Agremasho, two houses had the entrance chamber or *dehliz* painted by Osman Suleiman Saleh (Appendix

Figure 30
Saras, Saras-Tahali,
Agremasho, 1942, white
lime on mud, *dehliz*
paintings made by Osman
Suleiman Saleh for a
wedding

A, no. 13) for a wedding (Fig. 30). The painting, in white lime on mud, consisted of a band filled with geometric designs and a number of sitting ducks, facing right. Above the band were more sitting ducks, palm trees and crescents over peaks. The women's painting in this area was also composed of a horizontal band of geometric forms (Fig. 21u, v), surmounted by naturalistic images, like palm trees, crescents and flowers. But there were never any ducks painted by women, nor did the figural forms, except in one case (Fig. 21u), intrude upon the geometric band. Space division within the band was different. The women were concerned to preserve the traditional division into rectangles, while the male decorator introduced arches and areas divided by slanted crosshatching. Osman Suleiman Saleh also made some mud relief decoration, in the style of Abdoun Muhammad Fadl, builder. But he was described as a professional artist, not a builder or plasterer.

The greatest number of male professionals who imitated women's painting appear to have been in Gemai, Murshid, an area largely vacated by the time it

Plate 29
Gemai E., Murshid,
painting by Muhammad
Hamid Hassin. *Photo*
T. Higel

was examined. It is just possible that these artists were family members, bride-grooms perhaps, whose paintings occasionally copied that of women. One of the most accomplished painters signed his work, 'Muhammad Hamid Hassin' and the owner of the house was identified by inscription as Hassin. The artist could have been Hassin's grandson, as it is usual to call men by the name of their father and grandfather, with a first name which is new to them. This artist painted only naturalistic animals, palm trees, flowers and flags (Pl. 29) and omitted the geometrical band which was common to all those who signed themselves as artists: (Appendix A, nos 27–30)

'The artist Nasr ad-Din' (Pl. 36);
'the artist Shedad' (Pl. 36);
'the artist Ahmad Karafti' (Pls 31, 32);
'the artist Melik Muhammad Hasan' (Pls 33–35).

It may be that in Murshid sheikship, boys and young men who were family members produced informal painting or chalk graffiti, while artists who were

hired to do paintings adhered to the formalised geometrical band of the women, surmounted by representations of animals and objects.

One of the houses in Gemai, Murshid, Adurma, had a painting of flowers and a naturalistic gazelle pursued by a large lion. Here there was someone still living near by who told us that the painting was by one Ahmad Hasan Muhammad Khalil, called 'Tablet', who worked in the Ministry of Informa-tion and Labour in Khartoum, in the section for photography. He was thus

not a professional artist, but did the lion painting for the wedding of a relative. There was no decorative band underneath the figures. Another house with similar work, showing a crocodile and gazelle (Pl. 30) was painted in 1961 by a Muhammad Isa, who was also a relative of the house-owner and who avoided the use of a decorative band.

Of the four artists known by name, Ahmad Karafti and Melik Muhammad had individual styles which could be observed in a number of houses. Both of them painted crocodiles whose legs were shown extending both sides of the body (Pls 31–35), so that they looked as if they had been stuffed and attached to the wall, as in fact happened in some parts (Fig. 10a). Yet the crocodiles of the one were immediately distinguishable from crocodiles of the other, because they demonstrated different formulae for the toes, teeth and tails. The toes of Ahmad Karafti's crocodiles were outlined individually and attached to a circle at the foot, resembling petals attached to the centre of a flower, while the crocodiles' mouths were held open with two rows of separately marked teeth (Pl. 31). The tail curved upwards. The toes of Melik Muhammad's crocodiles were painted on the main portion of the foot, with no separating line (Pls 33–

Plate 32
Gemai E., Murshid, west entrance by Muhammad Suleiman 1942, with females' painting in mud made as a repair over the worn lower part of the wall, and painting by Ahmad Karafti visible in the interior. *Photo* T. Higel

Plate 33
Gemai E., Murshid, crocodile
by Melik Muhammad
Hasan. *Photo* T. Higel

Plate 34
Gemai E., Murshid, painting
by Melik Muhammad
Hassan. *Photo* T. Higel

35). The crocodiles' teeth were visible at the sides of their mouths, but not at the tips, which were held shut as if the creature were caught while snarling. The tails were held relatively straight with the body line, but nipped in slightly at the point of separation from the body, like the tail of a beaver. They were divided into segments and marked with circles or dots on each part. Ahmad Karafti painted other creatures as well, notably fish (Pl. 31) and birds, and fitted

87

Plate 35
Gemai E., Murshid, painting by Melik Muhammad Hasan, showing crocodiles, birds, basket lids and flags. *Photo* T. Higel

birds and flowers into the geometrical band, as did his colleague Osman Suleiman Saleh in Saras. As well as signing his work he inserted admiring comments, such as, 'Lovely crocodile, beautiful fish.'

Melik Muhammad preferred painting objects to animals and represented baskets, flags or fly-whisks (Pl. 35), and yellow circles which may have been ivory bracelets (Col. pl. 8). Curiously the fly-whisk flags were shown attached to the ends of crescents (Pl. 34). When this was done at one side only the result looked like a bird with a neck and head and, indeed, he also painted birds with curved, crescent-like bodies close to the same formula. The artists Shedad and Nasir ad-Din both signed one painting (Pl. 36), which was not very distinguished except for a frond-like plant in a pot. This plant was repeated in another painting bearing the name of Shedad, where pictures of basket lids intruded on the stylised band in the same formula employed by Melik Muhammad. Many more paintings, in a wide range of colour, appeared in the same village but they were so similar that it was not possible to determine who the painter was, or whether it was a man or a woman. The crescent-like bird and fly-whisk flags were frequently repeated (Pl. 37) and seem to have been a village formula rather than inventions of Melik Muhammad.

Plate 36
Gemai E., Murshid, painting signed by the artists Nasir ad-Din and Shedad. *Photo* T. Higel

It was unusual to find professional painting which so closely imitated women's art; this occurred only in Saras and Gemai. The phenomenon may be explained by a social habit of those parts described as follows: 'When a girl is married, she can decorate her house alone, or if she has money, she can bring someone special to do it' (at Gemai, Amka, *hillet* Amka Alibek).

This would seem to imply that in Gemai women were given greater freedom to hire and pay male artists on their own initiative than they were to the north and south of Gemai, where artists were hired and paid by men. The women might accordingly have selected artists who would have agreed to paint as they them-selves would have done. These artists could have been either professional painters who did only this sort of work or builders who counted this kind of

Plate 37
Gemai E., Murshid, anonymous wall painting where bird, crescent and fan motifs are made to resemble one another. *Photo* T. Higel

painting as one of their many skills. It is interesting to note that both Dawud Osman and Muhammad Suleiman, when working in their native territory of Gemai, produced painting closer to women's style than they did when working outside (Fig. 44a, b, d, f, h; Col. pl. 19).

CHAPTER FIVE

Professional Decorators North of Wadi Halfa

The areas with the largest amount of professional decoration, namely, Gemai, Ashkeit, Debeira East and Argin, all not far from Wadi Halfa, were regions which had unusually good transport facilities and could thus keep in easy contact with each other. Gemai, Ashkeit and Debeira were on the east bank of the Nile where regular *suq* lorries carried villagers to and from Wadi Halfa and its neighbouring east bank *omodiyas*. Argin, on the west bank, enjoyed daily bus service to a point opposite the Halfa town centre, where a car ferry took people across. Debeira West and Serra West, north of Argin, were less fortu-nate and outside any mainstream of cultural contact with other parts. The west bank of the Nile is a great depository for Saharan sand blown by the northerly winds. It was difficult to keep roads clear or to prevent motor vehicles from sinking into the sand. Beyond the range of the West Halfa-Argin bus, communication between the east and west banks had to be made by means of Nile sailing-boats. In this region deprived of communication there was almost no professional decoration. Yet Faras West was connected to the east bank by a regular ferry arrangement and thus had greater opportunities for communica-tion and exchange of ideas with east bank inhabitants than did Serra West and Debeira West, to its south. Correspondingly, Faras West had more decoration, but not so much as Gemai, Ashkeit and Debeira on the east bank, on the same side as Wadi Halfa's town centre, or as Argin. The Wadi Halfa town centre lacked mud relief decoration. The houses were mainly of brick and imitated Western European architecture.

The complicated mud relief which was typical of the Halfa region was started in the 1920s by men who were house-smoothers. Even so there is evidence that the earliest relief decoration made north of Wadi Halfa was produced by the house-owner or house-builder, as until recently was also the case further south. There was an old tradition that the walls of houses should be marked with small wild animals in relief. Usually the animals mentioned were crocodiles. However, a Nubian driver for the Wadi Halfa Resettlement Commission, between sixty and seventy years old, remembered his grandparent's house so decorated when he was a child, but with a much wider assortment of creatures. These were crocodiles, hyenas, foxes, pigeons, fishes, scorpions, snakes and any kind of animal with horns. Little of this could recently be seen. In Faras West there was a small animal over an interior doorway which might have been a hyena (Fig. 31c) while small mud crocodiles, stylised as a double cross as if seen from above (Fig. 31a, b) occurred sporadically south of the Second Cataract.[1] Scorpions in mud were reported to have been made years ago in Debeira West.[2] Although the Debeira scorpions were said to have been made by women, in most cases these relief figures of animals were added by the house-owner, and more recently on request by the plasterer and the builder. It was interesting that there was no mention of lions, since lions became extremely important in relief which was made later on.

Apart from hints that houses before 1920 were decorated with animals in relief, there was little memory of other decorations made at that date, except for saucer designs and the so-called 'women's art', which was not relief. The information we obtained was largely limited to Debeira, on the Nile east bank:

'The oldest houses, those of the forefathers, were not necessarily decorated with plates. There was no plastered decoration, or professional plasterer, either; the owner did it. At first it was plastered by hand, later they started using the *muhara* [trowel].'

'He remembers the old houses were very small and not decorated. However, they were decorated with plates.'

'Men of fifty to sixty remember that when they were born, the plates were there, but fewer.'

'He had no decoration in his house; he did not like it. But in 1913–14 his lady ordered the plates to be put up, and he found on his return (from Egypt) that all the saucers to the teacups were absent.'

'The oldest houses they remember were less decorated. They were smaller, not so high-walled as the new ones. They were built stronger, but poorly

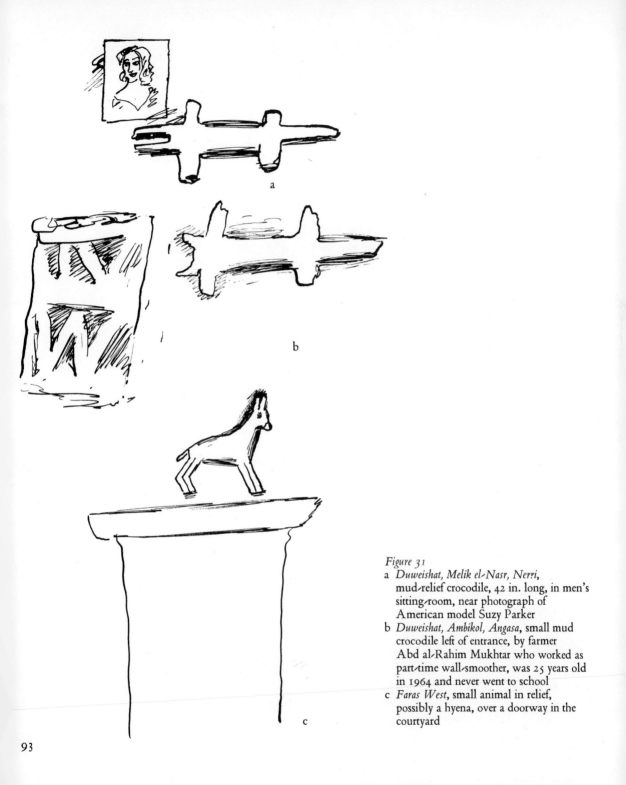

Figure 31

a *Duweishat, Melik el-Nasr, Nerri*,
  mud-relief crocodile, 42 in. long, in men's
  sitting-room, near photograph of
  American model Suzy Parker

b *Duweishat, Ambikol, Angasa*, small mud
  crocodile left of entrance, by farmer
  Abd al-Rahim Mukhtar who worked as
  part-time wall-smoother, was 25 years old
  in 1964 and never went to school

c *Faras West*, small animal in relief,
  possibly a hyena, over a doorway in the
  courtyard

decorated. The owner's father, Husain Haikal, remembers that in 1914 his house was decorated with plates and only a little relief.'

'At first they had no white painting [relief work cut into white lime?]. The builder put the plates out all alone.'

'Decorations started in 1896 when there was a kind of specialisation or division of the building work; a builder, somebody to smooth the wall, and other work. (About the same time) china plates used by women appeared. Before plates, women used shells, big shells which have different shapes. Plates appeared with Europeans, after they conquered the area. Before that, people used plates of red earth, which they put above the walls, not on the wall. They put many other things on the wall, like wooden plates. And when a woman gave birth to a boy, they put the sign of the cross on the wall above his head, and a flag on top of the house. All these decorations were meant to divert the attention of the visitor to the house.'

(This information was reported at a meeting with the *omda* Salhin of Debeira and local notables.) Additional information was obtained in Ashkeit and Argin:

'Before men started making paintings and relief, the women used to put up shells and dishes of woven palm leaves and wood, and sometimes they used to draw figures [with or on?] the shells. This kind of thing was only done by women, and was not the independent masculine profession it became later on' (from Ashkeit).

'The lockmaker Ahmad Suleiman, fifty-five to fifty-seven years old, got lockmaking from his father and grandfather. But his father's earliest lock types were plain, not decorated as they are now. The door was very rough wood then, and small, and the house entrances were not decorated. Later they wanted to decorate the locks to go with the nice decoration' (from Argin).

'Before Ahmad Batoul, a plasterer called Gowhar made a little decoration to help the ladies. The house was decorated with women's art only, at the time the housewife came to Nubia from Egypt in 1924. Ahmad Batoul was called to plaster and decorate in 1934, and Hasan Arabi in 1945' (from Argin).

The art of relief decoration north of Wadi Halfa may be said to begin with Ahmad Batoul (Appendix B, no. 3). His work typifies all decoration made in the 1920s and 1930s (Figs 32, 33), although there were other decorators practising at the time. These others copied and elaborated his designs. The most original of them were undoubtedly Jabir Bab al-Kheir (Appendix B, no. 4) and his student, Hasan Arabi (Appendix B, no. 6), who superseded both Batoul and Jabir and who introduced new inventions which extended the technique. These principal artists and their schools will be considered in chronological order.

Ahmad Batoul was said to be born in 1912, and he died in 1955. His birthplace was north of Ballana in Egyptian Nubia. Some time before his tenth birthday the family moved to Argin in the Sudan, where his brother Abdu was born in 1922. If we regard the date of his birth, supplied by his brother, as being correct, it means that he began to decorate when he was fifteen years old, since the earliest decoration found to be by him was clearly dated to 1927 (Fig. 32a–f). By 1950, when he would have been thirty-eight years old, he was already superseded in the field and no longer worked. The date of his birth may not be correct, because he was said by some to have been in his fifties when he died, and older than ten when he came to Argin.

Ahmad Batoul learned all he knew about plastering in the Sudan. He presumably learned from the builder Saleh Mirghani, who was thought to be a Dongolawi (man from Dongola), and who employed Batoul at an early age. The plastering job was essentially that of working with mud. The mud mixture used was composed of Nile silt, donkey dung and sand. The donkey dung was thought to make the surface strong and waterproof. In Nubia dung was used in a smaller proportion to the sand mixed with it than in the central Sudan, where rain occurred, and people went to greater pains to make house walls waterproof. The initial mixture of silt, dung, water and sand was allowed to settle for a few days until the sediment reached a desirable consistency, when the water was poured off and it was ready to spread over the unfinished walls. Before the 1920s only one layer was applied into which plates were set, but later on a second layer came to be added to certain parts of the wall into which decoration could be cut and plates inset. A small amount of adhesive was applied to hold them in place, as described in Ashkeit:

'The women asked the plasterer to decorate, and to place the plates. He charges extra for putting up the plates, and uses a small amount of cement for fixing them into the mud. When there is no cement, he will use mud.'

'The plasterer fixes the plates into the wall with a smooth, yellow or creamy-coloured sand, brought down when the rain runs in torrents in the desert. These torrents come down every few years. The boys go out and collect the mud, which is easy to mould, sticky and good for fixing.'[3]

By the time Ahmad Batoul started to work it had become the job of the plasterer, rather than the builder, to set dinner-plates or saucers into the mud walls, when requested to do so by women. The first innovation made by

Ahmad Batoul was that he not only fixed the plates but offered to make some special mud relief decoration around them, thus saving the women the necessity of decorating in paint. It is generally agreed that Ahmad Batoul's relief replaced women's painting in those areas of Argin, Debeira East and Ashkeit where he worked, and that it was the earliest relief decoration to be done:

'Ahmad Batoul was the first to do decoration in the area, and all the others succeeded him. The decoration before was made by women, and it was just smoothing (plastering). Ahmad Batoul came from Upper Egypt, Ballana, and started this work. Women used to paint by colours which they brought from the mountains. When Ahmad Batoul came from Ballana and started this work, some people laughed at him and criticised him, because this is the work of women' (from Argin).

'Ahmad Batoul made the decoration. At that time (1927) he was very young. He is the first man to begin the decoration. He was living both at Argin and Debeira East, and had two wives, one at each place. Most of his earliest work is at Argin' (from Debeira East).

'Before Ahmad Batoul, houses used to be decorated by women. The person who used to smooth the wall would also draw a small crocodile on the door against the evil eye. Also horns used to be put on top of the door, [sometimes] made out of mud' (from Debeira East).

It may be observed that most women's painting visible in 1964 was performed inside the house, usually in rooms where the wedding ritual took place, and that there was little to be seen on the façades. Thus the insistence that Ahmad Batoul's relief designs replaced women's decoration may seem curious, for although there were many reliefs by him in the men's marriage-room, or *diwan* (Fig. 32c, l, m; Fig. 33b, e), his major endeavours were applied to the outside of the houses (Fig. 32a, g, k, q, r; Fig. 33a, d, f–j). Yet in the regions of Debeira West and Serra West, where professional relief decoration had never gained ascendancy over women's art, the women not only put plates over the outer doorways but also painted the door surrounds in earth colours, in a variant form of women's painting type B (Fig. 23n, o). It is very likely that some such habit also obtained in Serra East, Debeira East, Ashkheit and Argin, and was replaced by relief designs of the sort made by Batoul which at first, in 1927 and 1928, featured a central peak or dome flanked by verticals or hook forms (Fig. 32a, g), which is a marked characteristic of women's painting type B (Fig. 23).

A chronology of Batoul's style shows that his earliest work not only demon-strated a borrowing of the motifs used by women but also a definite interaction

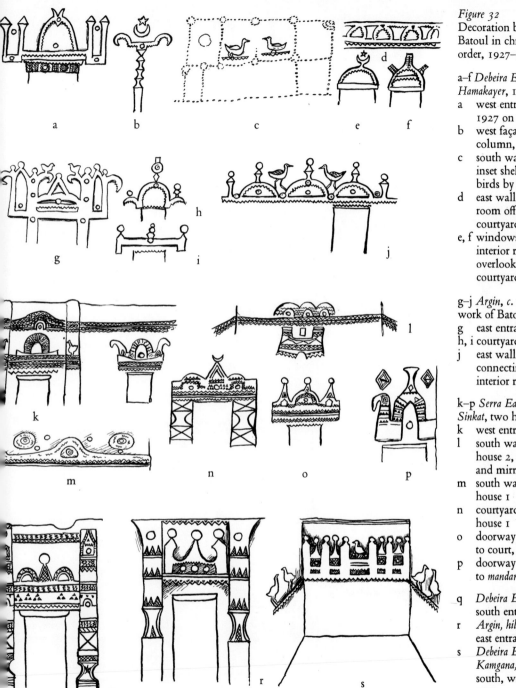

Figure 32
Decoration by Ahmad Batoul in chronological order, 1927–35

a–f *Debeira East, hillet Hamakayer,* 1927

a   west entrance, date 1927 on carved lintel
b   west façade, inscribed column, crescent, star
c   south wall, *diwan,* inset shells by women, birds by Batoul
d   east wall, interior room off main courtyard, frieze
e, f windows from the interior room 'd', overlooking the courtyard

g–j *Argin, c.* 1927, earliest work of Batoul in Argin

g   east entrance
h, i courtyard doorways
j   east wall and doorway connecting two interior rooms

k–p *Serra East, hillet Sinkat,* two houses *c.* 1928

k   west entrance, house 1
l   south wall, *diwan,* house 2, inset saucers and mirror
m   south wall, *diwan,* house 1
n   courtyard doorway, house 1
o   doorway from *dehliz* to court, house 2
p   doorway from *dehliz* to *mandara,* house 2

q   *Debeira East, Hassa,* south entrance, 1930
r   *Argin, hillet Torad,* east entrance, 1934–5
s   *Debeira East, Hassa, Kamgana, diwan* east, south, west walls, 1933

97

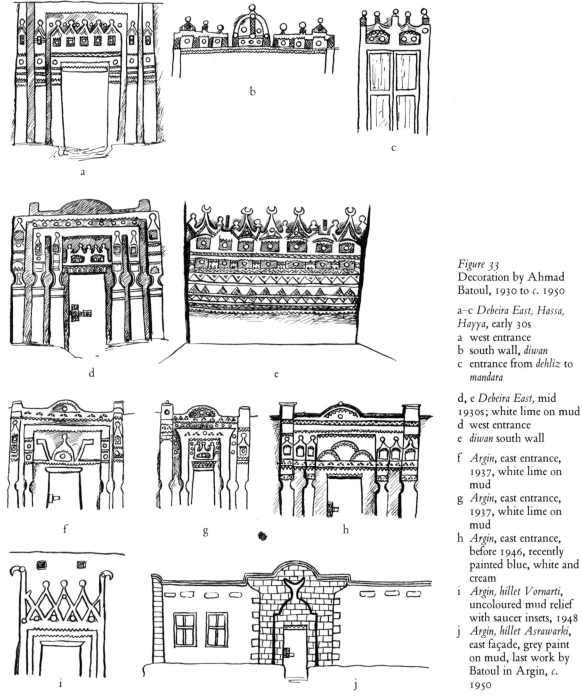

Figure 33
Decoration by Ahmad
Batoul, 1930 to *c.* 1950

a–c *Debeira East, Hassa,
Hayya,* early 30s
a west entrance
b south wall, *diwan*
c entrance from *dehliz* to
   mandara

d, e *Debeira East,* mid
1930s; white lime on mud
d west entrance
e *diwan* south wall

f *Argin,* east entrance,
   1937, white lime on
   mud
g *Argin,* east entrance,
   1937, white lime on
   mud
h *Argin,* east entrance,
   before 1946, recently
   painted blue, white and
   cream
i *Argin, hillet Vornarti,*
   uncoloured mud relief
   with saucer insets, 1948
j *Argin, hillet Asrawarki,*
   east façade, grey paint
   on mud, last work by
   Batoul in Argin, *c.*
   1950

between the women's and plasterer's art. The relief made in 1927, which is the earliest known, was on a house in Debeira; *hillet* Hamakayer, which was built and decorated in 1927 and had the date carved on a door lintel (Fig. 32a). The work was very crude, in plain mud with no white lime surface to the design. It lacked finesse, and seemed to be the effort of a beginner. One of the arches surmounting the doorways had an attached crescent at the top mounted on a pole (Fig. 32e). This feature could definitely have been borrowed from women's painting type B (Fig. 23g, t, v). Another tympanum designed by Batoul was given verticals each side (Fig. 32a), which differed from the women's painting (Fig. 23 o) only in that there were two verticals instead of one. These verticals did not extend to the ground either side of the door, and in no way could be seen as the inscribed columns flanking the doorway which they later became in Batoul's reliefs designed during the 1930s (Fig. 33d, f). An interior room had been marked with a horizontal decorative band of repeated domes (Fig. 32d), which is the main characteristic of women's painting type B. However, instead of rising above the band as in women's painting, the domes were superimposed upon it, showing the creation of new designs by superimposing old forms one on top of the other which was always a characteristic of Batoul's work. Some women's art existed in this house and took the form of a frieze of small Nile shells made in the *diwan* (Fig. 32c). In the centre of this frieze there was introduced a pair of birds made in mud relief standing on zigzag ground lines, which became a keynote of Batoul's later style (Fig. 32k, s). The frieze must have been composed by women working together with Batoul, because both techniques, the relief and the shell pattern, needed to be made when the wall was still wet.

In the 1920s Ahmad Batoul was not paid for his relief decoration, which he performed as a service to the housewife. Yet by 1931 he was receiving extra payment for relief, over and above what he was paid for plastering the house (Appendix B, no. 3). At the same time Batoul's style rapidly changed. By the 1930s he had developed a series of decorative formulas, largely based upon the multiplication of arches and peaks attached to a horizontal base line. Their derivation from women's painting type B was disguised. Whereas in 1928 Batoul had retained the simple arches used by women, elaborating them only by covering the surface with numerous zigzag bands (Fig. 32k–n), in the 1930s he changed the shape of the arch altogether. In place of the round arch, he substituted an elegant series of peaks between poles surmounted by knobs (Pl. 38; Fig. 32s; Fig. 33c–e). The round arch was retained for the inside of the peak (Fig. 33c, g). Rows of such peaks were used over one doorway (Pl. 38; Fig. 33a) whereas previously one peak would have been enough (Fig. 32g). They also served as a patterned band in the *diwan* (Fig. 33e) where the white lime

surfacing made them stand out as a lacy silhouette. This would have been visible even to one who had just stepped out of glaring sunlight in the courtyard and looked at the most dimly lit wall of the *diwan*.

Batoul's use of the inscribed column showed marked development in the early 1930s. In the Debeira house of 1927 there were two kinds of inscribed columns; those which were simple verticals to either side of the entrance arch (Fig. 32a), and another, which was a single inscribed column on the outside wall not far from this door (Fig. 32b). This column was extremely curious. Its form, never again used by Batoul, consisted of stacked-up, concave units terminating in two hooks above which were a crescent and a star. It was oddly reminiscent of a certain kind of monument found in the southern Nilotic regions of the Sudan, the funeral markers or 'tally posts' of the Bongo tribe, where each unit signified an animal killed and therefore represented an additional virtue to the credit of the deceased.[4] The Bongo tally posts were often surmounted by animal horns. Wherever Batoul may have acquired this motif, he did not retain it for long although hints of it appear in his later work. In the 1930s his exterior doorways were flanked by as many as three inscribed columns

Plate 38
Ashkeit, west entrance by Ahmad Batoul, early 1930s. Features typical of Batoul are the multiple peaks over the entrance and the three inscribed columns to each side

on each side, sometimes joined at the top to form a kind of box enclosure for the door (Pl. 38; Fig. 33a, d, f–h). The side columns had peaks of the same sort as over the door, superimposed upon them and giving a kind of false window or lantern effect (Pls 38, 39). Underneath these 'windows', each column was given one concavity, like a nipped-in waistline (Fig. 33d, f–h). This peculiar detail could be seen to derive from the single column of his 1927 work, only the three concavities had been reduced to one. In Batoul's very late decoration in Ashkeit he used two concavities per column instead of one (Pl. 40).

In 1928 Batoul introduced the incising of a mud surface to look like imitation brick or stone (Pl. 41). This was never an important element of his art although he returned to it in his final work (Fig. 33j). However, it was always popular with his followers who found it easy to do and in the late 1940s and 1950s younger artists decorated façades with imitation stonework, to the exclusion of all other design. A cook employed in Wadi Halfa, called Mekki, made a number of uninspired doorways in Argin of this kind. The design was particularly popular for doorway surrounds which were painted rather than made in relief. The Saras builder, Kasbana Hasan Taffoul, picked up the idea when

Plate 39
Ashkeit, west façade by Ahmad Batoul *c.* 1930. The decoration incorporates an unusually large number of saucers, of which some are orange and turquoise lustre

he worked in Halfa itself in 1955 and carried it back to *hillet* Bishangi in Saras, Semna, where he used it to decorate his own house with painted doorway surrounds in black, red, yellow and green (Pl. 42).

Throughout the 1930s, the complexity of a relief pattern depended to some extent on how much the artist was paid, and on the degree to which he wished to please his employer, but principally on the number of saucers which the householder provided to set into the design. The design was essentially a surround for a display of saucers, used in greatest numbers in the mid thirties when from twenty to forty saucers would appear on a single façade (Pl. 39). By the late 1930s, artists had developed a different kind of complication in design which was made by adding pattern elements rather than by multiplying the number of saucers. Certain methods of surface elaboration which were used to build up a complex design unit were invented by Batoul and, again, copied by minor artists who imitated him.

From 1928 onwards, Batoul used a triangular punch to remove the interior portions of a zigzag edging (Fig. 33f–h). This triangular punch could also be used to enliven a plain surface by scattering triangles over it, punched out in groups of three (Pls 41, 43). The taste for groups of hollowed-out triangles used as surface elaboration may have derived from a kind of brick openwork patterning to be seen on walls throughout Nubia, both in Egypt and the

Plate 40
Ashkeit, west façade by Ahmad Batoul made shortly after the 1946 flood. It is unique in having two concavities on each column flanking the door, instead of one, as was usual. Sitting-room windows were blocked up in winter and unblocked during the summer heat

Plate 41
Ashkeit, façade entrance by
Ahmad Batoul, 1928,
white-lime relief on mud.
This is the earliest known
example of imitation
stone-work, punched-out
triangles and surface
hatching used on mud
relief. *Photo* J. Shiner

Plate 42
Saras, Semna, Bishangi,
the decorator Kasbana
Hasan Taffoul by the
door of his own house,
decorated with imitation
brickwork in 1955

Sudan (Fig. 25a, d). The patterns, made by leaning sun-dried bricks one against the other to form a row of peaks on top of which a flat layer of brick was laid, were used along the tops of walls and to fill in windows (Fig. 31b). The hollow triangles as employed by Ahmad Batoul in relief designs were copied by three minor artists working in Batoulian style: Khamis from the South (Appendix B, no. 5), Babikr al-Mansuri (Appendix B, no. 9), and Abd al-Aziz al-Amin from Sukkot (Kosha) who died young (Appendix B, no. 13).

Plate 45
Debeira E., hillet Hayya,
interior doorway to
diwan decorated by
Khamis from the south in
1934, using a triangular
punch to cut the designs

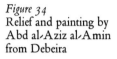

Figure 34
Relief and painting by
Abd al-Aziz al-Amin
from Debeira

a, b *Debeira East, hillet Fadros*
a   exterior west entrance, mud relief
b   *diwan*, south wall, upper forms in relief with coloured bands painted along the top; images below painted in red and blue

c–e *Ashkeit*
c   west entrance, painting in colours, ochre, terra-cotta, blue, on lime-white ground; no relief except band at the top
d, e doorways in central courtyard, relief painted in ochre, terra-cotta, blue

f, g, h *Debeira West, hillet Nag el-Kenuz*
f   courtyard, relief decoration behind a water stand, uncoloured
g   interior room, painting in terra-cotta, earth-green, no relief
h   *dehliz*, lower design: relief; upper design with flags; painting in terra-cotta, earth-green

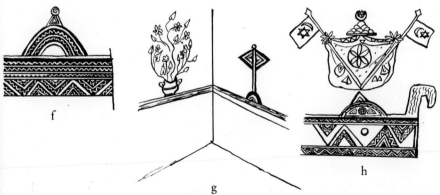

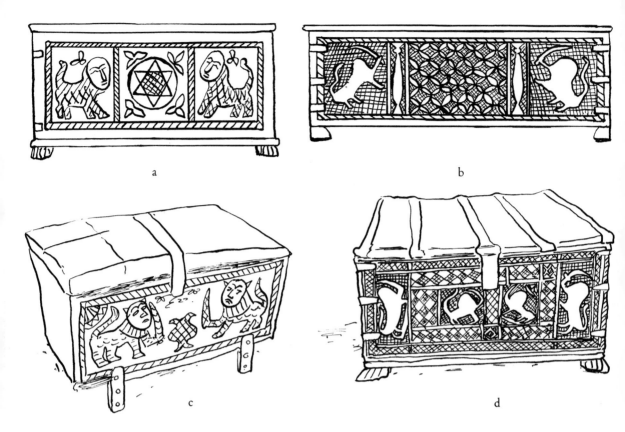

a

b

c

d

Khamis alone placed the triangles in varying arrangements of numbers (Pl. 45), while Abd al-Aziz al-Amin and Babikr al-Mansuri slavishly followed Batoul's patterning of triangles in groups of threes. Of these artists, Abd al-Aziz al-Amin was the most original because he added freestyle painting to the relief, featuring his personal insignia, a double flag (Fig. 34b). He also invented certain semi-anthropomorphic shapes which he used to vary the pattern of the relief (Fig. 34a, b).

Between 1928 and 1935 Batoul began to fill in the surface of his relief designs with areas of lightly scratched lines, forming cross-hatching (Fig. 33b, e) and at the same time he introduced lions carrying swords (Pls 46–48). Both these motifs may have been borrowed from Egyptian marriage chests, imported in numbers during the earlier part of this century and highly prized (Fig. 35). The chests displaying lions with swords were thought to come from Alexandria; the lions were either given a hatched coat or were shown without features on a ground surface of cross-hatching. The earliest lion said to have been made by Batoul was in Debeira, Hassa, Kamgana, in 1933 (Pl. 46). It lacked ears,

Figure 35
Egyptian chests decorated with lions, some human-faced, some carrying swords

a *Debeira East*, chest belonging to great-grandfather of house owner
b *Ashkeit*
c *Kosha, Farka*, chest in old house dating 1912
d *Akasha, Ukma*

and was much cruder than his later examples. It is possible that it was not intended to represent a lion but Antar, an Arab hero depicted as a lion with the head of a man. This identification was made by some of the inhabitants of neighbouring houses in Debeira. The human-headed lions often seen on wooden chests from Egypt lacked identifying inscriptions.

Lions made by Ahmad Batoul in the later 1930s were given not only ears, but also eyes made from broken pieces of red glass or plastic bracelet, and teeth from bits of porcelain (Pl. 48). Ahmad Batoul's rival, Jabir Bab al-Kheir, when discussing the introduction of lions with swords, mentioned this addition of teeth and eyes in another material than mud:

'Ahmad Batoul came from Egypt and introduced lions. We laugh at Batoul sometimes saying these lions carry a sword and lions cannot carry a sword. Afterwards Batoul made this a distinct feature of his art to compete with us; then I made this painted lion, not with a sword but with a gun, to overcome this competition. Ahmad Batoul took lions from newspapers and magazines

Plate 46
Debeira, Hassa, Kamgana, west façade by Ahmad Batoul, 1933, showing lions with swords which may represent the Arab hero Antar, depicted as a lion with the head of a man

Plate 47
Ashkeit, west façade by
Ahmad Batoul, 1938.
Photo J. Shiner

Plate 48
Ashkeit, detail of Pl. 47.
The lion's eyes are made
from broken red plastic
bracelet, while his teeth
are porcelain fragments

Plate 49
Ballana, Egyptian Nubia,
lion made by Abdu
Batoul in imitation of
those by his brother
Ahmad. Detail of Pl. 77

from Egypt.[5] Then he said, 'No lions without teeth and eyes', and started
putting them in specially. Lions carrying a sword are a sign of King Farouk,
King of Egypt and the Sudan in the 1940s.

'Lions died with Ahmad Batoul. I introduced men shooting lions as
competition to Batoul. As I like firearms and shooting, I introduced crocodile
shooting as competition to the lion with the sword, and also lion shooting'
(Pl. 60; Col. pl. 11).

An inconography new to house façade decoration, consisting of lions with
swords (Pls 46–49), men shooting lions (Pl. 60; Col. pl. 11), men shooting lions
with swords (Fig. 47) and men shooting crocodiles (Fig. 47; Pls 68–70, 79,
84) may here be seen to have developed as the result of competition between

artists. Rivalry led the artists to experiment with additions to established formulae, and to make new combinations of accepted patterns. Even so, the popularity of lions on Nubian house façades may have related to the existing tradition of decorating houses with wild animals in relief.

After 1940 the work of Ahmad Batoul became simpler, and no longer included lions (Fig. 33i, j). Reports of householders state that he began to be extremely temperamental about his work, and this led them to prefer other artists. He became angry when people complained about the slowness with which he worked:

'Ahmad Batoul first began the work but he was very slow finishing it and left them waiting for some days. Then when they asked him to finish up his work, they quarrelled and he left the work unfinished. Hasan Hawa [the east bank name for Hasan Arabi] then came and completed the job' (at Ashkeit).

Ahmad Batoul may have left himself open to criticism by householders about his working methods, since he always let them watch him as he worked. Hasan Arabi protected himself from criticism before a job was complete by never allowing anyone to watch him work. Nor did he allow people to enter the room where work was in progress until the decoration was complete.

Even in Batoul's apparent decline after 1940, he maintained an inventiveness in his art. A late doorway in Argin, made in about 1948 (Fig. 33i), abandoned the stock side-column formula and reintroduced the horn-like hooks of his very early work produced before 1930 (Fig. 32b, g, h, k, p). He combined the hooks with a totally new departure: the overlapping of sharp peaks outlined in relief, to form a kind of net.

At every stage in Batoul's career, his inventions were taken over by other artists. This was freely admitted by Hasan Arabi, who said:

'Ahmad Batoul introduced new things. I used to develop his ideas, and Dawud Osman would carry them further. Then Ahmad Batoul started changing his method. For instance, he began using cement, the imitation of stonework, and the dome and the crescent, doing these things in a new way. But he failed, because his stone pieces weren't popular. Dawud and I both did the same thing only better, since we arranged the stones in a pattern and coloured them. I made them in Argin, as squares of white lime and yellow, outlined by a red and blue line. I did this about 1956, shortly before I became tired and left the field, and Ahmad Batoul died.'

Considering Ahmad Batoul's success, it is not surprising that he soon had competitors. The two earliest were the builder Saleh Mirghani (Appendix

a

b

c

d

B, 2), for whom he first worked, and the firearm-lover, Jabir Bab al-Kheir (Appendix B, 4). It is possible that the work of Mirghani may antedate that of Batoul, and may therefore not originally have been in competition. The *diwan* of a house in Debeira, said to have been decorated for a wedding in 1923 (Fig. 36), and two façades in Ashkeit, *hillet* Hakmanerki (Pls 50–52), dating from 1939, appear to be by the same hand. They show strong personal characteristics, such as circles outlined by a zigzag, thick, curved-topped columns surmounted by a crescent, and a kind of floating unit, a band of decoration, rounded at the ends, which is suspended over the rest of the composition. Yet only the doorways of 1939 are known for certain to have been made by Saleh Mirghani. If the 1923 work had been definitely attributed to him, it would have been clear that he had been the first person to make large-scale mud relief in the Halfa region. Ahmad Batoul would then have learned to do relief decoration by working with him. Instead, it seems that Batoul was largely self-taught.

113

Figure 36
Debeira East, anonymous decoration said to have been made in 1923, possibly by Saleh Mirghani

a south entrance into *diwanin hasil*
b east wall of the *diwan*, with entrance to the outside, and matting wall
c west wall of the *diwan*, southern portion
d south wall of the *diwan*, with inset saucers, plates and a mirror. Most of this house except the diwan was destroyed in 1946

Most of Saleh Mirghani's work, apart from the 1939 doorways, is so close to the style of Batoul that, except for a few details, it is difficult to distinguish the two artists. Saleh Mirghani made birds with rounded backs like those of Batoul (Fig. 32s), but with very long necks like the birds of Hasan Arabi (Fig. 41). He never depicted crocodiles or lions. Hasan Arabi described him in a few words:

Plate 50
Ashkeit, hillet
Hakmanerki, west
façade by Saleh
Mirghani, 1939. *Photo*
A. Potter

'Saleh Mirghani was from Debeira and is now in Kerma. He worked with me a few days in decorating a *diwan*, but couldn't keep up with me. He was a builder first, and used to build from stones, sand and mud. But he did not continue building because of the competition. He worked on building before Ahmad Batoul came, and Ahmad Batoul did only the smoothing. The generation of Ahmad Batoul, Saleh Mirghani and Jabir Bab al-Kheir started first with smoothing, and then turned to decorating. They all appeared between 1930 and 1931 in Debeira. They say that women did some of the decoration, without colours, before then.'

With the 1940s and 1950s, Saleh Mirghani fell into harder times. He was not successful as an assistant to other artists. His last dated job of decoration was in Debeira West, Hassa, Kenuz. It consisted of a peak and two verticals, out-lined in saucers (Fig. 11d). Inside the peak was a large Red Sea shell, and two triangles made out of zigzags scratched into the mud. There was no relief.

Plate 51
Ashkeit, hillet
Hakmanerki, detail of
Pl. 50

Ahmad Batoul and Saleh Mirghani were of Nubian origin whereas Jabir Bab al-Kheir was of southern slave extraction, much darker and with more negroid features than most other inhabitants of Debeira. He was not a slave himself but was the son of a slave. He had been born in Debeira East in the house of his 'patron' which he decorated with 'a woman's head with horns, just for fun' (Pl. 53).

Jabir Bab al-Kheir was the first of the artists we have mentioned which it was possible to interview in person, and he provided some details about how he was trained. He said that he began work as one of a team of house-decorators. The work used to be divided. The head of the team was allotted one-quarter of the work, and the remainder of it was given in smaller proportions to the others. Jabir was the only person to tell us that such a system had obtained, although other artists mentioned that they had been helped by students, or that they had been the student of someone else. It may be that Jabir's team of house-decorators was the same as a group of students working in combination with an established

Plate 52
Ashkeit, hillet
Hakmanerki, west
façade by Saleh
Mirghani, 1939, made
adjoining that in Pls
50, 51

Colour Plate 11
Debeira E., interior wall painting made for a wedding, depicting a man luring a lion with meat while another man, not shown, shoots the lion from behind. Work of Jabir Bab al-Kheir, 1947 (pp. 122–4)

Colour Plate 12
Debeira East, diwan south wall, 1947, painting by Jabir Bab al-Kheir (pp. 124–5)

Colour Plate 13
Argin, the decorator
Hasan Arabi standing by
a *diwan* entrance painted
by him *c.* 1942
(pp. 127–51)

Plate 53
Debeira E., birthplace of
Jabir Bab al-Kheir, west
entrance decorated by him
c. 1940 with the horned
head of a woman. *Photo*
J. Shiner

artist, who functioned as head of the team. Jabir claimed that he worked in this way for one year, after which he turned to building and became a builder.

'Then', as he said, 'I became a wall smoother, and then turned to wall decoration, to which I introduced colour.'

All decoration made by Jabir al-Kheir which can be given any date, was done between 1929 and 1948. After that time he fell out with the community, lost his working tools and retired in considerable poverty. In 1964 he was found living in an undecorated hovel and practising land cultivation. He had worked at decoration only long enough to earn money to buy one cow, and he had never gained enough money to afford a wife. Nevertheless, he was the only artist of the older generation whose work had shown no signs of repetition or decline, and when commissioned to produce a crocodile in the New Mexico Expedition house in Wadi Halfa, he was proven to be in the full vigour of his art (Pls 54–56; Col. pl. 9). A shy man, he could only be persuaded to make the crocodile with the direct persuasion of the Halfa region *nazir*, into whose

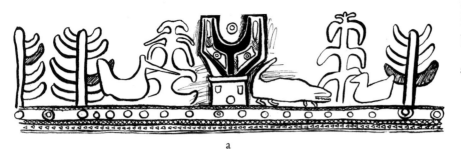

a

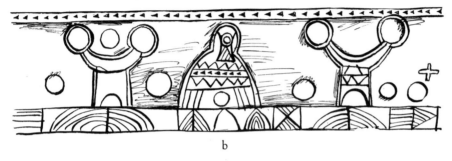

b

c

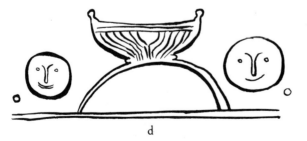

d

Figure 37
Relief and painting by Jabir Bab al-Kheir, in house interiors

a *Serra East, hillet Abdinirki, diwan,* 1929, band and central motif; relief, surrounding ducks, crocodile, plants, painting in red and blue

b *Debeira East, hillet Shabka, diwan* south wall, 1944, uncoloured relief, featuring what the artist called a sphinx

c *Debeira East, hillet Kukoma, diwan* south wall, 1945, paler mud relief over darker mud, with a human figure in the middle

d *Debeira East,* doorway in *mandara* leading to the *dehliz,* 1947, painting in blue lines

Plate 54
Wadi Halfa, Museum of New Mexico Expedition house, 1964. Jabir Bab al-Kheir working in Nile mud and sand to make the wall relief of a crocodile

Plate 55
Wadi Halfa, Museum of New Mexico Expedition house, completed crocodile made in March 1964 by Jabir Bab al-Kheir

Plate 56
Wadi Halfa, Museum of New Mexico Expedition house, detail of Pl. 55

Plate 57
Argin, early work of
Jabir al-Kheir made in
late 1920s. *Photo*
J. Shiner

house he had never before been called. Later on, he tried to return the money
he had been paid to the *nazir*. Although he had done no decoration between
1948 and 1964, he had always kept a small talismanic packet of green powder
paint in the pocket of his robe.

Jabir Bab al-Kheir took great pride in his work and held to his own strict
standards of how he wanted it to look. For these standards, he was willing to
suffer unpopularity. His art, according to the *nazir*, was not much admired in

Plate 58
Debeira E., hillet Shabka,
west façade by Jabir Bab
al-Kheir executed in 1944
without using inset
saucers as part of the
design

120

Debeira. It lacked regularity, and did not conform to local taste. It was closer to some Western taste, showing skilful arrangement and balance of abstract forms which appeared to be repetitive but which in fact never were (Fig. 40; Col. pls 10, 11). Jabir's earliest work (Fig. 50 l, o) resembled the early work of Batoul (Pl. 57; Fig. 32a, g, h) but, unlike Batoul, he retained the horn-like hooks (Fig. 32b, g, h) in certain of his later reliefs (Fig. 50r). The shapes represented, he said, horns when they turned up (Figs 38, 50 o), banana leaves when they turned down (Fig. 50r). When horns turning down surmounted inscribed columns (Fig. 50r), Jabir said the columns represented trunks of the banana

Figure 38
Debeira East, late work of Jabir Bab al-Kheir *c.* 1948, representing columns surmounted by horns

trees. When the horns turning up surmounted columns (Pl. 38), Jabir said the columns were 'pillars under the horns'. He continued, 'People don't ask for horns, I put them if I feel like it. Horns came with the beginning of this art.' Jabir also retained the 'tally post' division of a pole into concave units, which had been used by Ahmad Batoul in his early relief work (Fig. 32b) and then dropped. Unlike Batoul, Jabir marked these units on the surface of an inscribed column, and did not cut them in silhouette (Pls 58, 59; Col. pl. 10).

Designs employed by Jabir Bab al-Kheir in the late 1930s and early 1940s
included a cyclops form, like a head with one eye (Col. pl. 10; Fig. 37b, c; Fig.
40) and a circle with triangles following each other around the outside, like a
chain (Pl. 59; Col. pl. 10). Jabir said this kind of circle represented a water-
wheel. From 1944 onwards he refused to employ saucers, announcing that
they were old-fashioned and spoiled his compositions by having a different
surface texture from the rest of the relief; he preferred to cut plain white circles
instead. This, according to his clients, was too much to accept. They felt it was
more important to have saucers on doorways than to have relief designs, since
saucers were necessary to divert the evil eye. His clients also felt that he spent an
excessive amount of time on his painted work (Col. pl. 11). He had used an
especially small brush, and worked so carefully that his hands were often
swollen. In 1947, Jabir reported, a magician was employed to cast a spell on
him, with the result that he became ill and suffered for three months. His tools
shortly disappeared, and he decorated no more.

The interpretations given by Jabir Bab al-Kheir to the forms he used in his

Plate 59
Debeira E., hillet Shabka,
west façade by Jabir Bab
al-Kheir made in 1944.
The top motif represents
a water wheel between
trees

123

designs were different from interpretations given to them by people who lived in the houses where they appeared. For instance, in Debeira, *hillet* Kukoma, he made a *diwan* relief where the central image was a cyclops form, with a single eye (Fig. 37c). Jabir said that this represented a human figure, but the house-owner thought it showed a cake, like a bridegroom, made for the Prophet's birthday. It is the custom throughout the Muslim Sudan to make cakes on this occasion which are shaped in a number of different ways. Jabir also said that the images to each side of the human figure were domes, which he had put there to make the figure appear to be in the centre. But the house-owner believed them to be domed buildings, flanked by minarets.

Jabir was under the impression that most of his work was very close to nature. He said that his tree and flower forms were imitated from those he had seen when he was a gardener. He described the trees as being either banana trees (Fig. 50r), apple trees (Col. pl. 12) or rose trees (Fig. 37a; Col. pl. 12). Other motifs he claimed to have borrowed from pictures he had seen. One example of the cyclops form (Fig. 37b) was described by him as a sphinx which he saw in a newspaper. His most elaborate composition (Col. pl. 12), painted in 1947 in the same house as several others (Figs 37d, 39; Col. pl. 11), did indeed look as if he had been noting the figures arranged in registers which were depicted in ancient Egyptian art. He would have needed only to have travelled the few miles

Plate 60
Debeira E., interior wall painting made for a wedding, depicting a man luring a lion with meat while another man shoots the lion from behind. Work of Jabir Bab al-Kheir, 1947

124

between Debeira and Abu Simbel to have seen ancient Egyptian art, or he could have seen examples in smaller temples and tombs closer to Wadi Halfa. Yet everything in this Debeira painting, which he said represented such varied images as a man with a rifle shooting a bird, a man feeding a donkey from a table, a man in front of a woman, both holding oranges, another donkey, apple and rose trees and a dog, was, he claimed, copied from nature.

Jabir said that he composed by first decorating the centre and then placing things to the side. He said that the things to the side had no particular significance, but that the things in the centre did. In the composition just described (Col. pl. 12), the things in the centre were the man shooting, accompanied by his dog, and below him a dome, into which was fitted an apple tree. The importance of men shooting and apple trees was never commented upon by Jabir, but the importance of the dome was something on which he insisted. Every doorway composition, and preferably every other composition as well, had to have a dome in the middle. He said, in fact, that 'a dome and a circle' was required. In the works of Jabir where the central dome and circle could be discerned, it was clear that they represented a number of very different things. The 'dome' represented a sphinx (Fig. 37b), a vase (Fig. 37d) and what he said were the divided bow legs of a human figure (Fig. 50r). The 'circle', above the dome, represented a water-wheel (Pl. 59; Col. pl. 10), or a woman's head with horns (Pl. 53). It appeared from this that Jabir was talking about the shape itself, and not about what the shape depicted, when he said that things in the centre had significance while things to the sides did not.

One other shape thought suitable by Jabir for use in the centre of a composition was the crescent elevated upon a stem. He used it centrally in arrangements where the surrounding figures were birds, crocodiles and trees (Fig. 37a). In speaking of his *diwan* relief where the central image was a sphinx and the things to the sides were crescents on stems (Fig. 37b), he said, 'In this case the decorations to both sides of the sphinx could have gone in the middle.' Thus it appears that the shapes which Jabir found significant, insisting that they be placed in the centre of his arrangements, were those found in women's painting type B, namely, a dome (Fig. 23), sometimes surmounted by a circle (Fig. 23 o), and a crescent on a stem (Fig. 23g, t, w).

In one case, it was the image fitted inside the dome shape which was more traditional than those which were placed around it. In the house in Debeira painted in 1947, he placed a snake within an arched tympanum over the doorway from the *dehliz* to the *hosh* (Fig. 39). The tympanum was flanked by representations of lambs and trees. An iconographer would have attempted to explain the whole composition as hieratic, but Jabir's explanation was narrative, and as follows: 'The snake was in the tree. The lambs started to make

Figure 39
Debeira East, dehliz
doorway leading into
courtyard, painted by
Jabir Bab al-Kheir in red
and blue, showing a
serpent, lambs and two
trees, 1947

noises, and the snake went into his hole to hide. I saw snakes like this when I
was a gardener, and how they stayed around the sheep.'

In spite of Jabir's story, the snake was included among those animals which
functioned traditionally to deflect the evil eye, and therefore according to local
views deserved a position of greater importance than lambs, which had never
been so used.

Jabir claimed also to have made a composition of men playing football; but,
unfortunately, the house in Debeira East with this particular *diwan* was inhabited
by an Egyptian woman who consistently refused us entry. Eventually she took
an axe and hacked the design off the wall rather than let it be seen by us. The
nazir said that she was the second wife of a local Nubian, while the composition
had been made at the wedding of his first wife, who had died.

Figure 40
Debeira East, hillet Shabka,
west façade by Jabir Bab
al-Kheir, 1944, mud
lightened with white lime
on a darker mud ground

When making a façade decoration, Jabir himself did the decoration over the door but he sometimes allowed a student to make the surrounds. Such was the case with a doorway made in 1944 in Debeira, *hillet* Shabka (Fig. 40) which shows an original attempt to link side columns with the central doorway unit by means of overlapping shapes. One student employed by Jabir Bab al-Kheir was Hasan Arabi (Col. pl. 13) who, some time between 1937 and 1941, invented another way of linking the doorway compositions together, by super-imposing horizontal bands across the side columns (Fig. 41). The bands were made up of circles or saucers.

Ahmad Batoul's basic doorway formula had been an entrance flanked by up to three pairs of inscribed side columns which were joined only at the tops, by horizontal bands which linked the columns (Fig. 33a, d, f, g). In altering the formula and attempting to link the side columns in new ways, Hasan Arabi reduced Batoul's three pairs of columns to two main pairs (Fig. 41). The outer pair (a) were slightly taller than the inner pair (b). There was a third,

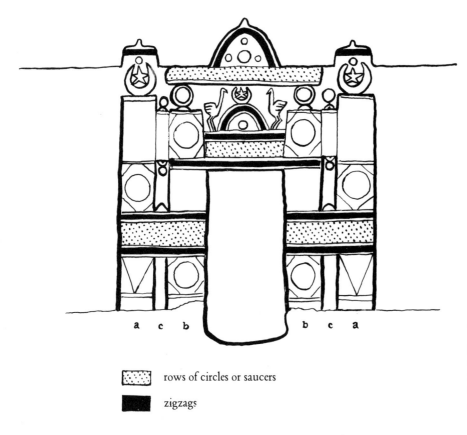

a c b   b c a

▨   rows of circles or saucers

■   zigzags

Figure 41
Constant features in the
formula for doorway
decoration which was
invented by Hasan Arabi
and used by him in
Ashkeit and Argin,
1941–5

subsidiary pair (c), which extended to the top of the inner columns (b) but not to the top of the outer columns (a), and which was placed between (a) and (b) for purposes of linking. It is possible that Batoul had also been trying to link two columns by placing a shorter element between them, but there were only two examples of this, in Argin (Fig. 33h) and Ashkeit (Pl. 38). Batoul had not pursued this idea, which was borrowed from him and developed by Hasan Arabi. Batoul had never adopted the notion of overlapping the vertical columns with thick horizontal bands, which was a basic feature of Hasan Arabi's work (Fig. 51).

Hasan Arabi's façade formula allowed for variation within a set arrangement, resulting in an overall impression of similarity among the doorways which were made in this way (Pls 61–4). The invariable features were, first, the lengths and placement of three pairs of columns. They formed the main verticals of the composition. Next there were three rows of circles and saucers which crossed the design horizontally from bottom to top. The lowest was the wide band of

circles joining columns (a) and (b). This lowest band began about halfway up the side of the door and below the termination of column (c). The next band was immediately over the door, underneath a rounded arch which was also invariable (Fig. 41). Above the arch and columns, to either side of it, there was a third band which seemed almost to be suspended at the top of the composition, in the manner fancied by Saleh Mirghani (Pls 50, 52). Like Mirghani's doorways, made in Ashkeit in 1939, the top band had slanted or rounded ends and was surmounted by another round arch which was silhouetted against the sky. Mirghani's doorways, which also boasted a horizontal band of saucers linking the two principal side columns, may well have been an impor﹣ tant influence in the development of Hasan's design. Unfortunately this cannot be evaluated, for it is not known to what stage Hasan had evolved this formula by 1939, from whence the Mirghani examples date.

A part from the vertical columns and horizontal bands of saucers, certain smaller details were invariable in virtually every doorway made by Hasan Arabi. The outer columns (a) were surmounted by crescents and stars, as was the central dome over the door. Columns (b) were surmounted by orbs placed on half﹣circles, and columns (c) were given orbs and half﹣circles at both bottom and top. The upper arch which was silhouetted against the sky had a zigzag

Plate 61
Ashkeit, hillet Ari, west façade by Hasan Arabi, 1942, made using his special formula for constructing patterned door surrounds

129

edging which surrounded an arrangement of at least three saucers placed round a
dinner-plate and set into uncoloured mud. The arch over the doorway was also
edged with a band of zigzags, but it was filled in with white lime. It had a
saucer set into the middle, on either side of which was frequently a small flag
(Pls 62, 64). Flanking the dome over the door were two long-legged and
long-necked birds. Columns (a) had large circles inscribed on them, about the
size of a basket lid for covering *kisra*. They were given different kinds of filling,
and were placed just above the lowest horizontal band of saucers. Columns
(b) were marked with two such circles, one below the band and one much
higher, to either side of the birds. The lower circle was often obliterated by wear,
because it was at the extreme bottom of the composition (Pls 61–4). Variable
features of the composition were other space fillings marked on the columns
themselves.

Hasan Arabi's doorway formula was imitated successfully by Abdu Batoul,
the younger brother of Ahmad Batoul (Col. pl. 18), and by Hasan Arabi's
friend and co-worker, Dawud Osman (Pls 67, 71; Fig. 43e), to make new doorway designs of great complexity. The most involved patterns were made by
Hasan himself. His ten most complicated designs were in Ashkeit (Pls 61–4,

Plate 62
Ashkeit, hillet Shartokija,
west façade by Hasan
Arabi

68). The formula was used from 1941 to 1945, when it was abandoned by most artists because it involved too much work.

Hasan Arabi was the first of a new class of artist who were full-time decorators rather than plasterers who happened to be able to decorate. At the height of his achievement, in Ashkeit in the mid forties, he engaged Ahmad Batoul to plaster the walls on which he was to work. He was born in Argin in 1909 – the same place where he was employed as bus conductor on the Argin–West Halfa bus at the time the inhabitants were moved to Khashm el-Girba. He enjoyed considerable social privileges, such as being able to order tea in virtually any house. In his youth he had worked in the Government railway yards at Atbara but, finding the pay too low, he turned to house decoration which proved more rewarding. His earliest work was made on an island which he called 'Ornarti', which seems to be Awwen-Arti in southern Argin. He said that this early work, which was all washed away in the Nile flood of 1946, had consisted of simple domes inscribed in a square over the door.

Plate 63
Ashkeit, hillet Ari, west façade by Hasan Arabi, 1944. The window to the left of the entrance was that of a shop selling tea, coffee and groceries. Unlike the doorway relief, the relief over the window was coloured in maroon, blue and gold

Hasan continued to work in Awwen-Arti until 1946, and it is possible that his doorway formula was first worked out there and was among the work which had been destroyed, since only one example existed in the Halfa region which showed a transition to the final phase. This was in Ashkeit (Pl. 65) and was said locally to have been made in 1933. In fact it was certainly later, since Hasan himself did not claim to start working round Wadi Halfa until after 1935. There was nothing else in Ashkeit made by him dating before 1941, when he said he began decorating there. In this particular doorway the three side columns were crossed by horizontal bands of saucers but the central columns (c) were not shortened. The whole doorway thus appeared to be a solid mass rather than a composition of articulated units. The surface was otherwise elaborated with nothing other than designs punched out with the triangular punch, featuring triangles in groups of threes, which is a Batoulian characteristic never visible in Hasan's major work.

The only other example seen of Hasan's early decoration, made before 1940, was also on the east Nile bank, in Debeira, *hillet* Arnaut, where the doorway was dated by the owner to 1935. The design consisted of a painted door surround of orange imitation brick, combining Batoulian punched-out triangles

Plate 64
Ashkeit, house of
Muhammad Ahmad
Sayyid, south façade
painted by Hasan Arabi,
1945 in colours of maroon,
dark blue, light blue,
ochre and white. He
added the colours only
after persuasion from the
house owner

Colour Plate 14
Ashkeit, hillet Sizki, diwan end wall decorated by
Hasan Arabi in 1942, during his 'geometric' phase
(pp. 4, 146–7)

Colour Plate 15
Ashkeit, doorway by Hasan Arabi, 1942, very like
the works of Dawud Osman but differing in
trademarks
(p. 138)

Colour Plate 16
Ashkeit, 1946, *diwan* painting resulting from Hasan
Arabi's 'Art Deco' phase, using the
step-pyramid motif elsewhere popular in the 30s
(pp. 134, 147)

Colour Plate 17
Ashkeit, diwan painting by Hasan Arabi in 1949,
during his 'Art Deco' phase
(p. 151)

*Colour Plate 18
Ashkeit, hillet Sorba,*
west façade by Abdu
Batoul, brother of
Ahmad Batoul, who
inset green ashtrays
bought in a Cairo
chain-store
(p. 153)

Colour Plate 19
Gemai East, Gemai, Said, dehliz painting by Muhammad
Suleiman in 1961 or 1962, featuring designs based on
hanging baskets
(pp. 154–5)

with the cyclopean forms of Jabir Bab al-Kheir. Although this early work of Hasan Arabi does not appear very accomplished, it seemed so to the local inhabitants. On the east bank of the Nile, in Debeira as well as in Ashkeit, he was known as Hasan Hawa, Hasan son of his mother Hawa, an acknowledgement that his mother was remarkable in having given birth to an exceptional son. This name was disliked by Hasan's wife who lived on the west bank, and was not used there, but on the west bank they knew another nickname for him. Hasan had been a twin. The souls of twins could enter into any cat which had not had its ears clipped at birth.[6] The cat then went round and stole food, demonstrating that it contained the soul of a twin by walking in a peculiar way. Hasan's soul had entered into cats so many times that they referred to him as 'Hasan *kedis*', or Hasan the Cat.

The development of Hasan Arabi's façade decoration seems to have been directed to some extent by his strong personal convictions about what effects were desirable in his work. Such convictions had also affected the work of Jabir Bab al-Kheir, and the taste of Hasan, like that of Jabir, diverged from that of the people for whom he worked. This divergence had led to Jabir's unpopularity, but Hasan seemed better able to convert people to his own taste. For

Plate 65
Ashkeit, early work of Hasan Arabi, before 1941, at a time when his doorway formula was still being developed.
Photo J. Shiner

instance, Hasan said that before using colours he had made relief in the natural tones of sand and mud. All this while people kept asking him to use colour, so so he first used white, and then colours on the outside of the house. But he came to the conclusion that colour did not look well on house exteriors, so he went against popular demand and reverted to using white lime silhouette on a dark mud background, as had Ahmad Batoul. After he 'deserted colours', as he put it, he became dissatisfied with coloured saucers because, when set in a white design, they did not make a homogeneous pattern. Since few saucers produced by the householders had no colour, he substituted white circles and crescents for the saucers (Pl. 61) and this, he claimed, was how saucers on the outside of houses came to be no longer used. And, he added, the people liked the absence of saucers. But he continued to employ colours inside the house because he said that people gathered together there, and it suited the gathering (Col. pl. 14). It in fact appeared that people liked anything that Hasan Arabi chose to do, and did not like what Jabir Bab al-Kheir chose to do, and that this had something to do with the personalities of the two men apart from their work. Apparently, the rejection of saucers which was said to have made Jabir unpopular, also accounted for Hasan's success.

Hasan Arabi's major decorative work belongs to the period between 1941 and 1946. Two phases may be distinguished: during the first, the designs are exclusively geometric (Col. pl. 14); in the second, the geometry is affected by features of the decorative style of the 1930s now known as 'Art Deco' (Col. pls 16, 17).[7] The principal forms characterising this second phase include concentric circles and light rays or parallel bands (Fig. 45a–c)[8], as well as the stepped pyramid which, because of the 1930s fascination with Aztec art, is thought to be Mexican rather than Egyptian in origin (Fig. 46; Ic, IIId; Col. pl. 16).[9] Further popular 1930s designs found in the art of Hasan Arabi are vines and flowers enclosed in sharp geometric outlines (Fig. 46, Ic, Id, IId, IIId),[10] and a background of angular shapes which seem to bear a remote affinity to the Bauhaus school of art (Fig. 46, Ib, IIIc; Col. pl. 17).[11] According to Hasan, he had taken these designs from imported tin boxes.

The 'geometric' phase lasted until 1943, and the Art Deco period from then until 1959. His façade decoration, however, was always primarily geometric. The only Art Deco manifestations it showed were zigzag patterns imposed on angular, irregular shapes (Pl. 62),[12] and rigid, rainbow-coloured bands forming large chevrons.[13] Such chevrons appeared on a Huntley and Palmers biscuit tin called the 'Mayfair' (Fig. 45g) and on advertisements for a kind of ginger nut biscuit called Johnny Ginger, current in the mid thirties. Hasan painted these chevrons in colour on columns (c) of a façade at Ashkeit (Pl. 64).[14] This was one of the few instances after 1940 when Hasan used colour

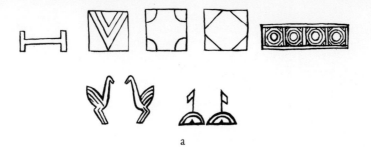

a

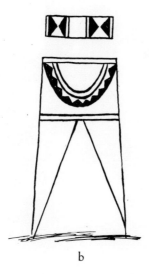

b

Figure 42
a Hasan Arabi,
  trademarks
b Dawud Osman,
  trademarks

on a house exterior, and its use was the result of strong insistence from the house⁄ owner.

During Hasan Arabi's geometric phase, he was assisted by Dawud Osman. Before 1941, when he was perfecting his doorway formula, he started to deco⁄ rate his façades with a double string⁄course just below the roof, giving the effect of a cornice (Pls 63, 65); and Hasan acknowledged Dawud's help in devising this: 'The decoration near the roof is called "*darabzin*". I myself and Dawud were the only people who used it, and we invented it together.'

In fact, however, although Hasan believed that he and Dawud Osman had invented this feature, it had been employed by Sayyid Ahmad Hogla (Pl. 28) as early as 1930. The examples of it were all in South Wadi Halfa. Dawud Osman must have seen Sayyid Ahmad's work, since it lay on the road along

*Plate 66
Ashkeit, hillet Jakkonona,
decoration at the south-
west house corner by
Dawud Osman, 1942,
showing his trademark
at the column base
consisted of an acute
chevron below a
semicircle*

which he travelled when he came north from his home in Gemai, Kokki
Islands, shortly after 1935.

The association between Hasan Arabi and Dawud Osman involved a
precise division of labour: Dawud Osman installed the horizontal line of
saucers, while Hasan Arabi provided the decoration in paint or relief. Together they devised trade-marks to distinguish their work whenever they operated

individually. Hasan Arabi's principal trade-mark was a pair of confronted, long-legged birds, separated by a dome (Fig. 41; Fig. 42a). He also used alternative trade-marks, such as a flattened letter H (Fig. 42a; Pl. 64), or a square with segmented corners (Fig. 42a). This square could in turn be filled with chevrons or flags; he explained that these were the tents and flags used to cele-brate the Prophet's birthday.[15] Dawud Osman's main trade-mark was an acute chevron within a rectangle, inscribed below a semicircle (Fig. 42b; Fig. 43d; Pl. 66) which he placed at the bottoms of each of the two pairs of thick side columns flanking the door which were demanded by Hasan's formula (Pls 69–71). Dawud's other trade-mark, placed virtually anywhere on the façade, was the X between parallel bars (Fig. 42b), the carpentry motif and sign of the builder-decorator, which was what Dawud initially had been.

Hasan Arabi's decoration always continued uninterrupted to the ground, whereas Dawud Osman explained that there was no point in decorating this

Plate 67
Debeira E., hillet Semesi,
Dawud Osman façade *c.*
1942, using an adaptation
of the doorway formula
invented by Hasan Arabi

part of the façade, because goats would rub up against it and ruin the design. Following damage by goats, women replastered the lower several feet of the façade with new mud, covering all the decorations up to that point (Pls 32, 38, 39, 41, 46, 47, 50, 53, 62–5). Dawud filled this area only with the simple acute chevron which became his trade-mark (Pl. 69; Fig. 43d) cutting it deeply into the surface so that some of the design would stay, even if re-covered with new mud (Pl. 67). His attitude did not influence Hasan Arabi, who was a perfectionist, and not deterred by the impermanence of his creations.

In 1942 Dawud and Hasan each produced a façade in Ashkeit which was almost identical to that made by the other, both displaying Hasan's doorway formula and a man shooting a crocodile (Pls 68–71; Col. pl. 15). Only by means of the different trade-marks used by each artist could the two works be told apart. A further, slight difference was that Hasan's figure of the hunter (Col. pl. 15) was more crudely drawn than that of Dawud (Pl. 70).[16] It was in fact his only known representation of the human figure, whereas Dawud made something of a speciality of depicting natural forms. He was said to have been the first to introduce the scene of the crocodile and hunter, in the mid 1930s. After his return to the Second Cataract in 1945, he produced automobiles

Plate 68
Ashkeit, west façade by Hasan Arabi in house with interior decoration by Ahmad Batoul. Hasan was assisted at this time, in 1942, by Dawud Osman, who produced a similar façade (Pl. 69)

Plate 69
Ashkeit, hillet Jakkonona,
façade made by Dawud
Osman in 1942, at a
time when he was
collaborating with Hasan
Arabi

139

Plate 70
Ashkeit, hillet Jakkonona,
detail of façade made by
Dawud Osman

in relief (Pls 72, 75) and later, in the 1950s and 1960, he painted antelopes (Fig. 44e), pin-up girls (Fig. 44b) and Mecca scenes (Fig. 44c). His work at that time had fallen under the influence of men's sitting-room art and *Hajj* painting.

Hasan Arabi's Art Deco phase, beginning in 1943, marked the end of his close association with Dawud Osman, and the styles of the two artists diverged. While Hasan developed his Art Deco style, Dawud experimented with a simplification of Hasan's doorway design; between 1945 and 1947 he intro-duced it into the region of the Second Cataract, where it could be seen in Gemai, *hillet* Diffinog (Pl. 73), and Halfa Degheim West, *hillet* Sheikh Abd al-Qadir (Fig. 43f), with a similar example in South Halfa dated 1947. Dawud began to pick out surface details in pink, and to add a vertical line over his circles (Fig. 43f; Fig. 44f). This had the effect that the circles were actually basket lids suspended on strings. Dawud had not done this north of Halfa where the custom of suspending baskets was out of date. By 1949 Dawud started painting instead of making relief. He decorated few façades, and those he did make (Fig. 44g) were given painted details. He concentrated instead on interior wall paintings characterised by a horizontal band of basket forms surmounted by naturalistic images (Fig. 44a, b, h), including modern automobiles taken from magazines. Of his former trade-marks, he retained only the X between parallel bars (Pl. 73; Fig. 44b, d, f, h). In 1960 he stopped decorating and went to work as a bricklayer in Atbara.

The Art Deco style of Hasan Arabi was largely executed in paint and not in

Plate 71
Ashkeit, hillet
Jakkonona, doorway
detail of the façade by
Dawud Osman shown
in Pls 66, 69, 70

Plate 72
Gemai, hillet Definok,
west façade by Dawud
Osman in 1947, with
white-lime reliefs of
automobile and bird.
Photo J. Shiner

140

Figure 43
Decorations by Dawud
Osman, 1935–46

a, b *Gemai, Amka Sharg,*
   1935, west entrance,
   south courtyard
   doorway in the house
   of the Sheikh of
   Amka, uncoloured
   mud relief
c   *Argin, hillet Rizga,*
   1939, east entrance,
   home of lockmaker
   Ahmad Suleiman,
   incised mud relief
d   *Gemai, Gemai, Nale*
   Matto, c. 1940 west
   entrance, mud relief
   covered with white
   lime, made for beauty
   alone
e   *Argin,* 1944, east
   entrance, mud relief,
   decorated areas
   covered with white
   lime
f   *Halfa Degheim West,*
   hillet Sheikh Abd
   el-Qadir, 1946, east
   entrance, mud relief
   coloured white, red
   and green
g   *Halfa Degheim West,*
   hillet Sheikh Abd
   el-Qadir, 1946, *dehliz*
   of house above,
   painted in pink, red,
   wine; slight relief

relief. According to Hasan he learned the technique of painting from women.
From 1945 he decorated interiors and abandoned façades, except for the occasional example of imitation stonework. He employed a new assistant, the lockmaker Khalil Saleh from Ashkeit (Appendix B, no. 10) who had formerly
been a student of Ahmad Batoul,[17] to help with the painting. Hasan first

a   b   c

d   e

f   g

a

b

c

d

e

f

g

h

Figure 44
Decorations by Dawud
Osman, 1947–55

a, b, c *Gemai, Gemai, Nale Matto*, interior room painted 1947 for a wedding, in terra-cotta, turquoise, yellow, orange and black; no relief

d *Gemai, Gemai, Kokki Islands*, 1949 only decoration in the home of Dawud Osman, *dehliz*, earth-red, blue, green, painting only

e *Gemai, Amka, Amka Alibek*, 1949, entrance to interior room, painted for a wedding, in red, blue and black

f *Gemai, Gemai, Diffinog*, 1952, painting in interior room, frieze painted with grey outlines filled with earth-red, apricot and gold; the circles are made to look like hanging-basket lids

g *South Wadi Halfa*, 1954–5, painting on a white-lime surface set out on a brown mud façade, in colours of red, yellow and blue

h *Gemai, Amka, Asheile*, 1959, interior room painted in red, blue, orange and black; automobile copied from a magazine. For this room and a simple band of decoration, type 'f', in the *mandara*, Dawud was paid £5

Plate 74
Gemai, hillet Diffinog,
detail of Pl. 72. The
bowl underneath the bird
is inscribed with the
signature of Dawud
Osman and the date
1947. *Photo* J. Shiner

Plate 75
Gemai, hillet Diffinog,
detail of Pl. 72; work by
Dawud Osman in 1947.
Photo J. Shiner

isolated the area to be decorated with white lime and drew the design in outline
using string dipped in paint. The string was stretched along the wall to mark
straight lines. Hasan drew around bowls or tin cans to make circles. He shaped
arches by using string stretched from a fixed point, like a compass. He mixed a
number of colours from earth or powder paint, each with its own brush, and
went round the wall marking all areas to be filled in with these as flat tones.

145

The painting of these areas was completed by Khalil Saleh. The more complex areas were painted by Hasan himself, occasionally employing a single tube of oil paint of unusual colour, such as bright orange, lavender or mint green.

By 1945 Hasan Arabi was being paid £3 to decorate an entire house. Servant's wages in Khartoum were, at the same time, about £6 a month. He could finish a job in three to five days of uninterrupted work, but not without strain. As he said about his decoration of a house in Argin: 'I worked very hard and lost my appetite for food, and started breathing heavily, and I prevented anyone from coming near me and I did this in five days.' The speed with which Hasan worked enabled him to earn more than any other decorator (Appendix B, no. 6). Even those who were later paid more, such as the Egyptian commercial artist Sabri, usually took some weeks to finish a complicated piece of work (Appendix A, no. 23). Although Hasan never allowed people to watch him work, if the housewife was kindly he was known to sing to her, telling her that he would make her a masterpiece.

The *diwan* painting of Hasan Arabi's Art Deco phase retained the same space divisions as those he had used before, but the designs filling the spaces were new (Pl. 76). The horizontal band encircling the *diwan* had, in his geometric phase, been marked with alternating basket-lid circles and vertical

Plate 76
Argin. The decorator Hasan Arabi stands in an abandoned, roofless *diwan* which he painted around 1945. The principal motif on the south, end wall is a crown between flags.
Photo J. Shiner

146

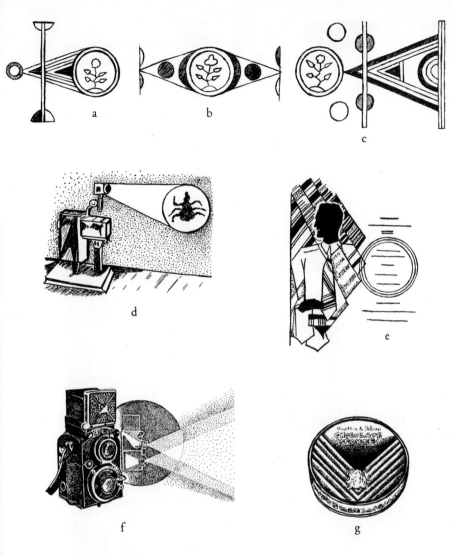

Figure 45
Hasan Arabi motifs
featuring circles combined
with cones of light or light
rays, and similar motifs in
pictorial and advertising
art of the 1930s

a, b *Argin, hillet Rizga,*
frieze made by Hasan
Arabi in *diwan,* 1945–6,
details
a south wall of *diwan,*
   motif painted in ochre,
   sienna, grey-green and
   blue, on white
b east and west walls of
   diwan, motif painted in
   the same colours as 'a'

c *Ashkeit,* motif from
   south wall of the *diwan,*
   1949, painted in dark
   red, pale blue, ochre
   and green on a white
   band, running
   horizontally
d Scientific illustration
   from *Al-Hilal,*
   Egyptian pictorial
   review, no. 10, Cairo,
   August 1938, p. 1197
e Advertisement for
   neckties, signed
   'Morelli', *Al-Hilal* no.
   7, 1935, p. 4
f Camera advertisement,
   L'Illustration, 91, no.
   4735, Paris, December
   1933, p. xxx,
   advertisements
g Biscuit tin, Huntley
   and Palmer's catalogue,
   *Huntley and Palmer's
   Xmas Biscuits and Cakes,*
   Reading 1934, p. 8,
   'Mayfair Tin'

bands (Fig. 42a; Col. pl. 14), such as were always retained by Dawud Osman
(Fig. 44). In his Art Deco phase the bands were still divided by vertical bars,
like those of a film-strip (Pl. 76), but the circles now became half-circles (Fig.
46, Ia, Ic), step-pyramids (Fig. 46, Ic; Col. pl. 16), or orbs (Fig. 45a–c; Pl.
76). One orb was filled with a flower while the other, smaller orb functioned as a
light source from which issued rays. These rays fanned out in a chevron to
strike the larger orb (Fig. 45a), which in certain variations even cast a shadow
to the side (Fig. 45b), or in others functioned as the source of the rays (Fig. 45c).
Such motifs of images in combination with light rays, influenced by pictures

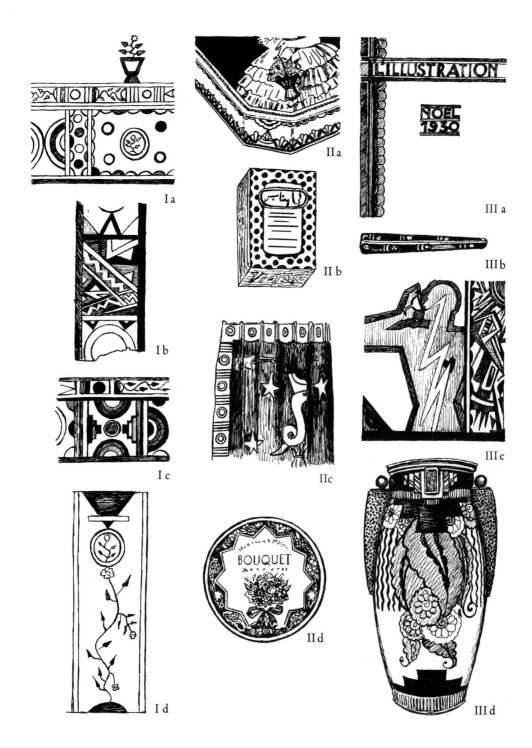

I a

I b

I c

I d

II a

II b

II c

II d

III a

III b

III c

III d

Colour Plate 20
Faras West, the Great
Cathedral, medieval
painting, early twelfth
century. Nubian prince
seated in the lap of Christ
wears a variant of the
Nubian Eparch's crown
(p. 165)

Colour Plate 21
West Degheim, Degheim North, Kenuz, painting of a holy
man's tomb (p. 170)

Figure 46

Typical motifs from Hasan Arabi's 'Art Deco' period, compared with things which he might have seen, and others which were made in the common style of the 1930s, called 'Art Deco'

Column I, *diwan* decorations by Hasan Arabi, 1946–9, which were painted on a horizontal white band marked on a mud ground: coloured areas were given incised outlines

Ia 1949, *Ashkeit, diwan* end wall, south, the same frieze as fig. 42c: coloured circles, half circles, circles between parallel bars, flower container, flower, vine

Ib 1946, *Ashkeit, diwan* east wall, framework for a cement water-pot holder, painted ochre, sienna, grey-green and dark blue on white: zigzags, erratic, angular shapes

Ic 1946, *Ashkeit*, end wall of *diwan*, south painted ochre, sienna, blue, grey: step-pyramid form, coloured parallel bands, rainbow arcs, undulating vine

Id 1946, *Argin*, west wall of main courtyard, entrance to *diwan*: undulating plant between geometric shapes, flower in a circle

Column II, images which Hasan Arabi might have seen

IIa Biscuit tin, 'Wistaria', catalogue, *Huntley and Palmer's Xmas Biscuits and Cakes* 1934, p. 6: half circles making a scallop border, scalloped rainbow arc, flower container with flowers

IIb Vitamin tablet package, 'Vi-Tabs', *Al-Mussawar*, Egyptian illustrated review, Cairo, 8 September 1939, p. 29: circles, half circles making a scallop border

IIc Pseudo ancient Egyptian wall hanging, from an illustration in *Al-Hilal* no. 7, Cairo 1935, p. 80: circles between parallel bars

IId Biscuit tin, 'Bouquet', catalogue, *Huntley and Palmer's Xmas Biscuits* 1934, p. 10: flower in a circle, zigzags

Column III images made in the common style of the 1930s, called 'Art Deco'

IIIa Magazine cover, *L'Illustration* 88, no. 4579, Paris 1930: scallop border, coloured parallel bands

IIIb Hair clip, *L'Illustration* 91, no. 4736, 1933, p. xxix, advertisements: circles between parallel bars

IIIc Book cover, *Savoy Cocktail Book*, 1930, after B. Hillier, *Art Deco*, p. 63: zigzags, erratic, angular shapes, scallop border

IIId French pottery vase with iron mounts, after B. Hillier, op. cit., p. 128: undulating plant between geometric shapes, the step-pyramid form, flower inside a hard-edged outline, circles, parallel bands

of the microscope (Fig. 45d) or camera (Fig. 45f), were common in illustrative art of the thirties. The motifs were used in other examples of advertising design where light was not being depicted (Fig. 45e, g).

The dome surmounting the horizontal band of the *diwan* had, in Hasan Arabi's geometric phase, been filled with circles between vertical bars (Col. pl. 14). The circles sometimes consisted of saucers, surrounded by yellow bands to make them shine. In his Art Deco phase Hasan no longer used saucers and the domes were filled with angular, abstract shapes and bands of tendrils (Fig. 51b). At the same time a substitution for this dome was introduced. It was the so-called crown of King Farouk (Fig. 51a, b; Pl. 76), a form marked with tendrils and angular shapes as was the dome. Like the dome it was surmounted by a crescent and star. It bore some resemblance to the actual crown of King Farouk as it was shown embroidered on the upholstery of his throne[18] (Fig. 51d) and depicted in cigarette advertisements[19] (Fig. 51e). The principal difference between the crown made by Hasan and the one depicted on Egyptian products was that Hasan's crown was combined with two Egyptian flags. Usually the flags were placed to each side of the base of the crown (Fig. 51b; Pl. 76), but sometimes they were mounted on to the body of the crown (Fig. 51a). In the latter cases, the object depicted was much closer to the objects represented in women's painting type B (Fig. 23i, j), where domed shapes surmounted by a crescent had flag-like hooks issuing from the sides. The crown motif was borrowed from Hasan Arabi by Khalil Saleh, his assistant, who placed it over the outer doorway of his own home in Ashkeit (Fig. 51c).

When asked about the source of his Art Deco motifs, Hasan Arabi said that he selected them from anything which suited his taste, such as towels or tin boxes, and that he composed them in any way he liked. It is not now possible to trace the motifs on Egyptian towels. The situation is different with tin boxes. Three kinds of tin box were frequently visible in Nubia: uniform Tate and Lyle Golden Syrup tins, large undecorated petrol tins, and decorative biscuit tins of assorted kinds. Of these, it is probable that the tin boxes chosen by Hasan Arabi as pattern models were biscuit tins, or similar containers of luxury foods. These containers had been designed by their manufacturers to be desirable objects in themselves, and were good reflections of whatever popular taste was the style of the moment.

The Huntley and Palmers Biscuit Company in Reading have exported biscuits in tins from 1827, and until the First World War they were the only large exporters of biscuits to Africa. After the Battle of Omdurman in 1898, when the Mahdist forces were defeated by the British near Khartoum, a Mahdist sword was picked up on the battlefield, the scabbard of which was held together by strips of metal cut from a Huntley and Palmers biscuit tin.[20] After 1920 other biscuit manufacturers became more important, but Huntley and Palmers continued to be the main exporter of biscuits to the Sudan.

The designs borrowed by Hasan Arabi from biscuit tins such as those made by Huntley and Palmers were already out of date at the time he worked. It was the tins of the 1920s and 1930s which showed designs reminiscent of Hasan's Art Deco style which he began only in 1943. Yet the discrepancy between the date of manufacture of the tins and the date when he made use of their decoration need not be a source of surprise. Decorative tin boxes, whatever their contents, are an expensive item on the Arab market. They would have been kept for some time on the shelves of Greek groceries in Cairo and Khartoum before being sold in the first place. Their purchasers would more likely have been the European employer of a Nubian cook or houseboy rather than the Nubian himself, who would eventually have received the tin as bakhsheesh. They might not have been brought back to his village for some years, perhaps not until he had finished employment. In the 1950s, newspapers and magazines replaced biscuit tins as design models for artists (Fig. 44a, h) and the date of the artists' work became closer to the date of their models.

The designs used by Hasan Arabi which may be located on biscuit tins were of two sorts: those which belonged to the late 1920s and early 1930s and those which dated from 1934 to 1939. Those of the late 1920s and early 1930s were somewhat frivolous, including flower forms, rainbows and coloured balloons, while those of the later 1930s were more severe, featuring angular, jagged shapes. All these designs stopped with the war years and did not reappear.[21] The principal flower used by Hasan Arabi was a single rose on a stem, placed within a banded circle (Fig. 46, Id; Col. pl. 17). He painted the same rose standing in an unusually shaped flower container (Fig. 46, Ia). In one case he combined the rose inside a circle with a flowering vine (Fig. 46, Id). The vine was compressed between two hard-edged, geometric shapes: a triangle above and a semicircle below. Flowers depicted on biscuit tins between 1931 and 1934, as on the Huntley and Palmers 'Bouquet Assorted' packaging (Fig. 46, IId), were enclosed within hard-edged, geometric shapes. Although Hasan may have seen other objects made in the 1930s where flowers were bounded in borders or compressed between geometric shapes[22] (Fig. 46, IIId), his flower within a banded circle probably related to the design of these tins. A 'Wistaria' tin design (Fig. 46, IIa), produced by Huntley and Palmers between 1934 and 1936 showed flowers which were less schematic, but which were placed inside a flower container which resembled that depicted by Hasan Arabi (Fig. 46, Ia). This same 'Wistaria' tin had a border of coloured half-circles such as were used by Hasan in combination with his flower container (Fig. 46, Ia).

From 1934 to 1939 Huntley and Palmers ran a series of tins designed to contain cocktail biscuits. The patterns on them usually had angular space division and jagged, overlapping shapes such as appeared elsewhere in the design of literature about cocktails (Fig. 46, IIIc).[23] Hasan Arabi seemed to be experimenting with this kind of angular shape on his early Ashkeit doorway (Pl. 65) which probably dated little, if at all, before 1941; but these erratic, angular shapes were not common in his work before 1942 (Pl. 62), and they were not painted in colours until his *diwan* designs of 1946 (Fig. 46, Ib; Col. pl. 17). He combined the angular shapes with coloured circles suggestive of coloured balloons depicted on biscuit tins of the late 1920s and early 1930s, and with rainbow arcs, or split concentric circles, in use at the same time (Col. pl. 17). Such coloured concentric circles linked the art of the 1920s and 1930s with the basket patterns traditional to Nubian wall decoration (Pls 9, 26, 27, 35; Col. pl. 8).

Figure 47
Decorations by Abdu
Batoul, 1943 to c. 1948

a *Serra West, Aksha*,
1943, white-lime relief
on mud, south-east
entrance; lion with
sword, crocodile and
man with gun all have
inset, red plastic eyes
from broken bracelets

b, c *Argin, hillet
Shawisharki*, 1944
b tympanum over east
entrance, painted in
red, yellow, grey and
white; the first time
Abdu Batoul used
colours
c *diwan* east wall, detail,
in relief, painted the
same colours as 'b'

d, e, f *Ashkeit, hillet Sorba*
(same house as Col. pl.
18), date unknown,
probably 1944–7, lighter
tone relief on darker mud
d tympanum over water-
pot stand, *diwan*
e south, end wall of
diwan, relief inset with
saucers and small
plates; mirror hung on
top
f courtyard doorway

g *Argin, hillet Rizga*, after
1947, south, end wall
of *diwan*, painted in
blue, gold and white on
mud, no relief

A number of younger artists competed with Hasan Arabi during his Art Deco period, after Dawud Osman had returned to the Second Cataract region around 1945. The most important ones were Abdu Batoul, a butcher in Argin and younger brother of Ahmad Batoul (Appendix B, no. 8; Pls 49,

77; Fig. 47), and Muhammad Suleiman from the Second Cataract (Appendix A, no. 14; Pls 1, 78–84; Col. pl. 18). Abdu Batoul continued the
punched-out triangles and lacy zigzags of his brother Ahmad, although they
had begun to go out of fashion at the time he started using them in 1943 (Fig.
47a). Yet he applied them in his own individual way. This was, at first, to make
the lower edge of the cornice follow the outline of regularly placed inverted
triangles (Fig. 47a). Later, in 1944, his forms became closer to those of Hasan
Arabi, more solid and edged with bands (Fig. 47c–f; Pl. 77; Col. pl. 18). The
peaks surmounting side columns and doorways (Fig. 47a), developed by his
brother, were abandoned in favour of the round arches preferred by Hasan
Arabi (Fig. 47c–g). Abdu retained the groups of three punched-out triangles,
but made them less lacy and more solid by attaching each one to an edging
band (Fig. 47c, e; Pl. 77). His distinguishing feature was a crescent and star
completely surrounded by a circle (Fig. 47c, e). His most notable doorway was
in Ashkeit, set with green ashtrays marked with the name 'Mahallat Saidanawi',
a chain store with branches in Cairo (Col. pl. 18). By 1947 he had abandoned
relief and his last work was done in blue and white paint (Fig. 47g).

Muhammad Suleiman, like Jabir Bab al-Kheir, was not highly regarded
north of Wadi Halfa. People implied that this was because he was an alien, a
Bedouin Arab who moved between Faras and the Second Cataract. Few
could say exactly where he lived. They also did not like the fact that his work was
not symmetrical, and they stated that only those people hired him who could
not afford someone better. His style was based on the X between parallel bars,

Plate 77
Ballana, Egyptian Nubia,
west façade by Abdu
Batoul in white lime and
colours of brown, blue
and gold on mud. The
work shows a synthesis
of the styles of Ahmad
Batoul and Hasan Arabi

characteristic of decorators who began as builders (Pl. 79), and who had origins in Saras or Gemai. An early dated relief, made in 1942, was in Gemai, sheikh‑ship Gemai, hillet Artinassi Island, Tino‑Tu. It consisted of a horizontal band on a *diwan* south wall. The band was made up of five rows of zigzags, which did not extend to the end of the wall on either side. At each end of the band and in the middle there was a vertical pole surmounted by a knob. This unexciting early work was rapidly improved upon in a whole complex of houses in Gemai East, Murshid (Pls 78–81) also dated 1942, where the inventive repertoire of shapes found in all the works of Muhammad Suleiman appeared for the first time. Men in crouching postures were depicted shooting at either a crocodile or a lion with a sword on the opposite sides of the doorways, which were embellished with asymmetric arrangements of relief and peach, turquoise and gold painted designs. The forms most characteristic of Muhammad Sulei‑man were a knob placed on an inverted V, as if on divided legs (Col. pl. 19), curious balloon‑like or pear‑shaped forms, possibly representing ostrich eggs, employed as terminals to side columns and arches, the X between parallel bars, and anthropomorphic peaks with uplifted elbows. Of these, the first three were already apparent in 1942 (Pls 78–81), while the third appeared in a painted *diwan* made in Serra West, sheikship Aksha, in 1943, and was predominant in the courtyard and doorway (Pls 82, 83) leading to a remarkable *dehliz* paint‑

Plate 78
Gemai E., Murshid, west façade decorated by Muhammad Suleiman in 1942. Cuts made into the white‑lime surface of the door surrounds are outlined in peach and ochre paint. The poem to the right of the entrance (Pl. 1) was written by the house‑owner on abandoning the house in 1964. *Photo* T. Higel

ing in Gemai East, Gemai, Said (Col. pl. 19), made in 1962.

Muhammad Suleiman moved north of Wadi Halfa about 1943 and worked there from time to time until 1956, when his last dated doorway occurs in Argin. In Faras East he built and decorated several houses from 1944 to 1946 (Pl. 84) and in one house allowed a group of schoolboys between nine and thirteen years old to fill in his outline drawing in the *diwan* with tones they produced from ground, coloured chalk. Although he returned to Gemai and worked there during 1945 and 1946, he went north again after the 1946 flood and took part in the rebuilding of damaged homes in Argin. While in Gemai he produced painting which was very close to the local women's painting (Col. pl. 19), featuring a horizontal decorative band with peaks, and pictures of basket lids to which he was always tempted to add an anthropomorphic neck (Col. pl. 19). People said that he painted only with a brush and made no use of artificial aids such as plates or string dipped in paint. This free-hand quality was apparent in all of Muhammad Suleiman's work and was the source of some scorn on the part of certain Nubians who viewed what he had done.

Muhammad Suleiman was the last artist to decorate houses around Wadi Halfa. Perhaps because he was a builder, whose art was always allied with his trade, he never abandoned the technique of mud relief as did Hasan Arabi, Dawud Osman and Abdu Batoul. His final example of it was cut in 1961 in the

155

Plate 80
Gemai E., Murshid, diwan
south wall by
Muhammad Suleiman,
made in 1942. The
relief is coloured in
places with pale green
and orange paint. *Photo*
T. Higel

Plate 81
Gemai E., Murshid, west
wall of the *diwan* in Pl. 80,
decorated in relief by
Muhammad Suleiman in
1942. The image on the
left is an extreme
stylisation of a man
shooting a gun. *Photo*
T. Higel

Plate 82
Gemai, hillet Said,
courtyard entrance to the
dehliz in Col. pl. 19,
painted by Muhammad
Suleiman in 1961–2.
The design resembles that
of the Christian period
doorway surround in Pl. 87.
Photo T. Higel

Plate 83
Gemai, hillet Said,
painting by Muhammad
Suleiman on a courtyard
wall near the doorway in
Pl. 82 and outside the
dehliz in Col. pl. 19.
Made in 1961–2. *Photo*
T. Higel

Plate 84
Faras East, hillet Siwe,
house built and decorated
on east façade by
Muhammad Suleiman
in 1946. *Photo* J. Shiner

Yugoslav Expedition house in Halfa Degheim West, *hillet* Sheikh Abd al-Qadir. After 1961 his movements and activities are unclear, but, by 1964, he had gone elsewhere.

In Gemai, Amka, it was said that he had gone to Khashm el-Girba, village 15, but in Duweishat, Ambikol, people were not sure:

'They say Muhammad Suleiman has now a boat to bring things from Kerma. Some say he is at Dufi, some at Akasha. They say also he is forty-five years old and has dropped decoration. His house is not decorated. They say he used to dig wells and one son works a sewing machine.'

CHAPTER SIX

The Iconography of Nubian Wall Decoration

It is clear that the elaborate relief decoration in villages surrounding Wadi Halfa was a twentieth-century phenomenon, and yet certain aspects of the imagery employed are not explained by reference to contemporary material. Thus, it is important to ascertain why the people felt it compulsory to place wild animals on the exteriors of their homes and why they were obsessed with the combination of dome, crescent and horns. These are questions which are not answered by the general characteristics of this art which copies objects which were formerly hung up as wedding decoration or to deflect the evil eye. Nor can the interpretation of the dome and crescent as the tomb of a holy man explain why the flags on each side of it are sometimes turned into 'banana leaves' or horns. For explanation it is necessary to examine the folklore and popular history of the region.

The animals with which it had been customary to decorate houses at the beginning of this century were the crocodile, hyena, scorpion, fox, pigeon, snake and any kind of animal with horns. The extent of power of the creatures in question varied considerably in modern Nubian thought. A basic difference was that some of them were thought to have supernatural power, while others were thought either to have no supernatural power, or else to have it in minimal quantities. In this second group were the scorpion, fox, pigeon and animals with horns.

The scorpion, fox and animals with horns could protect the community in some way. This they did by means of sympathetic magic which was probably related to one or more of their natural characteristics. The scorpion owned a death-dealing sting, so that a clipping of a scorpion (at Argin) or an image of it made of black cotton and put on the wall (at Faras West), was enough to counter the powers of evil. The fox had cunning and enjoyed easy childbirth; he therefore served as a birth amulet.[1] The horns of goats, bovines and wild antelopes protected the animal throughout its life, and so the horns were believed to have the power to protect houses where they were hung up after the animal had been killed.[2] The pigeon may have acquired some protective power as the result of its past association with the Christian cross; the cross was still the most powerful protective symbol in Nubia.[3]

The most dominant feature of crocodiles, snakes and hyenas was their supernatural power. In Nubia crocodiles could affect the fertility of women.[4] It was not stated that they were inhabited by ancestral souls, as believed further south along the Nile at Atbara,[5] but it was thought that they were inhabited by a certain kind of malignant spirit called *sahhar*.[6] Kitchener, during the reconquest of the Sudan, ordered that crocodiles in the Batn al-Hajar should not be shot, because of the existence of this belief.[7] Halfa region Nubians were, on the other hand, convinced that the souls of ancestors resided in snakes. Such snakes could be recognised by the tracks they left in the sand. There was also widespread agreement that snakes guarded the archaeological treasures which were being disturbed. Strange sounds heard in the night were either snakes bewailing their treasures being torn away, or night birds coming down to mate with hyenas (hyenas were considered to be all female and could not therefore mate with each other), or the Saracens rising from the sea. This last explanation, told us in 1964, was probably a reminiscence from the time of Muslim incursions into medieval Nubia. The final days before the flooding were times of supernatural unrest. Various accidents which befell the Polish expedition working on the medieval church at Faras were said to be the result of machinations of the resident snake.

Hyenas were greatly feared. They ate carrion and the flesh of the dead, and were unnatural: the idea that they were all female suggested that they were some kind of baleful female spirit. The hair from their necks could cure barrenness in women.[8] The dreadful stories about their attacking travellers who went alone in unsheltered places began to be transferred from them on to those dogs which managed to escape being shot by the police at the time the people and livestock were moved to Khashm el-Girba.

Of the animals listed as house decoration at the beginning of this century, the fox and hyena were no longer used in 1964, with one possible exception (Fig. 31c). The serpent was also infrequent, and only one example was seen (Fig. 39), although the local inhabitants implied that it was still in common use. On the other hand, a new animal with supernatural qualities had been added to the repertoire, becoming as important as the crocodile. This was the lion with the sword. It is quite likely that in Nubia this lion image was a borrowing from contemporary Islamic material, where it frequently appeared (Fig. 35).[9] Older Nubians thought it represented the Arab hero, Antar, or King Farouk, while younger ones thought it was the British lion. The motif of the lion with the sword was also known to be an image of Ali Ibn Abi Talib, the major person of the Muslim Shia sect. He was the cousin of the Prophet and married his daughter Fatimah; he possessed remarkable courage and was eventually murdered and elevated to importance by the Shia group after his death.

The Sudanese are not Shia, but the popularity of Ali and his two fierce sons is widespread in Egypt and the Sudan as an inheritance from the Fatimid Caliphs of Egypt, who were Shia.[10] The imagery was well known from prints that were sold in the markets. Ali was shown either as a fat man seated on a prayer mat, with lions carrying swords to each side, or as a lion carrying a sword. When he was shown anthropomorphically, the lions flanking him represented his two sons, Hasan and Husein, who imitated him in fighting power but could not excel his unique prowess. Sudanese today swear by the sharp sword of Ali 'karrar', Ali the fighter. A heretic once stood behind a tree and Ali sliced the tree and the heretic at one blow. On another occasion he cut off the head of a man so cleanly that the man did not notice, until Ali said to him, 'Just nod your head!' In the imagery of popular prints, a picture of a single lion with a sword was Ali, while two lions with swords were his two sons.[11]

A doorway in Ashkeit designed by Ahmad Batoul shows the central entrance flanked by two lions carrying swords (Pl. 47). This is one of the few examples which does not have a central dome over the door, suggestive of the tomb of a Muslim holy man or saint (Fig. 24). Instead there are two crossed flags, representing the flags of the holy man's particular religious group which are normally placed around his tomb or shrine of the same shape.[12] It would seem that the entrance itself is intended to signify the tomb, or Ali himself, since anything flanked by lions carrying swords may signify Ali. Although Ali Ibn Abi Talib is not an indigenous Sudanese saint, the Sudanese do have several saints called Ali.[13] The picture of one of them was put up over a doorway in a village in Kosha,[14] underneath the skull of a crocodile (Fig. 48). The crocodile in Nubia was thought to be awesome and spirit-filled, and it had the power to bring fertility to women. These features it shared with the tomb of the holy man, which was visited by women to bring them children. The cult of holy men's tombs is, in fact, the main aspect of Islam in which the Sudanese women actively participate.[15] The cult was particularly alive around Wadi Halfa

Figure 48
Kosha, Dal, Abdullando,
doorway constructed by
Ai Hasan Taffoul,
surmounted by crocodile
skull and picture of a
Sudanese Saint Ali

Plate 85
Halfa Degheim West, hillet
Sheikh Abd al-Qadir,
medieval church fresco.
Nubian ruler wearing the
Eparch's horned crown,
surmounted by a crescent
on a stem. Photo
M. Medić

where, as we have seen, representations of these tombs were painted on walls at weddings[16] (Fig. 23).

The holy man's tomb, or 'qubba' is built in the form of a domed structure (Fig. 24), sometimes surmounted by a crescent on a pole (Col. pl. 21).[17] This shaped tomb is widely used throughout North Africa,[18] but in the Wadi Halfa region it had antecedents in the Christian period. The crown of the Christian

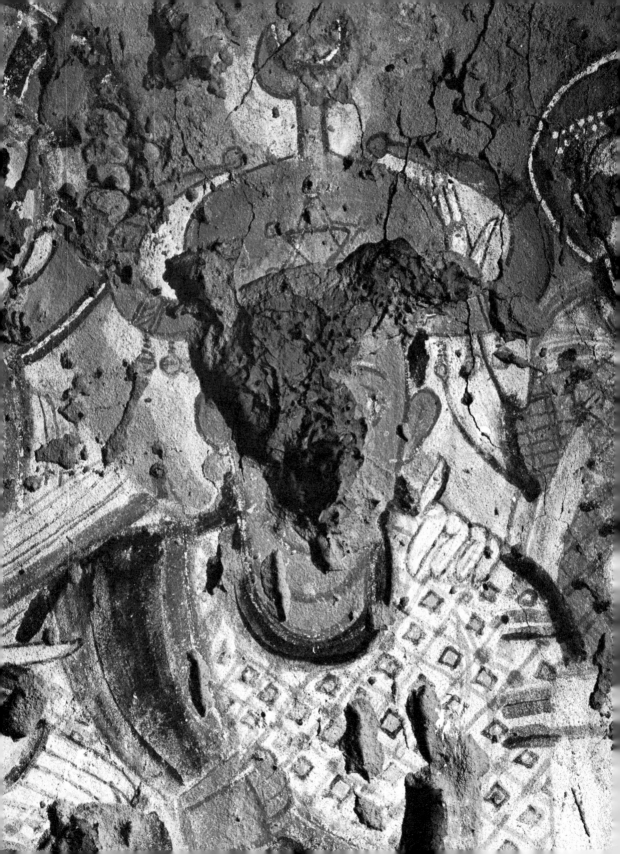

Plate 87
Faras West, the Great
Cathedral, medieval
painted doorway
surround depicting horns
on either side of the door.
The central feature may
represent a Christian period
tomb, shown over the
door as were tombs of
Muslim holy men under
Islam
Use of photo courtesy
K. Michalowski

Nubian king, who was called by the Greek title 'Eparch' of Nobadia, was a dome surmounted by a crescent on a pole.[19] Not only was it so depicted in the medieval frescoes of the churches of Faras[20] (Col. pl. 20) and Sheikh Abd al-Qadir[21] (Pls 85, 86), but it was also mentioned by an early traveller who described it in its full form when the dome was flanked by horns.[22] The pagan Funj of Sennar, south of Nubia, who held Dongola from the sixteenth century until 1776, invested their tributary kings with this kind of crown long after the break-up of the Nubian kingdoms.[23]

The crown worn by a Nubian boy prince in the medieval frescoes from Faras (Fig. 50b; Col. pl. 20) differed from that shown at Sheikh Abd al-Qadir (Fig. 50c). The former was a variant form, possibly signifying the boy's lack of adult power, and consisted merely of the dome without horns surmounted by a crescent on a stem (Col. pl. 20), thus resembling some modern Nubian doorway designs (Fig. 50f). It is interesting to compare this crown with the horned crown at Sheikh Abd al-Qadir (Pl. 86) and with a doorway decoration (Fig. 50a; Pl. 97) and tympanum (Pl. 88; Fig. 50t) at Faras church, both of which were

Plate 86
Halfa Degheim West, hillet
Sheikh Abd al-Qadir,
detail of Pl. 85.
Photo M. Medić

a

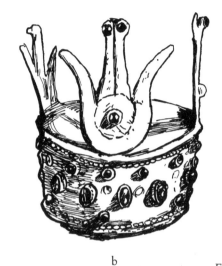

b

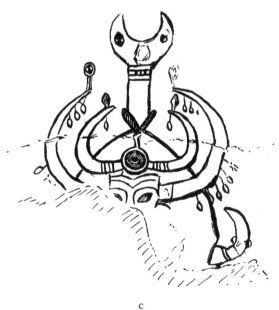

c

Figure 49
a, b *Ballana,* Egyptian
Nubia, X-Group
crowns, fourth–sixth
century, silver set with
semi-precious gems, after
W. B. Emery

a king's crown, crescent
on stem enclosing
feather motif from
Egyptian Atef crown;
horned ram at base of
stem

b queen's crown, horns
enclosing a disc, as on
Egyptian Isis headdress;
feathers surmounting
disc

c *Faras West*, medieval
fresco, Eparch's
crown, twelfth-century
fresco, after K.
Michalowski; crescent
on stem, horned animal
at base of stem, two
pairs of horns enclosing
a disc

painted with horns. On the tympanum the horns were at the top of the dome,[24] as was the crescent on the Eparch's crown, but they turned down instead of up and thus resembled the form described in modern decorators' terminology as 'banana leaves' (Figs 50r, 50s). The doorway at Faras had a rectangular painted surround, hatched and bordered with a band of circles (Fig. 50a). Three large orbs surmounted this rectangle. The central orb was slightly pear-shaped and painted on a small dome which was topped by a cross. The two horns at the outer edges of the rectangle were painted turning down, and looked like those sometimes painted by Hasan Arabi in his *diwan* decorations (Fig. 50h, m; Pl. 90). Hasan never called these shapes 'banana leaves' as did Jabir Bab al-Kheir; they remained unexplained. The shapes on the medieval door-way at Faras, which were strikingly like those used by Hasan, clearly represented horns (Pl. 87). Both medieval doorways and medieval crowns, therefore, resembled modern Nubian doorways in having domes and horns, while the crown had, in addition, the horned crescent on top of a stem or pole.

Both horns and crescent which appeared on the medieval Nubian crown were revered in Nubia before Islam. The horned skulls of bovines were put on ancient, C-group graves at Faras where there was, later in the time of Rameses II, a shrine dedicated to the cow goddess Hathor.[25] The cow goddess Hathor

Plate 88
Faras West, the Great Cathedral, medieval tympanum decoration surmounted by horns. Use of photo courtesy K. Michalowski

a b c d e f g h i j k l m n o p q r s t

Figure 50

Representations of horns, and crescents on stems surmounting a dome, which are found in both medieval and modern Nubian art

a   *Faras West*, Faras church, painted doorway, *c.* twelfth century; horns, central dome
b   *Faras West*, Faras church fresco, young prince wearing a form of the Nubian Eparch's crown with a dome surmounted by a crescent on a stem, twelfth century
c   *Halfa Degheim West, hillet Sheikh Abd el-Qadir*, church, fresco, Nubian Eparch wearing typical crown; horns, central dome surmounted by a crescent on a stem
d   *Faras West*, village doorway, anonymous, relief, suggestion of the horn and dome structure of doorway 'a'
e   *Ashkeit*, doorway by Abd al-Aziz al-Amin, 1947, painted relief; horns, central dome
f   *Debeira East*, doorway by Ahmad Batoul, 1927, relief; dome surmounted by a crescent on a stem
g   *Argin*, doorway, anonymous, house abandoned 1946, relief; dome surmounted by crescent on stem
h   *Ashkeit*, water-pot enclosure by Hasan Arabi; central dome, horns, orbs surmounting rectangular framework as in 'a'
i   *Debeira East*, abandoned house complex inhabited 1911, wall painting; dome surmounted by horns
j   *Debeira East*, doorway in relief by Ahmad Batoul, 1927; dome surmounted by horns
k   *Debeira East*, abandoned house complex, wall painting, dome surmounted by horns
l   *Argin*, doorway by Ahmad Batoul before 1930; earliest work in Argin, relief; horns
m   *Ashkeit*, water-pot enclosure by Hasan Arabi, *c.* 1941; central dome, horns
n   *Halfa Degheim E.*, doorway, mud relief, anonymous; crescent on stem surmounting a dome, flags in place of horns
o   *Argin*, house entrance by Jabir Bab al-Kheir, *c.* 1929; central dome horns
p   *Faras West*, anonymous relief, horns
q   *Faras West*, anonymous doorway relief, dome surmounted by horns
r   *Debeira East*, doorway by Jabir Bab al-Kheir, *c.* 1930, relief where the horns were identified by him as banana leaves on banana trees, and the central dome, with surmount, as a human being with upraised arms
s   *Argin*, doorway by Jabir Bab al-Kheir, *c.* 1929; horns
t   *Faras West*, church, tympanum decoration, dome surmounted by horns

and the ancient Egyptian moon goddess Isis, as well as rulers who adopted their attributes, were shown both at Faras and at Abu Simbel wearing the head-dress of the moon disc placed between horns (Pl. 89).[26] From the Ptolemaic period until the sixth century A.D., when Justinian ordered the cult to be suppressed, Isis was favoured in Nubia above other foreign deities. Each year the Nubians were permitted to remove the statue of Isis from her temple at Philae and take it for some time into their own land.[27] The Nubians did not abandon lunar deities with the coming of Christianity. Abu Salih writing in the thirteenth century mentions one Nubian town which had not only a well-built church overlooking the Nile, but also a pagan shrine in the town centre which contained 'an idol of a single piece which has a moon carved on the chest'.[28] Nubian rulers of the fourth to sixth century A.D., before their conversion, were already wearing a crown with crescent and horns, as found among the buried

treasures at Ballana and Qustal, north of Faras[29] (Fig. 49a, b). Here one crown showed the horns attached to an animal's head, that of a ram (Fig. 49a). This feature also occurred on another Christian medieval crown depicted at Faras (Fig. 49c) only at Faras the animal had double horns.[30]

It may be observed that while, by the Middle Ages, the representation of a dome shape combined with horns could be either a tympanum decoration or the crown of the Nubian king, later it was a tympanum decoration (Fig. 50e, i, o, p; Pl. 82), or the tomb of a holy man with the horns converted to flags (Fig. 50n; Col. pl. 21). It was also a traditional shape, with horn-flags (Fig. 23i, j), or banana leaves (Fig. 50 o, r), or even once more the crown of a king. One substitute for a central dome in the compositions of Hasan Arabi was a shape with a crescent on top known as the crown of King Farouk, which had been given flags instead of horns (Fig. 51a). In some cases the so-called crown was indistinguishable from the arched shape known as a dome. Khalil Saleh, who used the design over his own doorway (Fig. 51c), said:

> 'The shape over the door is just decoration. It is supposed to be a crown; I don't know whose crown it is. I wanted to make a crown, but didn't know which or whose. Other people put different kinds of crowns. The domes are crowns, sometimes.'

Plate 89
Abu Simbel, temple of Hathor, south wall, barque of the cow goddess. The figures wear variant forms of the crown with moon disc and horns

a

b

c

d

e

Figure 51
Recent Nubian and Egyptian
representations of a king's crown

a Hasan Arabi, *Argin*, 1945,
  painting on the *diwan* south wall
b Hasan Arabi, *Ashkeit*, 1946, *diwan*
  south wall
c Khalil Saleh, *Ashkeit*, entrance
  to own home, decoration over the
  door
d Farouk's crown as represented on
  his throne, news photo, *Al-Hilal*,
  vol. 48, Cairo 1939–40
e Crown depicted in a cigarette
  advertisement, *Al-Mussawar* 779,
  Cairo 1939

There is some evidence that the Nubians were very anxious to make the doorway a point of purification for those who set foot into the house. Their lintels were not infrequently carved with some inscription from the Quran, calling a blessing on whoever passed underneath and, presumably, keeping out devils and djinns. It would have been in keeping to identify the doorway with the presence of a sacred person, such as a saint or a holy man, who had considerable protective power and who would thus pass this power to the door and those who passed beneath. This might have been carried out by placing a picture of the holy man over the door (Fig. 48) or by changing the tympanum into the shape of that which contained his spirit or power; namely, his head-dress or his tomb. The door entrance itself could even symbolically replace the venerated person, as the door replaced the Prophet's cousin Ali in the iconographical arrangement where Ali is between his two sons who are shown as lions with swords. In all cases the person entering the house would pass under, or through (Fig. 23m), the purifying power or *baraka*[31] of the sacred person.

It is probable that Christianity was never such a personal religion to the Nubians as is Islam. Christianity, for the Nubian, implied that the subjects of adoration were foreign and white.[32] The conversion of Nubia to Christianity was peaceful; there was no call for martyrs to the faith, so there was no possibility of canonising Nubian martyrs. Islam, on the other hand, did not require its saints to have died for their faith, so that there are a number of Islamic saints and holy men who were Nubian, including the Mahdi himself. This is a major attraction of Islam over Christianity. Islam also has a wider appeal than had Christianity, which was directed towards the nobility. The Christian liturgy was strange to the average Nubian since it was conducted in Coptic or Greek, which they could not understand.[33] It is very likely that the village Nubian put most faith in supernatural, superstitious aspects of Christianity, power-containing signs and the like. In the same way, his ancestors under Egyptian and Meroitic rule had placed faith in amulets while priests gave their attention to the rich. Even today the women, who are largely excluded from Islam, place faith in amulets and that major power-source, the holy man's tomb.[34]

The Nubian Church was not strong and it is unlikely that it would have been able to restrain the pagan superstitions of its members. Nubian Christianity was on an outer fringe of the Christian world. Few other churches were interested in it. The Arab conquest of Egypt in 700 made a gulf between the Nubian Christians and their parent Coptic Church in Egypt. From this time, Nubia's elegant church painting slowly degenerated into folk art[35] and it may be assumed that the spiritual life of the average Nubian suffered a similar decline.[36] Yet there is no doubt that a strong faith in the merit of things from which power issued, whether the cross, the crocodile or things wearing horns, remained throughout.

Certain Christian views which might have been retained by the Nubians could have been unorthodox. The Nubian Church followed the Coptic Monophysite practice for all or some major part of its existence.[37] The Monophysites believed that Christ was of One Spirit with God the Father.[38] This notion could be combined with the prevalent Byzantine view that Christ's representative on earth, the Christian ruler, imitated the role of Christ,[39] thus making the ruler exceptionally close to God. To Africans, the idea would have resembled the familiar concept of cosmic kingship. The church at Faras, in its later phases, had some unique images of royalty: a Nubian prince was shown sitting on the very lap of Christ, as Christ sits on that of the Mother of God[40] (Col. pl. 20). The prince wore a version of the Eparch's Crown, in the form of a dome surmounted by a crescent (Fig. 50b). It may be presumed that to the Nubian, who felt that Christian saints were remote, being foreign and white, the Nubian king, who in Monophysite views could partake of the actual Spirit of God, was a better object of reverence because he was one of them, as were later Sudanese Muslim holy men. It is certainly true that when the Nubian kings became Muslim (which they did by marriage and matrilineal succession rather than by conversion) Nubian Christianity lost much of its appeal and the Christian community drifted over to Islam.[41] The imagery of the horned domed crown, however, like the cross itself, may have been too strong a power-source to be abandoned, continuing to dispense its force within the framework of Islam, while the form of the holy man's tomb adopted some of its characteristics.[42]

The earliest works of Ahmad Batoul and Jabir Bab al-Kheir, made in the 1920s, showed features which may have derived from long-standing local traditions. The dome and outward curving horn shapes (Fig. 32b, g, h, k, p; Fig. 50 o), as in the painted doorway and tympanum design at Faras (Fig. 50a, t), were visible in the work of both. The horn shapes were shortly afterwards abandoned by Ahmad Batoul, who came originally from Upper Egypt, yet were retained by Jabir, born locally in Debeira (Fig. 50r). It is interesting that these horns were most prominent in the work of Hasan Arabi (Pl. 90; Fig. 50h, m), the painter who used many sophisticated forms which were part of the international repertoire of design in the 1920s and 1930s (Figs 45, 46). Yet, unlike Ahmad Batoul and even Jabir Bab al-Kheir, who was of southern slave stock, Hasan Arabi was a local Nubian. His birthplace, Argin on the west bank of the Nile, was only a few miles south of Faras church.

Plate 90
Ashkeit, surround for a
water-pot stand designed
by Hasan Arabi in
1943, painted rust,
yellow, pale blue and
pale green. The bird
stands on a curved form
identified as a banana
leaf by decorator Jabir
Bab al-Kheir

CHAPTER SEVEN

Aftermath of Nubian Wall Decoration

Relief decoration of the sort which was typical in the region of Wadi Halfa is no longer made. This is partly due to different conditions in Khashm el-Girba, where most people of the Wadi Halfa region were moved in 1964, and partly because of the feeling of instability of those Nubians who have chosen to remain on the outskirts of the flood-ruined town of Wadi Halfa, in temporary shacks which form a new community. Yet the move from ample mud dwellings around Wadi Halfa to cramped concrete houses in Khashm el-Girba is not the complete explanation for the abandonment of this art. The technique was already dying out some years before the move took place. In the 1950s, the only decorators who were still making relief and not purely painted designs were those, like Muhammad Suleiman and the Taffoul brothers, who came from south of the Second Cataract where the technique had never become so refined and where it did not so quickly become out of date.

Even some forms of purely painted designs had begun to die out around Wadi Halfa by the late 1950s. No façade decoration of any sort was being made. It was said in Argin: 'The custom of making painted or relief decoration out-side the house is becoming old, and people are now satisfied with decoration inside the house only.' Yet it is possible that wall painting may have some future in Khashm el-Girba. Unlike mud relief, it can be applied to any surface. Jabir Bab al-Kheir, partly as a result of this study, resolved to try to continue his work in Khashm el-Girba; he was capable of producing competent painting (Col. pl. 11). It is not yet known whether or not he has succeeded to do so in his new environment.

Some attempt has been made at Khashm el-Girba to adapt old customs to the new way of life. Abdulla Sabbar, an architect born in Ashkeit, went to Khashm el-Girba for the first Id festival, following Ramadan, since the people had been moved. His account was as follows:

'It was the custom in Ashkeit for the entire village, men and boys, to progress from certain house to certain house, these houses being small community gathering places, one for each small area. The men used to go in a straight line from place to place, as the village was laid out in a straight line along the Nile, and they stopped to have coffee in each selected house in the order in which it came. This they did all day. In Khashm el-Girba they wanted to retain this custom, but unfortunately, the village was laid out in a square. This led to a long discussion among the men as to which was the most important aspect of the custom, the order of the houses or the straightness in which people moved. They decided that the straightness was more important, and arranged to bisect the square, divided into groups, so that each group went in a straight line.'

Abdulla Sabbar also noticed a certain amount of painted decoration in Khashm el-Girba, most of it by women. The designs differed from those in their original home of Ashkeit.[1] There were few traditional motifs in which geometric shapes appeared, possibly because these had been patterned on the medium of cut mud relief. Instead the paintings showed a new interest in plant forms, in which the people may have expressed their nostalgia for the palm trees which do not grow in Khashm el-Girba, and for the lush banks of the Nile. Neither do the flat-topped hills of the type which surround Wadi Halfa exist there for the land is totally flat. There is, however, one hill forty kilometres away and the people make regular excursions to look at it.

Where known, the rates at which individual decorators were paid is given. These sums may be compared with the salaries earned by servants working in Khartoum, many of whom were Nubian and the employers of the decorators mentioned below. In the 1940s, servants working for Europeans were paid between £5 and £8 per month. By 1964, servants working for Europeans were paid between £12 and £18 a month. Servants working for Sudanese were paid on a lower scale, and in 1964 there were still some of them earning as little as £5 per month. At that time the Sudanese pound was worth slightly more than the pound sterling. It was divided into piastres, of which there were 100 to the pound.

The measure by which decorators were paid was either the metre or the *diraa* which was the equivalent of 58 cm.

* Certain decorators whose work was insignificant, are not referred to in the text.

** Only a few of the decorators who are mentioned in the text were still to be found in the area, and were available for interview.

A: *Decorators of South Wadi Halfa*

1. HAMID*
   occupation: builder
   years active: 1920

ethnic group: Shaiqiya or Lubatab
birthplace: Central Sudan
approximate life span: unknown
area of work: Kosha, Farka, where he made a raised band of mud relief round the doorways of houses he built
residence: the South

2. AHMAD DVIZ JAROUN*
occupation: not clear
years active: 1930
ethnic group: Mahas Nubian
birthplace: unknown
approximate life span: unknown
area of work: Saras, Saras⁄Tahali, where he decorated one doorway with a crocodile similar to Fig. 31a, b, and a four⁄legged animal on a zigzag base line
residence: Saras, Saras Tahali

3. SAYYID AHMAD HOGLA** (Pl. 28)
occupation: before 1929, smith at the Sudan Railway dock in Wadi Halfa
1929–64, builder, labourer on archaeological excavations
1942, lockmaker
years active: 1928–46
ethnic group: Arab
birthplace: Halfa Degheim E., *hillet* Majareb
age: born about 1910
area of work: Halfa Degheim
residence before the flooding: Halfa Degheim E.
residence afterwards: Atbara

4. OSMAN AHMAD KHALIL, called OSMAN AHMAD NAGGASH
(Fig. 25a–c; Fig. 28c)
kin: father of Ibrahim Osman
occupation: builder, carpenter, decorator
teacher of: Ibrahim Osman
co⁄worker with: Kasbana Hasan Taffoul, who worked with him four years helping him build
years active: 1924–63
ethnic group: Mahas Nubian
age: elderly in 1964
area of work: Kosha, Farka and Mugraka
1952 Saras, Saras⁄Tahali
1954–60 Kosha, Dal
1956 Kosha, Serkamatto
residence: Kosha, Farka, Gjinengurka
rate of pay: 150 piastres to decorate the front of a house which he did not build. The decoration was made after 1938

178

5. IBRAHIM OSMAN (Fig. 25d; Fig. 26a)
kin: son of Osman Ahmad Khalil
occupation: builder, carpenter, tin-cutter
years active: 1962–4
ethnic group: Mahas Nubian
age: unknown
area of work: Kosha, Farka, Gjinengurka, where he decorated his own house
    (Fig. 25d)
        1962–4 Kosha, Serkamatto, Deshna
residence: Kosha, Farka, Gjinengurka

6. MUHAMMAD EL-TAYIB*
occupation: builder
years active: 1934–54
ethnic group: Nubian; unknown if Mahas or Dongolawi
birthplace and residence: Kerma, hillet Nuzul
age: born 1919(?)
area of work: 1934–54 Duweishat, Melik el Nasr and, reputedly, Kerma and Wadi
    Halfa
rate of pay: for the decoration of a crocodile (type of Fig. 31a, b) and a bird on a
    zigzag ground line made in the *dehliz* of a house which he built in 1934, he was
    paid nothing. The house-owner said, 'He wasn't paid for the decoration as it was
    for himself.' By 1954 he was receiving payment for decoration; namely, for
    plastering and decorating the *mandara* of a house which he had built in 1952 in
    Duweishat, Melik el-Nasr, Geiya. For plastering including decoration, he was
    paid $6\frac{1}{2}$ piastres the *diraa*. Plastering without decoration would have cost less.
    The designs consisted of window surrounds, two birds and a rabbit, and looked
    like the early work of Batoul (Fig. 32k–p)

7. ABDOUN MUHAMMAD FADL** (Fig. 27b; Fig. 28a, b)
occupation: farmer who turned to building and decoration
co-worker with: Muhammad Beshir, plasterer, who decorated some houses which
    Abdoun built
years active: 1934–54
ethnic group: Mahas Nubian
age: born 1904
area of work: 1934–54 Saras, Atiri
        1939–45 Saras, Saras-Tahali; also Atbara and Wadi Halfa
residence before the flooding: Saras, Saras-Tahali, Sorbar
residence afterwards: Kerma
rate of pay: when he made uncoloured relief decoration to finish off a house which
    he had built, he was paid nothing beyond the price of building. When the
    decoration was coloured he was paid for his labour, although the house-owner
    provided the red earth colour which was popular for colouring house exteriors
    in Saras

8. DAWUD OSMAN (Figs 42b, 43, 44; Pls 66–7, 69–75)
occupation: builder, decorator, bricklayer
co-worker: Hasan Arabi, 1940–3
years active: 1935–60
ethnic group: Mahas Nubian
age: born 1919
birthplace: Batn al-Hajar, specifically Gemai, Kokki Islands
area of work: 1935–64 Gemai, East and West
      1942 Ashkeit
      1939–44 Argin
      1955 South Halfa or Halfa Degheim, East and West
residence before the flooding: Gemai, Kokki Islands (Fig. 44d) and Argin
residence afterwards: 1964 Khashm el-Girba, village 54
      1964 Atbara, Sudan Government Engineering Department, bricklaying section
rate of pay: he was paid more when his relief decorations were coloured than when they were not (at Gemai, Amka, when he decorated a house in 1949). In 1959 at Gemai, Amka, Asheile he was paid £5 to decorate two rooms, one being a *mandara* (Fig. 44h). These decorations were painted, without relief, and the house-owner provided the colours

9. MAHMUD MUHAMMAD OSMAN, called MAHMUD ITNAN (Figs 8e, 27a)
occupation: builder and decorator
competitor with: Abdoun Muhammad Fadl, who worked in the same area
years active: 1939–59
ethnic group: Mahas Nubian
birthplace: Saras
age: unknown
area of work: 1939–52 Saras, Saras-Tahali
residence before flooding: Saras, Saras-Tahali, Mushra, in a house he decorated in 1943
residence afterwards: Abri, working as builder
rate of pay: he was given no pay for uncoloured relief decorations which he added to embellish a house he had built. However, when he finished the building, the house-owner was expected to give him some baksheesh. In one case (Fig. 27a), in 1948, he decorated two doorways in a house which had been built by another builder in 1942. It was said that he did not ask for a specific amount of money, but when he had finished, the house-owner gave him 60 piastres

10. DAWUD SULEIMAN ABDULLA*
occupation: builder
years active: building from 1924, decoration work undated
ethnic group: Kenuzi Nubian
age: dates unknown, dead by 1964
area of work: Aswan and Saras, Saras-Tahali, Sorbar, where he came to live after 1924. There is only one house decorated by him, and it is in the 'Saras' style of

Abdoun Muhammad Fadl and Mahmud Itnan (Fig. 28a–c), with decoration painted in red earth colour

11. OSMAN KHEIRI* (Figs 209, 25d, Col. pl. 1)

occupation: builder

co-workers: Ibrahim Osman, who decorated a house built by Osman Kheiri (Fig. 25d), and Ali Muhammad Abakr, who did carpentry, pierced tin work and mud relief in houses which he built

years active: 1939–63

ethnic group: Mahas Nubian

approximate life span: birth date unknown, died 1963

area of work: 1939 Kosha, Farka

1954–7 Saras, Saras-Tahali, where he built the house in Col. pl. 1 in 1954 and decorated it in 1957

1957–8 Kosha, Dal

residence: unknown

12. ALI MUHAMMAD ABAKR** (Fig. 26b)

occupation: farmer, carpenter, decorator, tin-cutter

co-worker of: Osman Kheiri, for whose houses he did carpentry and some decoration

years active: 1940–63

ethnic group: Mahas Nubian

birthplace: Kosha, Serkamatto

age: elderly in 1964

area of work: 1940–63 Kosha, Serkamatto

residence: Kosha, Serkamatto, Karbin. In 1964 he was living in a two-room house unit as in Fig. 3c, with additions for kitchen and goats; the only decoration was a doorway painted by a schoolboy son

rate of pay: for doors, windows, cut tin decoration and general house fittings in a house built by Osman Kheiri, as well as mud relief, he was paid £30 in 1944. For a lock made in 1960 he was paid 25 piastres, and for an *angarib* bed with decorated legs, £2·50. He was paid 10 piastres for making a simple mud relief surround for a cupboard which was hollowed out of the wall

13. OSMAN SULEIMAN SALEH (Fig. 30)

occupation: artist-decorator

years active: 1942–52

ethnic group: Mahas Nubian

area of work: Saras, Saras-Tahali

other information: unknown

rate of pay: for making a band of relief consisting of zigzags and the X between parallel bars, and for colouring it with red earth colour, he was paid £1·50 in 1952. The band ran along the top and down the corners of a house in Saras, Saras-Tahali, Agremasho, which had been built by Mahmud Itnan in 1940. The red earth colour had been brought from the mountains and cost the house-owner 30 piastres for one tin

14. MUHAMMAD SULEIMAN AHMAD GRASHA, called MUHAMMAD ARAB (Pls 1, 32,
    78–84; Col. pl. 19)
occupation: builder, decorator
years active: 1942–62
ethnic group: Bedouin Arab
age: born *c.* 1919(?)
birthplace: unknown
area of work: 1942 Gemai, Gemai, Artinassi Island
                1942–62 Gemai E., Murshid
                1943 Serra West, Aksha
                1944 Gemai, Amka
                1946, 1954 Faras East
                1956 Argin
                c. 1960 Halfa Degheim West
residence before the flooding: said to be (a) Faras; (b) Saras
residence afterwards: reported in Serra West, Aksha, to be Ballana, Upper Egypt;
    reported in Gemai, Amka to be Khashm el-Girba, village 15; reported in
    Duweishat, Ambikol, to be Kerma, Dufi (? unlocated) or Akasha
15. KASBANA HASAN TAFFOUL** (Pl. 42)
    kin: brother of Ali, Himad and Saleh Hasan Taffoul
    Son of Hasan Taffoul of Semna, a carpenter, maker of artificial limbs and metal
    tools, saddle-maker, boat-builder, house-builder and decorator, who died in
    1939. Grandson of a member of the Tafulab tribe at Semna, who was a fisherman
occupation: builder and decorator
co-worker with: his brothers, at different times
influenced by: Osman Ahmad Khalil and Mohammad Diyyab Mohammad, both
    of whom were older than Kasbana. He 'copied some of their styles and then
    digested them to make his own style'
ethnic group: Mahas Nubian of the Tafulab tribe
age: born 1926
birthplace: Saras West, Semna, Kuddai
area of work: 1946, 1950 Duweishat, Melik el-Nasr
area of work: 1950–58 Saras, Semna
                1954 Wadi Halfa
                1955, 1956 Duweishat, Ambikol
                1959 Akasha, Ukma
                1960 Kosha, Dal. He also worked in Khartoum, and Khashm
                el-Girba where he helped build the Government buildings
residence before the flooding: Saras West, Semna, Bishangi. His own house (Pl. 42),
    with façade, courtyard doorways and *mandara* painted in colours, was the most
    elaborate decoration he made
residence after the flooding: Khashm el-Girba
rate of pay: 1950 For decorating the inside and outside of the mosque in Saras,

Semna, Bishangi he was paid £1·50. Because it was a mosque, he did not want more money. The interior painting, in gold ochre on white, resembled a kind of women's painting type A (Fig. 22n)

1955 For building work in Duweishat, Ambikol Island, Kasbana was paid 30 or 40 piastres the *diraa*, depending on how far the site was located from water. Water was necessary to mix with the mud. If the builder carried water he charged more for building. Otherwise water was brought by the house-owner. For plastering work with decoration, Kasbana was paid 5 or 5½ piastres the *diraa*. For plastering without decoration, he was paid 2½ or 3½ piastres the *diraa*

1959 In Akasha, Ukma, Iere, Kasbana was paid 13 piastres the *diraa* for building the house, and an additional £2·50 for plastering and decorating the front façade

16. ALI HASAN TAFFOUL (Fig. 48)

kin: brother of Kasbana, Himad and Saleh Hasan Taffoul

occupation: builder and decorator

co-workers: his brothers, particularly when they all worked together in Wadi Halfa in 1954

years active: 1944–64

ethnic group: Mahas Nubian of the Tafulab tribe

age: born between 1926 and 1930

birthplace: Saras West, Semna, Kuddai

area of work: 1944–58 Saras, Semna, where he painted façades earth red, or filled space with incised zigzags and the X between parallel bars
1954 Kosha, Dal (Fig. 48)
1962 Kosha, Serkamatto where he principally decorated cupboard surrounds in simplified imitation of those made by his younger brother, Saleh Hasan Taffoul (Fig. 29)

residence: Kosha, Dal, Jedid

rate of pay: in Kosha, Serkamatto, he was paid 25 piastres for each cupboard surround which he made during 1962

17. HIMAD HASAN TAFFOUL

kin: brother of Kasbana, Ali and Saleh Hasan Taffoul

occupation: builder

years active: 1952–5

ethnic group: Mahas Nubian of the Tafulab Tribe

age: born between 1926 and 1930

birthplace: Saras West, Semna, Kuddai

area of work: Kosha, Dal; and Wadi Halfa in 1954

residence: unknown

18. SALEH HASSAN TAFFOUL** (Fig. 29)

kin: youngest brother of Kasbana, Ali and Himad

occupation: builder and decorator

co-workers: his brothers, particularly in 1954 when they all worked in Wadi Halfa.
He did not join his brother Kasbana in Khartoum. Further, Saleh worked four
years with Osman Ahmad Khalil in Farka, as a building assistant

influenced by: the work of Osman Ahmad Khalil of Farka;

favourite decorators in order of preference: Osman Ahmad Khalil, Ibrahim Farum from
Abri, Natig Khalil from Farka, Sabri

ethnic group: Mahas Nubian of the Tafulab tribe from Semna

age: born 1930

birthplace: Saras West, Semna, Kuddai

area of work: 1954 Wadi Halfa

        1954–64 Kosha, Dal

        1957–63 Kosha, Serkamatto and Akasha, Kulb

        He also worked in Abri

residence: Kosha, Dal, Saide, in a house which he neither built nor decorated
except for one *manwara* cupboard for which he made the surround

rate of pay: for building he was paid by the *diraa*, but for making *manwara* cupboards
(Fig. 29), he was paid 50 piastres for big ones, 40 piastres for middle-sized ones,
and 25 piastres for small ones. He frequently made *manwaras* in houses which
he did not build, such as that of the Sheikh of Serkamatto (Fig. 29b), where he
was paid 60 piastres per *manwara*, and where he cut the image of a dog in relief,
above one such cupboard

19. AHMAD OSMAN*

occupation: decorator

co-worker of: the builder Mahmud Suleiman. Mahmud was brother to the owner of a
house and café in Saras which were built by Mahmud in 1952 and which are
the only known buildings decorated by Ahmad Osman

years active: 1952

ethnic group: unknown

age: unknown

area of work: Saras East, Saras-Tahali, Alifenti

rate of pay: for decorating inscribed columns at the house corners, colouring them
red and marking them with zigzags and the X between parallel bars, and for
making a doorway in the style of other houses in Saras (Fig. 28a) he was paid
180 piastres in 1952. He was paid an additional 120 piastres for decorating two
such inscribed columns on the café which adjoined the house. In this case, the
red earth colour was provided by the decorator. He needed four tins of colour
to decorate both buildings, and this cost him £1, leaving him £2 profit for his
work

20. MUHAMMAD BESHIR*

occupation: farmer, builder and plasterer, or smoother

co-worker of: Abd el-Jabir who helped him build, and Abdoun Muhammad Fadl
for whom he was the smoother and decorator when Abdoun worked on Mugufil
Island

years active: 1923 as builder

                1957 as smoother and decorator

ethnic group: Mahas Nubian

age: born 1904

area of work: 1923–57 Saras, Atiri, Mugufil Island, where he also farmed

residence: Saras, Atiri, Mugufil Island

rate of pay: For zigzags, simple arches over doorways and the X between parallel bars, all incised into the mud without relief, he was paid nothing. He made it in the course of his smoothing work, and was not asked to do so by the house, owner. The people said that decoration was his own idea because he liked his work to appear better and 'draw more people'

21. OSMAN MUHAMMAD KHAWLA*

occupation: smoother

co-worker: the builder Saleh el-Fadl Medani

years active: 1958

area of work: Duweishat, Ambikol, Angasa

other information: unknown

rate of pay: for mud relief window surrounds consisting of zigzags and a row of triangles, he was paid nothing. It was said, 'he is the person who smooths the house and he doesn't get paid for the decoration'

22. NUGUD ABDULLA*

occupation: unknown

co-worker: the builder Muhammad Idris Abdulla from Duweishat, Ambikol, Abermatto, for whom he decorated one house on completion of the building

years active: 1958

ethnic group: Dongolawi Nubian

age: unknown

area of work: Duweishat, Ambikol, Abermatto, where he decorated two doorways on one house. One doorway had mud relief zigzags and the other was given a smooth mud surround surmounted by a crescent on a stem

residence: Dongola

23. SABRI (Fig. 19; Pls 20–3)

occupation: commercial artist, possibly trained in Italy

years active: 1959–64

ethnic group: Egyptian

age: born around 1924

birthplace: Cairo

area of work: 1959 Gemai, Kokki Islands

                1960 Kosha, Dal

                1961 Kosha, Serkamatto

                1962 Kosha, Farka

                      Kosha, Mugraka

                He also worked in Abri and Dongola

residence before the flooding: Abri; Gemai, Kokki Islands; Kosha, Farka

residence afterwards: Dongola

rates of pay: in 1959, on Kokki Islands, he decorated more than five *diwans* for 270 piastres (£2·70) per *diwan*

In 1960, in Kosha, Dal, Aro, he was paid £8 to decorate a men's sitting-room (*mandara*), and he finished it in seventeen days. Sabri brought his own roller and brushes, but the house-owner provided colours

In Kosha, Farka, Kurkur, he was paid £5 to decorate a *mandara* (Fig. 19c, d). Paints were provided by the house-owner and the work took one month

24. SAYYID ABD EL-HAMID*

occupation: smoother

co-worker: the builder Abd el-Rahman Muhammad

years active: 1959

ethnic group and age: unknown

area of work: Duweishat, Melik el-Nasr, Nerri, the only known example of work being the house of the Sheikh of Melik el-Nasr

residence: unknown

rate of pay: The incised arches or domes over the door and windows to the men's sitting-room, each arch edged with triangles, raised the price of smoothing to 12 piastres the metre. Without decoration, smoothing would have been cheaper

25. OSMAN OSHI*

occupation: smoother

years active: 1960

ethnic group and age: unknown

area of work: Saras, Atiri, Mugufil Island, where he replastered and decorated a house built in 1923 by Muhammad Beshir

residence: Saras, Saras-Tahali, Sorbar

rate of pay: for incised decoration without relief, consisting of a dome over the door, zigzags and the X between parallel bars, he was paid nothing. It was said, 'For such decoration he doesn't get anything. It is just for showing off and gaining customers'

26. ABD AL-RAHIM MUKHTAR (Figs 21l, 31b)

occupation: farmer, part-time smoother

years active: c. 1960

ethnic group: Mahas Nubian

age: born 1939

area of work: Duweishat, Melik el-Nasr, Nerri

27. NASR AD-DIN (Pl. 36)

occupation: artist

area of work: Gemai E., Murshid

other information: unknown

28. SHEDAD (Pl. 36)

occupation: artist

area of work: Gemai E., Murshid

other information: unknown

29. AHMAD KARAFTI (Pls 31, 32)

    occupation: artist

    area of work: Gemai E., Murshid

    other information: unknown

30. MELIK MUHAMMAD HASAN (Pls 33–5, Col. pl. 8)

    occupation: artist

    area of work: Gemai E., Murshid

    other information: unknown

For Muhammad Saleh and Muhammad Mahmud Abd al-Rahim, both from Saras, whose work is only known in the Wadi Halfa district see Appendix B, 11 and 12

B: *Decorators of North Wadi Halfa*

1. GOWHAR

    occupation: house-smoother

    years active: before 1927

    area of work: Argin

    other information: unknown; he is said to have done some decoration to help the ladies, but none of it survived until 1964

2. SALEH MIRGHANI (Fig. 36?, Pls 50–2)

    occupation: builder until *c.* 1930, after which he was a decorator and house-smoother until 1960

    co-workers: Ahmad Batoul, who plastered houses built by Mirghani *c.* 1925. Later, between 1939 and 1944, Mirghani became a decorator's assistant to Batoul. About the same time he also assisted Hasan Arabi

    years active: 1924?–60

    ethnic group: accounts vary, said to be

        (a) Dongolawi Nubian

        (b) Mahas Nubian, with father from Saras West, Shoboka, and mother from Upper Egypt

    birthplace: accounts vary, said to be

        (a) Dongola

        (b) Debeira

    age: unknown

    area of work: 1924?, 1945 Debeira East

               1932 Argin

               1939–46 Ashkeit

1960 Debeira West
unknown time Faras East
residence before the flooding: Debeira
residence afterwards: Kerma

3. AHMAD BATOUL (Figs 32, 33; Fig. 50f, j, l; Pls 38–41, 43, 44, 46–8)
kin: older brother to Abdu Batoul
occupation: house-smoother (plasterer) and decorator
co-workers: Saleh Mirghani, for whom he worked as plasterer and who later worked
    for him as decorator's assistant and Hasan Arabi, whom he assisted in 1946
teacher of: Khalil Saleh
              Abdu Batoul
competitor with: Jabir Bab al-Kheir
                   Hasan Arabi
years active: 1927–48
ethnic group: Nubian from Upper Egypt
birthplace: said to be
    (a) Wadi el-Allaqi
    (b) Wadi el-Arab (by his brother)
    (c) Ballana
age: born *c.* 1912, died 1955
area of work: 1927–33 Debeira East
                unknown dates Faras East
                1928 Serra East
                1929–47 Ashkeit
                1935–47 Argin
residence: Debeira East and Argin, with a wife in both places, that is, on both sides
    of the Nile
rate of pay: in Debeira, c. 1930, he was paid for plastering by the metre, but if the
    houseowner wanted decoration along with the plastering, he paid Batoul slightly
    more per metre. The houseowner also paid extra if Batoul was to set the chinaware
    into the mud
        In Debeira, *c.* 1931, he was still paid for plastering by the metre, but a special
    contract was made for decoration: £2 or £3 per house

4. JABIR ABDULLA BAB AL-KHEIR** (Figs 37–40; Fig. 50, o, r, s, Pls 53–60;
Col. pls 9–12)
occupation: gardener, farmer, house-smoother, builder, decorator
teacher of: Hasan Arabi, *c.* 1935
competitor of: Ahmad Batoul
                 Hasan Arabi
years active: 1929–47
ethnic group: Negro from the Southern Sudan, of slave extraction
birthplace: Debeira E.
age: born *c.* 1910

area of work: 1929 Serra East
Faras West
1929, 1932, 1935–47 Argin
1929–47 Debeira East

residence before the flooding: Debeira East, in an undecorated house

residence afterwards: Khashm el-Girba

rate of pay: in Debeira, *c.* 1944, he made one contract with a house-owner for decorating the outer doorway (Col. pl. 10), and another for decorating the interior. He was paid £3 for both pieces of work together, and given food and drink for the time he took. The house-owner also provided white lime, which in this case was not enough. Jabir diluted the lime with mud and made the centre of the doorway pure white and the surround a paler beige

5. KHAMIS FROM THE SOUTH (Pl. 45)

occupation: house-smoother and decorator

co-workers: the builder Rihan from the South and another builder, also from the South, who was a Manasiri man from the Abu Hamed area. He worked with them as their plasterer in 1934. The two builders may have been one.

influenced by: Ahmad Batoul, Hasan Arabi, who claimed that Khamis tried to copy him but couldn't. It is true that in 1942 Khamis attempted to imitate the Hasan Arabi doorway formula on a house in Ashkeit, but did not copy it exactly

years active: 1934–46

ethnic group: Dongolawi Nubian

birthplace: Dongola

age: unknown

area of work: Ashkeit

residence before the flooding: Debeira E., where he had married

residence afterwards: Kassala (near Khashm el-Girba)

6. HASAN ARABI** (called HASAN HAWA on the east Nile bank) (Figs 41–2; Figs 45, 46; Fig. 50h, m; Pls 61–5, 68; Col. pls 13–17)

occupation: until *c.* 1935, railway worker in Atbara
1935–59 decorator
1959–64 conductor on the Argin–West Halfa bus

co-workers: *c.* 1935 Jabir Bab al-Kheir, whose student he was said to have been
c. 1940–3 Dawud Osman
after 1943 Khalil Saleh
1946 Ahmad Batoul, who worked with Hasan in a house in Ashkeit where Ahmad Batoul prepared the sand and mud surface, and Hasan made the actual decoration.
unspecified time in the early 1940s: Saleh Mirghani

years active: 1935–59

ethnic group: Mahas Nubian

birthplace: Argin

age: born 1909

area of work: 1935 Argin, Awwen-arti
    Debeira East
    1941–59 Ashkeit
    1942–59 Argin
    unknown dates: Ballana and Adindan in Upper Egypt
residence before the flooding: Argin
residence afterwards: Khashm el-Girba
rate of pay: c. 1941 in Debeira, a contract was made for decoration of the house
    following replastering to celebrate a wedding. Hasan was paid 5
    piastres per metre, which amounted to £5 in all. The owner of the
    house brought the colours, which were red, yellow, blue and white
    1942 in Ashkeit, Hasan was paid £7 to decorate the house before a
    wedding. Hasan worked for fifteen days to complete the decoration and
    was brought food and drink at the expense of the houseowner
    1945 in Argin, Hasan was paid £3 for decorating a *diwan*, which he did
    in three to four days
    1946 in Ashkeit, Hasan decorated the house of the son of Khalil Saleh,
    and was assisted in this by Khalil Saleh, who did part of the work for
    no charge. Hasan was paid 3 piastres per metre of decoration, and
    earned £3 in all. He completed the work in three days

7. SALEH, A MANSURI*
occupation: builder who did his own smoothing and decoration
years active: 1935
ethnic group: Sudanese from south of Dongola
birthplace: central Sudan, age unknown
area of work: Faras East, where he built and decorated one house. The decoration
    consisted of a *diwan* relief of a mosque, later painted in colours by the people of the
    house. They painted it in stripes and small chequers because the paint they obtained
    was in small quantities
residence: unknown

8. ABDU BATOUL** (Fig. 47; Pls 49, 77; Col. pl. 18)
kin: younger brother of Ahmad Batoul
occupation: until 1947 house-smoother and decorator
    1947–64 butcher in Argin
student of: Ahmad Batoul
influenced by: Ahmad Batoul, Hasan Arabi
years active: 1940–7
ethnic group: Nubian whose parents came from Upper Egypt
birthplace: Argin
age: born 18 May 1922
area of work: 1940–7 Ashkeit
    1943 Debeira West, Serra West, Aksha
    1944–after 1947 Argin

unknown dates: Faras West, *hillet al-Tira*
Ballana, Upper Egypt (Pls 49, 77)
residence before the flooding: Argin, in a house decorated over two doorways with simple incised arches lined with triangles, and over one doorway, a stuffed antelope's head
residence afterwards: Khashm el-Girba

9. BABIKR AL-MANSURI
occupation: house smoother
influenced by: Ahmad Batoul
years active: 1944
ethnic group: Sudanese from south of Dongola
birthplace: central Sudan
age: unknown
area of work: Ashkeit
residence: unknown

10. KHALIL SALEH** (Fig. 51c)
occupation: carpenter, decorator's assistant
student of: Ahmad Batoul
co-worker: Hasan Arabi
years active: 1945–7
ethnic group: Mahas of the Uliqi tribe, originally not from the Halfa area
birthplace and age: unknown
area of work: Ashkeit
residence before the flooding: Ashkeit
residence afterwards: unknown
rate of pay: As a decorator's assistant he was at first paid 4 piastres for one day's work. As he became more accomplished (and worked independently?) he was paid up to £1 a day
For making a wooden door he was paid £2

11. MUHAMMAD SALEH (Fig. 28d, e)
occupation: builder, smoother
years active: 1947, after the 1946 flood
ethnic group: Mahas Nubian
birthplace and residence: said to be from
(a) Saras, Saras-Tahali
(b) Saras, Atiri
(c) Abri
age: dead by 1964
area of work: Debeira East

12. MUHAMMAD MAHMUD ABD AL-RAHIM*
occupation: builder?, smoother
influenced by: Saras-style work (Fig. 28)
years active: 1946, 1947, after the 1946 flood

ethnic group: Mahas Nubian
birthplace and residence: Saras
area of work: Ashkeit, Argin

13. ABD AL‑AZIZ AL‑AMIN (Fig. 34: Fig. 50e)
occupation: smoother, decorator
co‑worker: a builder from Manasir, for whom he did smoothing
influenced by: Ahmad Batoul
years active: 1947, 1956?
ethnic group: Mahas Nubian
birthplace: Sukkot (Kosha)
age: unknown, but died young
area of work: Debeira East
         Debeira West, hillet Nag el‑Kunuz
         Ashkeit
residence: Debeira East

14. MEKKI
occupation: decorator
         cook in a Wadi Halfa restaurant
years active: c. 1950–60
ethnic group: unknown
birthplace and age: unknown
area of work: Argin, where he decorated façades exclusively with imitation stone‑
  work and brickwork
residence before the flooding: Wadi Halfa

For Dawud Osman and Muhammad Suleiman, who both worked north of Wadi
Halfa but even more so south of that town, see Appendix A, nos 8 and 14

Notes

PREFACE

1. Ahmad Muhammad Ali al-Hakim was responsible for taking down field interviews in villages from the Egyptian border to Gemai, south of Wadi Halfa. All remarks from this area which are given as quotations in the text are quoted from his Arabic field notes, as translated by Abdulla Sabbar and Nabil Shehabi. His own work on the subject, in Arabic, is: Ahmad Muhammad Ali al-Hakim, *al- Zakharif al mi'mariya wa talawaruha fi mantigat Wadi Halfa* (Architectural Decorations and their Development in the Wadi Halfa District), Sudan Unit Occasional Papers No. 1, University of Khartoum, October 1965.

Mustafa Ibrahim Taha interviewed villagers from Gemai through Farka. Quotations from people of this area are given as he himself translated them into English from his own Arabic notes, or occasionally as he translated them on the spot. His article derived from this field material is: M. I. Taha, 'The Art of Making Manwaras in Nubia', *Sudan Notes and Records* (hereafter *SNR*), XLIX, Khartoum 1968, pp. 155–7.

Other articles written by members of this Sudan Unit field project are: W. Merrill, 'The Wooden Locks of the Halfa region', *SNR* XLV, 1964, pp. 29–34; M. W. Cavendish, 'The Custom of Placing Pebbles on Nubian Graves', *SNR* XLVII, 1966, pp. 151–6; and M. Wenzel, 'A Note on the Cat-Lore of Nubia', *Folklore* 75, London, summer 1964, p. 121. Photographic documentation of the field project is located in the archives of the Sudan Unit, University of Khartoum. Xerox copies of the five volumes of field drawings made during the project are deposited with the Sudan Unit, Khartoum, and with the Smithsonian Institution, office of Anthropology, Washington D.C.

INTRODUCTION

1. W. Kidd comments on Khashm el-Girba from the point of view of urban planning in 'Comment', *Urbanization*, Magazine of the Faculty of Architecture, Ahmadu Bello University, Zaria, vol. 7, 1967–8, pp. 8–9:

'It was decreed that the population of Wadi Halfa should be moved to Khashm el-Girba, an area some 700 miles away in the south-east part of the country near the Ethiopian border. This was a district with a different climate, a different indigenous population and a potential for a different agricultural economy. Even more drastic was the change in the architectural environment. Wadi Halfa was developed in the organic way common to the mud constructed settlements of the Middle East and North Africa. It was untidy, interesting, plastic and, above all, human. Khashm el-Girba on the other hand was a new settlement based on grid-iron plans which when translated into reality became a drab collection of rows of blockwork houses – tidy, dull, rigid and quite inhuman.'

CHAPTER ONE: THE NUBIAN PEOPLE, THEIR HOMELAND AND HOMES

1. J. S. Trimingham, *The Influence of Islam upon Africa* (hereafter Trimingham, *Africa*), London 1968, pp. 22, 23.
   J. S. Trimingham, *Islam in the Sudan* (hereafter Trimingham, *Sudan*), London 1965, pp. 5, 6.
   W. Y. Adams, 'Continuity and Change in Nubian Cultural History', *SNR* XLVIII, Khartoum 1967, p. 18.
   B. G. Trigger, *History and Settlement in Lower Nubia* (hereafter Trigger, *History*), Yale University Publications in Anthropology, 69, New Haven 1965, p. 16.
2. P. L. Shinnie, *Medieval Nubia*, Khartoum 1954, p. 2.
   R. Herzog, *Die Nubier*, Berlin 1957, pp. 22, 23.
   Adams, op. cit., p. 18.
3. Trimingham, *Sudan*, pp. 53, 63, 65.
   F. Ll. Griffith, 'Pakhoras-Bakarâs-Faras in Geography and History', *Journal of Egyptian Archaeology* (hereafter *JEA*), XI, London 1925, pp. 265, 266, 268. Historical evidence implies that the kingdom of Dunkulah or Dongola comprised two large provinces, the southern one called Makuria or El-Mukurrah, in which the principal capital of Dongola lay, and the northern called Nobadia or El-Maris, where the capital was Faras.
4. R. Keating, *Nubian Twilight*, London 1962, fig. 63. South of the Second Cataract this costume began to be modified, and by Farka had been replaced by shorter dresses worn with a large coloured head-shawl. Examples of the southern garb are given by Herzog, op. cit., figs. 30, 31 and frontispiece.
5. J. L. Burckhardt, *Travels in Nubia*, London 1819, pp. 46, 58, 141.
6. H. Dafalla, 'Notes on the History of Wadi Halfa Town', *SNR* XLVI, 1965, p. 17.
7. Count Gleichen, *The Anglo-Egyptian Sudan*, London 1905, vol. 1, pp. 23–5.
   A. and W. Kronenberg, 'Preliminary Report on the Anthropological Field Work in Sudanese Nubia, 1964', *Kush* XIII, Khartoum 1965, p. 205, n. 1.
8. Dafalla, op. cit., *SNR* XLVI, 1965, p. 22.
9. The southernmost periphery of the Mahas, south of Kosha or the area also called Sukkot, is a region given the general title of Mahas, or Mahass. This region lay south of the area examined in our study.
10. Trimingham, *Sudan*, p. 8. Nubians of this group are called Dongolawi Nubians, and as such they will be mentioned in this text.
11. The differences between the so-called Fadicca dialect and the Mahas dialect are very slight, and according to recent field researches of Herman Bell, there is insufficient evidence to assign the Fadicca to a precise geographical location. The matter is discussed by R. Lepsius,

Nubische Grammatik, Berlin 1880, pp. 456–9, who has preferred to regard the Fadicca as being of one linguistic unit with the Mahas.

12. Trimingham, *Sudan*, pp. 7, 68, 79, 83, 84.

    P. M. Holt, *A Modern History of the Sudan*, New York 1961, p. 213.

    In Sudanese Nubia the Kenuzi tribe are often called 'Shellali' after Shellal, near Aswan, from where many of them came. The Kenuzi dialect is very similar to the Danaqla dialect, and the Nubians often say that they are the same. A possibility that they are in fact closely related is discussed by W. Y. Adams, 'Post-Pharaonic Nubia in the Light of Archaeology III, Epilogue: The Coming of Islam', *JEA* LII, 1966, pp. 153–5.

13. The Kenuzi who settled in Debeira West lived in barrel-vault houses, an early type of building used in the Christian period and before. It was retained in Egyptian Nubia but not in the Sudan. Life in Egyptian Nubia was less disrupted by the coming of Islam than it was in Sudanese Nubia, and early building traditions survived there when they did not survive in the Sudan. Ibid., *JEA* LII, 1966, p. 154.

    The Kenuzi method of building barrel-vault houses is described by G. S. Mileham, *Churches in Lower Nubia*, Philadelphia 1910, vol. 11, p. 9.

14. I am grateful to the Royal Danish Embassy, London, for the precision of this information.

15. Arabic and Nubian plurals are not given in the present text. An 's' ending has been added to some Arabic or Nubian words to form a plural, as is usually the case when these words are adopted into English speech.

16. This place-name system does not appear to have held in the early nineteenth century, before Muhammad Ali's Egyptian conquest in 1819, when Burckhardt visited Nubia. At that time the names which are at present attached to *omodiyas or sheikhships* were taken to be names of different dried-up river valleys, or *wadis*, of which Wadi Halfa is the only surviving example. The native authorities also had different titles, including that of *melik*, or king. At the same time, there were larger, apparently tribal or linguistic divisions, also called *wadi*, which included the regions named above. Thus 'Wady el Kenous', obviously the Kenuzi region, extended from Aswan to Es-Sebu, in Upper Egypt, and 'Wady Nouba' included all country south of Es-Sebu to the northern limits of Dongola.

    Burckhardt, op. cit., pp. 7, 25, 43.

    Trigger, *History*, p. 13.

17. Trimingham, *Sudan*, p. 7.

18. Griffith, op. cit., pp. 265, 266. Precise boundaries for Maris are seldom given in the sources.

19. Trimingham, *Sudan*, pp. 53, 64, n. 1.

20. Ibid., p. 59.

    W. B. Emery and L. P. Kirwan, *The Royal Tombs of Ballana and Qustal*, Cairo 1938.

    L. P. Kirwan, 'Prelude to Nubian Christianity', *Mélanges offerts à Kazimierz Michalowski*, Warsaw 1966, pp. 126–7.

21. B. G. Haycock, 'Towards a Better Understanding of the Kingdom of Cush (Napata-Meroe)', *SNR* XLIX, 1968, pp. 7–9.

    P. L. Shinnie, *Meroe, a Civilization of the Sudan*, New York 1967, pp. 30–57.

22. Trimingham, *Sudan*, pp. 36, 66.

    K. Michalowski, 'Open Problems of Nubian Art and Culture in the Light of the Discoveries at Faras', E. Dinkler, editor, *Kunst und Geschichte Nubiens in Christlicher Zeit* (hereafter *Kunst und Geschichte*), Recklinghausen 1970, p. 17.

    S. Jakobielski, 'Some Remarks on Faras Inscriptions,' *Kunst und Geschichte*, pp. 29–32.

23. Adams, op. cit., *SNR* XLVIII, 1967, pp. 10–12, 19.

W. Y. Adams, 'Post Pharaonic Nubia in the Light of Archaeology II', *JEA* LI, 1965, pp. 161–8.

W. Y. Adams, 'The Nubian Campaign: Retrospect and Prospect', *Mélanges offerts à Kazimierz Michalowski*, pp. 21–5.

B. G. Trigger, 'The Cultural Ecology of Christian Nubia', *Kunst und Geschichte*, pp. 354–5.

24. Trimingham, *Sudan*, pp. 76–7.
   Trimingham, *Africa*, p. 23.

25. K. Michalowski and G. Gerster, *Faras, die Kathedrale aus dem Wüstensand*, Cologne, Zürich 1967, Pl. 11.

26. G. W. Hewes, 'Gezira Dabarosa: Report of the University of Colorado Nubian Expedition, 1962–3 season', *Kush* XII, 1964, p. 181, fig. 3.
   P. L. Shinnie, 'The University of Ghana Excavation at Debeira West 1963', *Kush* XII, 1964, p. 211, fig. 3; p. 213, fig. 4.

27. Burckhardt, op. cit., pp. 58, 140, 141.
   F. S. Ensor, *Incidents on a Journey through Nubia to Darfoor*, London 1881, pp. 4, 5.

28. Burckhardt, op. cit., pp. 55, 141, 212, 213.
   H. Light, *Travels in Egypt, Nubia, Holy Land, Mount Libanon and Cyprus*, London 1818, p. 82.

29. Grace M. Crowfoot, 'A Note on the Stringing of Sudanese Beds and Stools', *Dryad Quarterly* III, No. 1, January–March, Leicester 1933, pp. 12–19.
   Herzog, op. cit., fig. 25.

30. Ensor, op. cit., p. 21.

31. Ibid., p. 24.

32. Count Gleichen, *With the Camel Corps up the Nile*, London 1888, pp. 22, 262.

33. Gleichen, *Anglo-Egyptian Sudan*, vol. 1, p. 85.

34. Trimingham, *Africa*, pp. 95, 96.

35. Ibid., p. 35, map 5. Berber is slightly north of the point on the Nile indicated as Al-Abwāb on Trimingham's map of State and trade routes. This route was also available for Muslim missionaries entering the Sudan from the Hijaz. Ibid., p. 24.
   I. M. Lewis, ed., *Islam in Tropical Africa*, London 1966, Chapter II, Y. Fadl Hasan, 'The Penetration of Islam in the Eastern Sudan', pp. 145, 146.

36. Burckhardt, op. cit., p. 141.

37. Adams, op. cit., *JEA* LII, 1966, p. 153.

38. Burckhardt, op. cit., pp. 43, 69, 70, 80.
   Trimingham, *Sudan*, pp. 83, 88.

39. Ibid., pp. 88, 89.
   G. A. Hoskins, *Travels in Ethiopia*, London 1835, pp. 201, 202.

40. Dafalla, op. cit., pp. 9–10.

41. Gleichen, *Anglo-Egyptian Sudan*, vol. 1, pp. 7, 22, Dafalla, op. cit., p. 18.

CHAPTER TWO: HOUSE DECORATION: SOURCES AND DESIGN

1. In the early nineteenth century, the custom of hanging up food containers as wall decoration extended further south along the Nile than Nubia.

Burckhardt, op. cit., p. 270: 'The ladies of Damer adorn their sitting rooms with a number of large wooden bowls or dishes hung against the wall like so many pictures.'

2. Abdulla Al-Tayib, 'The Changing Customs of the Riverain Sudan – III', *SNR* XLV, 1964, pp. 18, 27.
Sudan Almanac 1967, Central Office of Information, Republic of the Sudan, Khartoum 1966–7, p. 219.
A. M. Blackman, 'Some Egyptian and Nubian Notes', *Man* X, II, London 1910, p. 29.

3. Around Wadi Halfa, Kenuzi immigrants from Egypt were the only people still putting basket lids on the wall, and placing rolled-up mats on wall-pegs (Abdullah Sabbar, Ashkeit).
G. Gerster, 'Nubia before the Flood', *The Sunday Times Colour Magazine*, 11 June, London 1964, p. 28, shows basket lids as wall decorations in Egyptian Nubia. A less elaborate arrangement in the same area, very like decoration south of the Second Cataract, has been photographed by Violet Macdermott in Aniba (Pl. 9).

4. Burckhardt, op. cit., p. 146, mentions that bread in Nubia was served off basketry plates. Abdulla Al-Tayib, op. cit., pp. 27, 28, remarks the recent custom of serving food on metal trays covered by a *tabag* lid, but notes that in the regions with which he was familiar, the food was originally served not on another *tabag*, but in a wooden bowl under a basketry lid.

5. In the Christian period, crosses protected graves, and were marked horizontally on the mud superstructures above the grave.
W. Y. Adams, 'Sudan Antiquities Service Excavation at Mienarti 1963–64', *Kush* XIII, 1965, pp. 169, 170, Pl. XXXVII, fig. 8b.

6. The male professional pot-maker was Khalil Saleh of Kosha, Farka, Farkenkonj, where he had a kiln for making fired pottery, such as water-pots or *zeirs*, in which work he was assisted by an elderly woman called Sitt al-Benat Hamid. These *zeirs* were carried north on Nile boats and many were sold in the Batn al-Hajar region, where they were identified as being '*zeirs* from Sukkot'. Storage-pots were not fired, and were constructed by Khalil Saleh in the same way as they were made by housewives on the very spot where they later stood. North of Halfa, in Ashkeit, the only professional storage-pot makers were local women, usually widows such as Sitt al-Benat Hamid who wished to earn a little money.

7. Abdulla Al-Tayib, op. cit., pp. 20, 21, describes the cooking process, which is illustrated by G. Gerster, 'Threatened Treasures of the Nile', *National Geographic* 124, No. 4, Washington, October 1963, p. 601.

8. Trimingham, *Sudan*, p. 73.

9. Personal communication from Margaret Shinnie.
Burckhardt, op. cit., p. 270.

10. Trimingham, *Africa*, pp. 71, 132, n. 31, and Trimingham, *Sudan*, pp. 180, 182–3, mention certain *jirtiq* beads worn in the Sudan as protection during perilous moments such as circumcision, marriage and the seventh month of pregnancy. The Nubian marriage beads fulfil a similar function, and their protective powers may account for the prominent position they are later given on the house walls. Abdulla Al-Tayib, op. cit., p. 19, describes certain circumcision ceremonies in the Sudan as miniature celebrations of the wedding ceremony; in some cases the boy was dressed to appear like a girl and made to wear the long coral wedding necklace, as well as other beads of magical value.

11. Trimingham, *Sudan*, p. 31, confirms that these titles are used loosely in the Sudan to mean any West African, although there exist an estimated 80,000 Nigerians in the Sudan. They are mainly pilgrims who, on return from Mecca, have settled in the Sudan, or who are

working there to earn money to travel further, and, presumably, sell cowries as one of their occupations.

12. In Duweishat, Duweishat, Showerta, the bride went to the river on the seventh day, but in Duweishat, Melik el-Nasr, Turmukke, it was the second day.

13. The termites are called 'white ants', and are extremely rapacious. F. S. Ensor, op. cit., p. 37.

14. Hoskins, op. cit., p. 194, Pl. 37, shows hanging nets in use in a Dongola house.

15. In Duweishat, Melik el-Nasr, it was claimed that the local craft of making wooden bowls died out about 1935, when similar bowls began to be brought from Omdurman.
In Kosha, Dal, Jedid, a bowl of this sort was said to have been brought from Fasher in Darfur Province, towards the borders of Chad, about 1914.
The wooden bowl as generally used throughout the Sudan is described and illustrated by Abdulla al-Tayib, op. cit., pp. 18, 27, 28.

16. *Sudan Almanac* 1967, p. 222, states that *sunt* acacia is stronger than *haraz*. But the Wadi Halfa Nubians found that *sunt* was attacked by dry rot, and cicadas for breeding. Preference was there given to another kind of acacia wood, called *fara* in Nubian and *atil* in Arabic. The wood was hard, easy to chisel, and withstood dry rot.

17. W. Merrill, 'The Wooden Locks of the Halfa Region', *SNR* XLV, 1964, p. 30, figs. 2, 5; p. 32, fig. 6.

18. P. L. Shinnie, *Medieval Nubia*, Khartoum 1954, p. 13.
W. Y. Adams, 'An Introductory Classification of Christian Nubian Pottery', *Kush* X, 1962, pp. 249, 272–5.
Some of the pottery was made at Faras.
W. Y. Adams, 'The Christian Potteries of Faras', *Kush* IX, 1961, pp. 30–43.
G. T. Scanlon, 'Slip Painted Pottery from Wizz', *African Arts/Arts d'Afrique* II, No. 1, Los Angeles 1968, p. 11, fig. 6, p. 12, fig. 9.

19. Amalgro and others, 'Excavations by the Spanish Archaeological Mission in the Sudan', 1962–3 and 1963–4, V, 'The Christian Site of Abkanarti', *Kush* XIII, 1965, p. 92, Pl. XIX, fig. 3. Abkanarti is in the Second Cataract region.

20. Shinnie, *Medieval Nubia*, pp. 13, 15, figs. 7, 8. Peter and Margaret Shinnie have further discovered birds on eighth- and ninth-century pottery of Debeira West, which they have kindly brought to my attention.

21. Amalgro and others, op. cit., VI, 'The Christian Settlement of Ad-Donga', *Kush* XIII, 1965, p. 94, fig. 8a.
Ad-Donga is at North Argin.
K. Michalowski, *Faras, fouilles Polonaises 1961–1962*, Warsaw 1965, p. 65, fig. 5.

22. A Christian period pot decorated with scorpions was found in Debeira West by Peter and Margaret Shinnie, and is as yet unpublished.

23. Adams, op. cit., *Kush* X, 1962, p. 268, figs. 4, 6.
Ibid., p. 257, figs. 8, 9, p. 267, fig. 15.

24. Amalgro, op. cit. 'V', *Kush* XIII, 1965, p. 92, Pl. XIX, fig. d.
U. Monneret de Villard, *La Nubie Medioevale*, vol IV, Cairo 1957, Pl. CLXXXII, figs. 21, 22.

25. In Kosha West, Dal, Jedid, the flesh of a rayfish was put on the front door to drive out devils attracted by a woman in labour.

26. Trimingham, *Africa*, pp. 46, 47.
Trimingham, *Sudan*, pp. 24, 25.

27. This information was provided by Dr Omar Osman, University of Khartoum.

28. Some smaller crocodiles seen are in fact Monitor lizards, or *waranas*, as described by Gleichen, *Anglo-Egyptian Sudan*, p. 309.

29. The head of a cow could be put up to drive out the evil eye if a woman was giving birth to a child (Kosha, Dal, Jedid).

30. J. Gwyn Griffiths and Ibrahim Ahmed Ibrahim, 'The Use of Plates and Saucers to Decorate Houses in Lower Nubia and Upper Egypt', *SNR* XXI, 1938, pp. 217-20.
A. M. Blackman, op. cit., *Man* X, 11, London 1910, p. 29. Here the *omda* of Dehmit, in Egyptian Nubia, is quoted as saying that saucers were introduced into his region by Nubian servants working in hotels and European houses, from about 1895.
W. S. Blackman, *The Fellahin of Upper Egypt*, London 1927, p. 30.
W. B. Emery, *Nubian Treasure*, London and Southampton 1948, p. 16.

31. A. M. Blackman, op. cit., *Man* X, 11, p. 29.
Herbert Cole, University of California at Santa Barbara, has observed that when the Nigerian Ibo sunk plates into the mud walls of their *mbari* earth goddess shrines, they first called the building by its name, which meant 'the town eats'. The plates were so deeply sunk into the wall that they were seldom visible; one saw only the holes where they had been put. H. M. Cole, 'Mbari is a Dance', *African Arts/Arts d'Afrique* II, no. 4, Los Angeles 1969, p. 46.

32. W. S. Blackman, op. cit., pp. 30, 224.
Griffiths and Ibrahim Ahmed Ibrahim, op. cit., pp. 217-20.

33. Ibid., pp. 219-20.

34. See p. 94.

35. The name *haleb* is thought to derive from *Aleppo*, from where the gipsies are believed to have come (at Ashkeit). Fortune-telling by gipsies using shells gathered on the shores of the Red Sea is described by Burckhardt, op. cit., p. 465.
Some varieties of Red Sea fancy shells, such as were carried by gipsies to other parts, are given by W. Reed, 'A Study of Marine Fisheries in the Sudan', *SNR* XLIII, 1962, pp. 3, 10.

36. The *dom* palm (*Hyphaene thebaica*) provided leaves for making mats, sandals and baskets, but is a variety different from the date palm.
Gleichen, *Anglo-Egyptian Sudan*, p. 84.
Trigger, *History*, p. 15.

37. Merrill, op. cit., pp. 29-34.

38. K. Michalowski, op. cit., p. 78, fig. 47. Here a form of rosette is put between parallel bars which could be stylised to an X (Fig. 9f).
The X between parallel bars is itself seen on a Christian period key, obviously intended for a similar kind of lock as was used in Nubia recently. Mileham, op. cit., p. 53, fig. 11.

39. Merrill, op. cit., p. 32, figs. 9, 10.

40. Boards of fairly uniform shape, used for learning the Quran, appear not only in Nubia, but in many parts of the Muslim world.
H. Stannus, 'Alphabet Boards from Central Africa', *Man* X, 18, 1910, pp. 37, 38.
Abdulla Al-Tayib, op. cit., pp. 15, 18.

CHAPTER THREE: ART OF THE NUBIAN FAMILY

1. Gerster, op. cit., *The Sunday Times Colour Magazine*, 11 June 1964, pp. 23, 26, 27.
Gerster, op. cit., *National Geographic* 124, No. 4, 1963, p. 617.

A survey of house decoration in Egyptian Nubia has been undertaken by Armgard Grauer, Germany, who writes (personal communication):

'In the Egyptian area house decoration and wall painting may be divided into three groups:
1. The Kenuzi area (from Aswan till about es-Sebu). Here are the most rich wall painting and the most elaborate architectonic decorations. Most of the wall painting is done by women, while the architectonic decoration is carried out by the house-builders, but not by specialists. The mud relief, as found further south, is hardly to be seen in this area.
2. The district between es-Sebu and Ballana in the South, including the Wadi el-Arab. In this region one finds only occasional painting and architectonic decoration.
3. The frontier district, which shows nearly the same style as around Wadi Halfa.'

2. M. Swithenbank, *Ashanti Fetish Houses*, Accra 1969, pp. 16–20, 32, 36–42, etc.
3. D. Duerden, *African Art*, London 1968, p. 37, Pl. 37.
4. Trimingham, *Sudan*, pp. 191ff., 215.
5. Hélène Danthine, *Le Palmier-dattier et les arbres sacrés, dans l'iconographie de l'Asie occidentale ancienne*, vol. II, Paris 1937, Pl. 90, figs. 598, 599, 600.
6. Muhammad Osman Fadl also painted a duck, crescent and cross, in the house interior. It was reported: 'The *wizza* [duck] is a bird he likes, and that's why he drew it. He can't draw any other bird. All the colours he bought in the market. When he drew the crescent and the cross, he wanted to draw a crocodile, but it came out badly, and that's why he abandoned the idea.'
7. W. S. Blackman, op. cit., p. 30, mentions saucers and *Hajj* painting as the only house decoration visible in Upper Egypt up to the time she wrote, in 1927.
8. 1 Pound Sudanese (LS.) = 100 piastres tariff = 1,000 milliemes = £1 0s. 6d. *Sudan Almanac* 1967, p. 106.
9. Hasan Beshir was a Shaiqiyya who featured prominently in the military government of General Aboud, which was overthrown in the autumn of 1964, at the same time as our investigations.
10. Information from N. Shehabi.
11. Trimingham, *Africa*, pp. 46, 47.
12. Ibid., p. 3.
13. In Saras, Semna, Sindas, it was said that most mosques did not have minarets; the minarets, when they appeared, dated to post-1948.
14. In Iraq, according to Muwaffak al-Hamdani, University of Khartoum, people make special marks of mourning at Ashura for Ali Ibn Abi Talib, cousin of the Prophet, who was murdered at that time. The marks are made on their faces, and not on their houses. Ashura is the tenth night of the Muslim New Year. Although it is not a fixed festival, moving round the year as does Ramadan, it is that to which many African practices connected with the New Year have become connected. Such practices were meant to ensure prosperity throughout the New Year (Trimingham, *Africa*, p. 66). It is possible that the Ashura marks of the Nile Valley may be the survival of some such practices, rather than anything related to the culture of Islam.
15. M. W. Cavendish, 'The Custom of Placing Pebbles on Nubian Graves', *SNR* XLVII, 1966, p. 152, fig. 1. Burckhardt, op. cit., p. 35.

CHAPTER FOUR: PROFESSIONAL DECORATORS
SOUTH OF WADI HALFA

1. Margaret Shinnie has kindly permitted access to her sketches of such gateways in and around Dongola.

2. The wooden lock used throughout Nubia was the so-called Laconian lock, which spread from Greece north into Europe and south along the Nile into the Sudanic Belt region, after Hellenistic or Roman times. It was not known to the ancient Egyptians. Those locks south of the Second Cataract were an older, simpler type where the key entered the body of the lock (Fig. 9c), and where the lock was only lightly decorated, if at all. This kind, still found in many remote areas, is that discovered in the Monastery of St Epiphanius at Thebes. (H. E. Winlock and W. E. Crum, *The Monastery of Epiphanius at Thebes*, New York, Metropolitan Museum of Art, Egyptian Expedition Publications vol. III, part 1, New York 1926, pp. 57–9, fig. 19.) Such locks frequently serve as an inner bolt, requiring a hole in the door for the passage of one's hand to insert the key (Pl. 17). A similar lock with corresponding door hole is clearly described in Apuleius, *Metamorphoses* IV, 10. A thief puts his hand through the door hole in order to open the lock and has it nailed to the door by the householder, who is inside.
   North of the Second Cataract the lock was a new type, more heavily decorated, with the key entering the crosspiece of the lock, not the main body (Fig. 13b).
   Merrill, op. cit., pp. 29–34.

3. Certain circle repeats and elongated diamonds placed vertically on the string-course borders, just under the roof, made by Sayyid Ahmad Hogla (Pl. 14), resemble the repeated uraeus snakes on Meroitic architraves, whose heads are surmounted by discs.
   K. Michalowski, *Faras, fouilles Polonaises 1961*, Warsaw 1962, p. 81, fig. 13; p. 85, fig. 21.

4. The three brothers were Kasbana Hasan Taffoul, Himad Hasan Taffoul and Ali Hasan Taffoul. Ali and Kasbana made some decoration of a rudimentary kind, Himad made little or none at all. Their father had been a house-builder, boat-builder and maker of wooden limbs for those who were maimed.

5. M. I. Taha, 'The Art of Making Manwaras in Nubia', *SNR* XLIX, 1968, pp. 155–7.

6. I am grateful to T. Higel for the photographs of inscriptions which demonstrate this conclusion.

CHAPTER FIVE: PROFESSIONAL DECORATORS
NORTH OF WADI HALFA

1. Small mud crocodiles of the type described appeared in
   Saras, Atiri, Farki,
   Duweishat, Ambikol, Angasa,
   Duweishat, Melik el-Nasr, Nerri.
   In Duweishat, Ambikol, Farhana, they said the custom of making crocodiles had once existed, but had been stopped while on Ambikol Island, *hillet* Gnjere, the same was said although one crocodile was still visible. South of Duweishat, in Kosha, mud crocodiles were no longer seen but instead crocodile skulls were frequently set into the mud over doors.

2. Information provided by M. Shinnie.

3. Gleichen, *Anglo-Egyptian Sudan*, vol. 1, p. 86, demonstrates how rain may fall in heavy

local showers in the hills east of Wadi Halfa towards the Red Sea, when it does not fall in the vicinity of the Nile (see Fig. 1). The water is carried off by a number of shallow *wadis*, whose beds contract as they reach the rocky belt near the Nile, so that the water descends in torrents. This is also described by Burckhardt, op. cit., p. 10.

4. A. and W. Kronenberg, 'Wooden Carvings in the South Western Sudan', *Kush* VIII, 1960, pp. 274–6. The Bongo tally posts are divided into both concave and convex units.

5. I have not been able to find lions with swords in Egyptian newspapers and magazines, but have had access to none before 1933.

6. M. Wenzel, 'A Note on the Cat-Lore of Nubia', *Folklore* 75, summer 1964, p. 121. A. M. Blackman, op. cit., *Man* X, II, p. 26.

7. B. Hillier, *Art Deco of the 20s and 30s*, London 1968.

8. Ibid., pp. 8, 28, 29, 93, 95–7, 119, 126, 149, 159.

9. Ibid., pp. 44–9, 122.

10. This characteristic of the art of the 1930s is not remarked by B. Hillier, but is visible in his illustrations, ibid., pp. 61, 91, 97, 127, 128, while other naturalistic representations surrounded by hard-edged, geometric forms are typified by his frontispiece.

11. Ibid., pp. 11, 82, 158, and illustrations on pp. 63, 119.

12. Ibid., pp. 63, 125, 164.

13. Ibid., p. 164.

14. Keating, op. cit., fig. 30. This house of Muhammad Ahmad Sayyid in Ashkeit, north of the Second Cataract, is incorrectly located by R. Keating, who states that it is 'on the Second Cataract'.

15. Trimingham, *Africa*, p. 66.

16. Gerster, op. cit., *The Sunday Times Colour Magazine*, 11 June 1964, pp. 22, 23, reproduces Hasan Arabi's doorway representing a crocodile hunt, as does Herzog, op. cit., fig. 34.

17. Khalil Saleh claimed to have been the first student of Ahmad Batoul, but this in no way affected his style, which was almost totally derived from that of Hasan Arabi.

18. *Al-Hilal*, vol. XLVIII, Cairo 1 December 1939, gives a news photograph, p. 144, showing King Farouk seated on this throne.

19. *Al-Mussawar* no. 779, Cairo 15 September 1939, p. 27.

20. The sword and scabbard are now in the Huntley and Palmers archives, which will shortly be housed in the Reading Civic Centre, with documentary material in the Reading University Library, Department of Economics. I am grateful to Michael Paxton, Huntley and Palmers Public Relations Officer, for this and other information concerning the history of tin box design.

21. See the catalogues, *Huntley and Palmers Xmas Biscuits and Cakes*, as issued annually in Reading from 1925 to 1940.

22. Hillier, op. cit., p. 128.
Art Deco motifs appeared to a very limited extent in Egyptian newspapers and magazines, such as *Al-Hilal* and *Al-Mussawar*, but not before 1935 (Fig. 45e, fig. 46, IIc). Some advertisements using these motifs were signed by artists with Italian names (Fig. 45e), and may have been a sign of the influence of Italian advertising art in Egypt, as mentioned on p. 60. The Egyptian use of Art Deco motifs was extremely shortlived, and they were replaced in 1937 by a kind of sober line drawing combined with photographs which was retained throughout the war years. By 1939 only a few Egyptian container designs showed Art Deco characteristics (Fig. 46, 11b) and these were presumably first designed about 1935.

23. Ibid., p. 63.

CHAPTER SIX: THE ICONOGRAPHY OF
NUBIAN WALL DECORATION

1. A. M. Blackman, 'The Fox as a Birth-Amulet', *Man* IX, 4, 1909, pp. 9, 10.
   A. M. Blackman, op. cit., *Man* X, 11, 1910, p. 26.
2. The protective symbolism of horns is discussed by J. H. Turnure, 'Etruscan Ritual Armor: Two Examples in Bronze', *American Journal of Archaeology* 69, no. 1, January 1965, pp. 46, 47.
3. The pigeon was represented at Faras West in association with the cross (Fig. 13a), although the images were said to have had no meaning.
4. A. E. Robinson, 'The Cult of the Crocodile', *American Anthropologist* 34, Menasha Wisconsin 1932, p. 550.
5. Information from Muhammad Ibrahim Shoush, University of Khartoum.
6. The notion that crocodiles contained *sahhar* spirits was held both in Nubia and south of Nubia, around Merowe. The mother of M. I. Shoush, living in the village Mora Urkuri near Karima, *omodije* Shaiqiyya, was once near the river when a crocodile emerged from it and pursued her, avoiding all other women. This was thought to be because the *sahhar* spirit was attracted by her magnificent gold jewellery.
7. Trimingham, *Sudan*, p. 177.
8. Blackman, op. cit., *Man* X, 11, 1910, p. 26.
9. A. Sabra, Warburg Institute, London, can remember seeing lions with swords painted on walls in Cairo and Alexandria. There is, however, no evidence that these popular images derive from the flag and seal of Iran, where the lion with the sword has been represented for about 200 years. The Iranian lion is depicted with a rising sun behind his head and, according to the Iranian Embassy in London, lacks religious significance. Iran, unlike Egypt, officially follows the Muslim Shia sect. Iranians frequently title the chief figure of that sect, Ali Ibn Abi Talib, the 'Lion of God'. Yet the Iranian government does not officially relate this symbolism with the lion depicted on their flag and seal.
10. Trimingham, *Africa*, pp. 7, 8.
    The Fatimids gained control of Egypt in A.D. 969, and maintained friendly relations with the Christian Nubians. R. Oliver, ed., *The Middle Ages of African History*, London 1967, Chapter 1; Shinnie, *Medieval Nubia*, p. 6.
11. Information from Muhammad Ibrahim Shoush, University of Khartoum, and Hasan Zaroug, University of London.
12. A. M. Blackman, op. cit., *Man* X, 11, 1910, p. 28.
    Sometimes rags which had been in contact with someone who needed the saint's blessing were attached to sticks. These sticks were planted in the walls of the shrine for such a purpose, and they, too, resembled flags.
    Trimingham, *Sudan*, p. 145.
13. Ibid., pp. 94, 137, 139, 154, 197-8, 234-5.
14. Kosha, Dal, *hillet* Ari, also called Seli Farki.
15. Trimingham, *Sudan*, p. 25.
16. In Gemai, south of Wadi Halfa, where the women's painting type B began to develop, there also existed customs of divination connected with a saint's tomb as well as beliefs concerning the power of a dead body over the fertility of women.
    A. and W. Kronenberg, 'Preliminary Report on the Anthropological Field Work in Sudanese Nubia, 1964', *Kush* XIII, 1965, p. 209.

17. Trimingham, *Sudan*, pp. 142, 143, describes the usual shape of such a tomb. The crescent surmounting the dome was more common in women's painting type B than it was on actual holy men's tombs of the Sudan. Yet it appeared on the Mahdi's tomb in Omdurman, from whence it was, however, removed to the Khalifa House Museum where it may be seen today.

18. Trimingham, *Africa*, pp. 134, 135, n. 54, equates saint worship in the north-east part of Muslim Africa with spirit worship in Negro Africa. In parts of Negro Africa, as among the Mande, the founder of a village becomes a 'power' like a saint. Instead of in a saint's tomb, his spirit is often thought to reside in a conical earthen erection.

19. Michalowski and Gerster, op. cit., pp. 42-4.
Michalowski suggests that this crown was borrowed from the Sassanids who, between the fourth and the seventh centuries employed a crown featuring a crescent on a stem.
R. Goble, 'Die sasanidische Krone', *Alte und moderne Kunst* 7, November–December, Vienna 1962, pp. 2-4, p. 5, figs. 9, 11–13. Yet the crescent surmounting a pole, often combined with horns and a dome at the base, was an ancient symbol used in pre-Islamic Africa, Arabia and the Near East which often related to cosmic kingship.
C. G. Picard, *Catalogue du Musée Alaoui*, collections puniques, vol. 1, Tunis 1955, Pl. XXXV, no. 227, Pl. XXXVI, nos. 231-2, Pl. LXXI, no. 585, Pl. LXXVI, no. 637, Pl. CXVII, no. 1016, Tableau II.
A. Grohmann, *Göttersymbole und Symboltiere auf südarabischen Denkmälern*, Vienna 1914, pp. 19-28, p. 33, fig. 70d; p. 39, figs. 88, 89.
H. Jänichen, *Die Bildzeichen königlicher Hoheit bei den iranischen Völkern*, Bonn 1956, pp. 37–41. Additional examples are given in a review of this work by K. Erdmann, *Bibliotheca Orientalis* XIII, Leiden 1956, pp. 255-6.
H. P. l'Orange, *Studies on the Iconography of Cosmic Kingship in the Ancient World*, Oslo 1953, pp. 43-7.
B. Segall, 'Notes on the Iconography of Cosmic Kingship', *The Art Bulletin* XXXVIII, New York 1956, pp. 76, 77, 79, fig. 5.

20. Michalowski and Gerster, op. cit., p. 43, Pls 13, 92.

21. J. Nešković and Milorad Medić, 'Šeik abd al Gadir', *Zbornik zaštite spomenika kulture* XVI, Belgrade 1965, p. 75, fig. 56.

22. Trimingham, *Sudan*, p. 87, n. 3. The Arab writer Abu Salih, who saw the crown at Faras or, as he called it, 'Bujaras the capital of the ancient region of Maris', wrote his travel account in 1208.

23. Ibid., p. 87.

24. Michalowski and Gerster, op. cit., Pl. 11.

25. F. Ll. Griffith, 'Oxford Excavations in Nubia', *University of Liverpool Annals of Archaeology and Anthropology* VIII, Liverpool 1921, pp. 77, 87, 88, Pl. XI, figs. 1, 2.
The C-group tombs at Faras show a practice of artificially deforming cattle horns so that one horn, instead of turning upwards, turns down.
P. Huard, 'A propos des bucrânes à corne déformée de Faras', *Kush* XII, 1964, pp. 63–81.
The custom of deforming cattle horns still survives elsewhere in the Sudan, and is thought to be of early Egyptian origin.
H. T. B. Hall, 'A Note on Cattle Skulls Excavated at Faras', *Kush* X, 1962, p. 61.
At Argin, horned skulls were buried inside of C group tombs.
Amalgro and others, op. cit., I, 'The Group Cemetery at Argin South', *Kush* XI, 1963, p. 178.

26. S. Curto, *Nubia, storia di una civiltà favolosa*, Novara 1965, Pl. 243, 245, 248, 253, 255, 256.

27. Trimingham, *Sudan*, p. 46.
   Shinnie, *Meroe*, p. 50.
   A. J. Arkell, *A History of the Sudan*, London 1955, p. 179.

28. E. Quatremère, *Mémoires géographiques et historiques sur l'Egypte, et sur quelques contrées voisines*, vol. II, Paris 1811, p. 34.

29. Emery, *Nubian Treasure*, Pl. 12, 14, 15, 16.
   Emery and Kirwan, *The Royal Tombs of Ballana and Qustal*, vol. I, pp. 182–6, vol. II, Pls 32–5. Arkell, op. cit., p. 182, fig. 22.
   The structure of the crowns appears to be a combination of the feather and ram's horn *atef* crown, worn by the Ptolemaic rulers of Egypt, and the moon disc and cow's horn headdress worn by both Isis and Hathor.
   Curto, op. cit., Pls 54, 58, 291.

30. Michalowski and Gerster, op. cit., Pls 13, 92.

31. Trimingham, *Sudan*, pp. 128, 131, 135, 138, 141, 142. It is possible that sacred tombs depicted over doors pre-date Islam, and that the central shape in Pl. 87 represents one such.

32. Ibid., pp. 76–8.

33. Ibid., pp. 66, 76.
   S. Jakobielski, 'Some Remarks on Faras Inscriptions', *Kunst und Geschichte*, p. 31.
   M. Krause, 'Zur Kirchen – und Theologiegeschichte Nubiens', Ibid., p. 78.

34. Trimingham, *Sudan*, pp. 25, 180, 181.

35. The style may be compared between the eighth-century frescoes uncovered at Faras (Michalowski and Gerster, op. cit., Pls 27–33), and those of the eleventh and twelfth centuries (ibid., Pls 64–5, 69, 75–7).

36. Trimingham, *Sudan*, pp. 76–7.

37. M. Krause, op. cit., *Kunst und Geschichte*, pp. 71–86.
   Michalowski, *Faras*, Leyden 1966, pp. 6, 12, 20.
   Adams, 'Post Pharaonic Nubia II', *JEA* LI, 1965, p. 172.

38. *Dictionnaire de Théologie Catholique*, vol. X, 2, Paris 1929, col. 2216–46, Monophysisme, col. 2276, Monophysite (Église Copte).

39. O. G. von Simson, *Sacred Fortress*, Chicago 1948, p. 35.

40. Michalowski and Gerster, op. cit., Pl. 95b.

41. Trimingham, *Sudan*, pp. 71, 72, 79.
   A. and W. Kronenberg, 'Parallel Cousin Marriage in Medieval and Modern Nubia', Part I, *Kush* XIII, 1965, pp. 256–60.

42. Examples of African monarchs exchanging traditional aspects of kingship for Muslim characteristics of the holy man are given by I. M. Lewis, *Islam in Tropical Africa*, London 1966, pp. 36, 37.

CHAPTER SEVEN: AFTERMATH OF NUBIAN WALL DECORATION

1. D. R. Lee, 'The Nubian House: Persistence of a Cultural Tradition', *Landscape* 18, No. 1, Berkeley, Winter 1969, p. 39. Evidence is given to suggest that woodcarving, as well as painting, may have a future in Khashm el Girba as a form of house decoration substituting for mud relief.

BIBLIOGRAPHY

ABDULLA AL-TAYIB. 'The Changing Customs of the Riverain Sudan – III', *Sudan Notes and Records*, XLV, 1964, 12–28.

ADAMS, W. Y. 'The Christian Potteries of Faras', *Kush* IX, Khartoum 1961, 30–43.

ADAMS, W. Y. 'An Introductory Classification of Christian Nubian pottery', *Kush*, X, Khartoum 1962, 245–88.

ADAMS, W. Y. 'Post-Pharaonic Nubia in the Light of Archaeology, III', *Journal of Egyptian Archaeology*, LI, London 1965, 160–78.

ADAMS, W. Y. 'Sudan Antiquities Service Excavation at Mienarti 1963–64', *Kush*, XIII, Khartoum 1965, 148–94.

ADAMS, W. Y. 'The Nubian Campaign: Retrospect and Prospect', *Mélanges offerts à Kazimierz Michalowski*, Warsaw 1966, 13–30.

ADAMS, W. Y. 'Post-Pharaonic Nubia in the Light of Archaeology, III', *Journal of Egyptian Archaeology*, LII, London 1966, 147–62.

ADAMS, W. Y. 'Continuity and Change in Nubian Cultural History', *Sudan Notes and Records*, XLVIII, Khartoum 1967, 1–32.

AHMAD MUHAMMAD ALI AL-HAKIM. *Al-Zakharif al mi'mariya wa Talawaruha fi mantigat Wadi Halfa* (Architectural decorations and their development in the Wadi Halfa district), Sudan Unit Occasional Papers No. 1, University of Khartoum, October 1965.

Al-Hilal, Egyptian Pictorial Review, vol. XLVIII, Cairo, 1 December 1939.

Al-Mussawar, Egyptian Illustrated Review, No. 779, Cairo, 15 September 1939.

AMALGRO, M., F. PRESEDO, and M. PELLICER. 'Preliminary Report on the Spanish Excavations in the Sudan 1961–62 (b), the C-Group Cemetery at Argin South', *Kush*, XI, Khartoum 1963, 175–195.

AMALGRO, M., R. BLANCO CARO, M. A. GARCIA-GUINEA, F. PRESEDO VELO, M. PILLICER CATALAN, and J. TEIXIDOR. 'Excavations by the Spanish Archaeological Mission in the Sudan, 1962–3 and 1963–4, V, The Christian Site of Abkanarti', *Kush*, XIII, Khartoum 1965, 89–92.

APULEIUS. *Metamorphoses*, published as *The Golden Ass*, W. Adlington tr., Loeb Classical Library, London and Cambridge, Mass. 1958.

ARKELL, A. J. *A History of the Sudan*, London 1955.

ARKELL, A. J. *History of the Sudan to 1821*, London 1961.

BELL, H. *Place Names in the Belly of Stones*, Linguistic Monograph Series No. 5, Sudan Research Unit, Faculty of Arts, Khartoum University, Khartoum, December 1970.

BLACKMAN, A. M. 'The Fox as a Birth-Amulet', *Man*, IX, 4, London 1909, 9, 10.

BLACKMAN, A. M. 'Some Egyptian and Nubian Notes', *Man*, X, 11, London 1910, 29.

BURCKHARDT, J. L. *Travels in Nubia*, London 1819.

CAVENDISH, M. W. 'The Custom of Placing Pebbles on Nubian Graves', *Sudan Notes and Records*, XLVII, 1966, 151–6.

COLE, H. M. 'Mbari is a Dance', *African Arts/Arts d'Afrique*, II, No. 4, Los Angeles 1969, 42–51.

CROWFOOT, GRACE M. 'A Note on the Stringing of Sudanese Beds and Stools', *Dryad Quarterly*, III, No. 1, January–March, Leicester 1933, 12–19.

CRUM, W. E., see Winlock, H. E.

CURTO, S. *Nubia, storia di una civiltà favolosa*, Novara 1965.

DAFALLA, H. 'Notes on the History of Wadi Halfa Town', *Sudan Notes and Records*, XLVI, Khartoum 1965, 8–26.

DANTHINE, HÉLÈNE. *Le Palmier-dattier et les arbres sacrés, dans l'iconographie de l'Asie occidentale ancienne*, vol. II, Paris 1937.

Dictionnaire de Théologie Catholique, Vol. X, 2, Paris 1929, Col. 2216–46, Monophysisme; Col. 2276, Monophysite (Église Copte).

DUERDON, D. *African Art*, London 1968.

EMERY, W. B. and L. P. KIRWAN. *The Royal Tombs of Ballana and Qustal*, Cairo 1938.

EMERY, W. B. *Nubian Treasure*, London and Southampton 1948.

EMERY, W. B. *Egypt in Nubia*, London 1965.

ENSOR, F. S. *Incidents on a Journey through Nubia to Darfoor*, London 1881.

ERDMANN, K., see Jänichen, H.

FADL HASAN, Y., see Lewis, I. M.

GERSTER, G. 'Threatened Treasures of the Nile', *National Geographic*, 124, No. 4, Washington, October 1963, 587–621.

GERSTER, G. 'Nubia before the Flood', *The Sunday Times Colour Magazine*, London, 11 June 1964, 22–9.

GERSTER, G., see Michalowski, K.

GLEICHEN, COUNT. *The Anglo-Egyptian Sudan*, London 1905, vol. I.

GRIFFITH, F. LL. 'Oxford Excavations in Nubia', *University of Liverpool Annals of Archaeology and Anthropology*, VIII, Liverpool 1921, 65–104.

GRIFFITH, F. LL. Pakhoras-Bakarâs-Faras in Geography and History. *Journal of Egyptian Archaeology*, XI, London 1925, 259–68.

GROHMAN, A. *Götersymbole und Symboltiere auf südarabischen Denkmälern*, Vienna 1914.

HALL, H. T. B. 'A Note on Cattle Skulls Excavated at Faras', *Kush*, X, Khartoum 1962, 58–61.

GWYN GRIFFITHS, J. and IBRAHIM AHMED IBRAHIM. 'The Use of Plates and Saucers to Decorate Houses in Lower Nubia and Upper Egypt', *Sudan Notes and Records*, XXI, Khartoum 1938, 217–20.

HAYCOCK, B. G. 'Towards a Better Understanding of the Kingdom of Cush (Napata-Meroe)', *Sudan Notes and Records*, XLIX, Khartoum 1968, 1–16.

HERZOG, R. *Die Nubier*, Berlin 1957.

HEWES, G. W. 'Gezira Dabarosa: Report of the University of Colorado Nubian Expedition, 1962–3 season', *Kush*, XII, Khartoum 1964, 174–85.

HILLIER, B. *Art Deco of the 20s and 30s*, London 1968.

HOLT, P. M. *A Modern History of the Sudan*, New York 1961.

HOSKINS, G. A. *Travels in Ethiopia*, London 1835.

HUARD, P. 'A propos des bucrânes à corne déformée de Faras', *Kush*, XII, 1964, 63–81.

Huntley and Palmers Xmas Biscuits and Cakes, catalogues issued annually, Reading 1924–40.

IBRAHIM AHMED IBRAHIM, see Gwyn Griffiths, J.

JAKOBIELSKI, S. 'Some Remarks on Faras Inscriptions', E. Dinkler, ed., *Kunst und Geschichte Nubiens in Christlicher Zeit*, Recklinghausen 1970, 29–38.

JÄNICHEN, H. *Die Bildzeichen königlicher Hoheit bei den iranischen Völkern*, Bonn 1956, reviewed by Erdmann, K., *Bibliotheca Orientalis*, XIII, Leiden 1956, 255–6.

KEATING, R. *Nubian Twilight*, London 1962.

KIDD, W. 'Comment', *Urbanization*, Magazine of the Faculty of Architecture, Ahmadu Bello University, Zaria, vol. 7, 1967–8, 8–9.

KIRWAN, L. P. 'Prelude to Nubian Christianity', *Mélanges offerts à Kazimierz Michalowski*, Warsaw 1966, 121–8.

KIRWAN, L. P., see Emery, W. B.

KRAUSE, M. 'Zur Kirchen- und Theologiegeschichte Nubiens', E. Dinkler, ed. *Kunst und Geschichte Nubiens in Christlicher Zeit*, Recklinghausen 1970, 71–86.

KRONENBERG, A. and W. 'Preliminary Report on the Anthropological Field Work in Sudanese Nubia, 1964', *Kush*, XIII, Khartoum 1965, 205–12.

KRONENBERG, A. and W. 'Parallel Cousin Marriage in Medieval and Modern Nubia – Part I', *Kush*, XIII, 1965, 241–60.

KRONENBERG, A. and W. 'Wooden Carvings in the South Western Sudan', *Kush*, VIII, 1960, 274–81.

LAPIDUS, IRA M., ed., *Middle Eastern Cities*, Berkeley and Los Angeles 1969.

LEE, D. R. 'The Nubian House: Persistence of a Cultural Tradition', *Landscape*, 18, No. 1, Berkeley, Winter 1969, 36–9.

LEPSIUS, R. *Nubische Grammatik*, Berlin 1880.

LEWIS, I. M., ed., *Islam in Tropical Africa*. Part Two, II, Y. Fadl Hasan. 'The Penetration of Islam in the Eastern Sudan', 144–55.

LIGHT, H. *Travels in Egypt, Nubia, Holy Land, Mount Libanon and Cyprus*, London 1818.

L'ORANGE, H. P. *Studies on the Iconography of Cosmic Kingship in the Ancient World*, Oslo 1953.

MEDIĆ, M., see Nesković, J.

MERRILL, W. 'The Wooden Locks of the Halfa Region', *Sudan Notes and Records*, XLV, 1964, 29–34.

MICHALOWSKI, K. *Faras, fouilles Polonaises 1961*, Warsaw 1962.

MICHALOWSKI, K. *Faras, fouilles Polonaises 1961–1962*, Warsaw 1965.

MICHALOWSKI, K. *Faras*, Leyden 1966.

MICHALOWSKI, K. 'Open Problems of Nubian Art and Culture in the Light of Discoveries at Faras', E. Dinkler, ed., *Kunst und Geschichte Nubiens in Christlicher Zeit*, Recklinghausen 1970, 11–19.

MICHALOWSKI, K. and G. GERSTER. *Faras, die Kathedrale aus dem Wüstensand*, Cologne, Zürich 1967.

MILEHAM, G. S. *Churches in Lower Nubia*, Philadelphia 1910.

MONNERET DE VILLARD, V. *La Nubie Médiévale*, vol. IV, Cairo 1957.

MUSTAFA IBRAHIM TAHA, 'The Art of Making Manwaras in Nubia', *Sudan Notes and Records*, XLIX, Khartoum 1968, 155–7.

NEŠKOVIĆ, J. and M. MEDIĆ. Šeik abd al Gadir. *Zbornik zaštite spomenika kulture*, XVI, Belgrade 1965, 67–80.

OLIVER, R., ed., *The Middle Ages of African History*, London 1967.

PICARD, C. G. *Catalogue du Musée Alaoui*, Collections puniques, vol. 1, Tunis 1955.

QUATREMÈRE, E. *Mémoires géographiques et historiques sur l'Egypte, et sur quelques contrées voisines*, vol. II, Paris 1811.

REED, W. 'A Study of Marine Fisheries in the Sudan', *Sudan Notes and Records*, XLIII, 1962, 1–15.

ROBINSON, A. E. 'The Cult of the Crocodile', *American Anthropologist*, 34, Menasha Wisconsin 1932, 550.

SCANLON, G.T. 'Slip Painted Pottery from Wizz', *African Arts/Arts d'Afrique*, II, No. 1, Los Angeles 1968, 8–13, 65–9.

SEGALL, B. 'Notes on the Iconography of Cosmic Kingship', *The Art Bulletin*, XXXVIII, New York 1956, 75–80.

SHINNIE, MARGARET. *Ancient African Kingdoms*, London 1965.

SHINNIE, P. L. *Medieval Nubia*, Khartoum 1964.

SHINNIE, P. L. *Meroe, a Civilization of the Sudan*, New York 1967.

SHINNIE, P. L. 'The University of Ghana Excavation at Debeira West 1963', *Kush*, XII, Khartoum, 1964, 208–15.

SIMSON, O. von, *Sacred Fortress*, Chicago 1948.

STANNUS, H. 'Alphabet Boards from Central Africa', *Man*, X, 18, 1910, 37–8.

Sudan Almanac, 1967, Central Office of Information, Republic of the Sudan, 1966–7.

SWITHENBANK, M. *Ashanti Fetish Houses*, Accra 1969.

TRIGGER, B. G. *History and Settlement in Lower Nubia*, Yale University Publications in Anthropology, 69, New Haven 1965, 16.

TRIGGER, B. G. 'The Cultural Ecology of Christian Nubia', E. Dinkler, ed., *Kunst und Geschichte Nubiens in Christlicher Zeit*, Recklinghausen 1970, 347–78.

TRIMINGHAM, J. S. *Islam in the Sudan*, London 1965.

TRIMINGHAM, J. S. *The Influence of Islam upon Africa*, London 1968.

TURNURE, J. H. 'Etruscan Ritual Armor: Two Examples in Bronze', *American Journal of Archaeology*, 69. No. 1, January 1965, 39–48.

WENZEL, M. 'A Note on the Cat-Lore of Nubia', *Folklore*, 75, London, Summer 1964, 21.

WINLOCK, H. E. and W. E. CRUM. *The Monastery of Epiphanius at Thebes*, New York, Metropolitan Museum of Art, Egyptian Expedition Publications, vol. III, Part I, New York 1926.

INDEX

Nubian place-names in this index are given as recorded in my own field notation. Dr. Herman Bell has kindly provided corrections of these names based on his field survey of place-names from the Egyptian border through Kosha, Serkamatto. Corrected names appear in brackets and small capitals following the relevant word. Question marks indicate names not personally recorded by Dr. Bell.

A discussion of these names and a map showing Batn al-Hajar sites mentioned in this book can be found in H. Bell, *Place Names in the Belly of Stones*, Linguistic Monograph Series No. 5, Sudan Research Unit, Faculty of Arts, Khartoum University, Khartoum, December, 1970.

ABBREVIATIONS

Administrative divisions:
om., *omodiya* ('UMUDĪYYA)
sh., *sheikhship* (SHAYKSHIP)
h., *hillet* (HILLA)
E., East
W., West
Geographical but not administrative divisions:
e.b., east bank of the Nile
w.b., west bank of the Nile

Abd al-Aziz al-Amin, decorator (Appendix B, no. 13), 105–6, 108, 193
Abd al-Rahim Mukhtar, decorator-plasterer, farmer (Appendix A, no. 26), 186; Figs. 21l, 31b
Abd el-Jabir, builder's assistant, 184
Abd el-Rahman Muhammad, builder, 186
Abdelrahin Abddai, Sheikh of Serkamatto, Fig. 29b
Abdinirki (ABDĪIN IRKI), h., see *Omodiya* Serra, sh. Serra E.
Abdoun Muhammad Fadl, builder-decorator (Appendix A, no. 7), 78, 83, 179–81, 184; Figs 27b, 28a,b
Abdu Batoul, decorator-butcher (Appendix B, no. 8), 97, 130, 152–3, 155, 189, 191; Fig. 47; Pls 49, 77; Col. pl. 18
Abdu Hasan Fadl, bridegroom, artist, Fig. 15
Abdu Saber, house-owner, artist, 53; Col. pl. 5
Abdulla Ahmad Dijab, see Lockmakers
Abdulla Kheir al-Sid, see Lockmakers
Abdulla Sabbar, 176, 198 n. 3
Abdullando (ABDÚLLANDO), h., see *Omodiya* Kosha W., sh. Dal
Abermatto, h., see *Omodiya* Duweishat E., sh. Ambikol
Abkanarti, h. and medieval site, see *Omodiya* Gemai, sh. Amka
Aboud, General, 201 n. 9
Abri, town and om., see *Omodiya* Abri
Abu Hamed, town in Shaiqiyya country; see also Manasiri, 21, 190
Abu Salih, Arab writer, 205 n. 22
Abu Sarieda (ABU SARIIDA?), h., see *Omodiya* Kosha E., sh. Farka
Abu Simbel, 9, 125, 169
Abushuna (AB SHÚUNA), h., see OMODIYA Akasha, sh. Akasha
Acacia wood, 24, 35, 199 n. 16
Adhesive, used in wall decoration, 97
Adindan, Upper Egypt, 191
Adurma (ADÚRMA), h., see OMODIYA Gemai, e.b., sh. Murshid E.
Advertising art, 56, 149–50; Figs 45e–g, 46, 11a–d, 111a

Aeroplanes, 44, 54, 56, 59; Pls 20, 21; Figs 14, 19d
Aesthetic judgments or opinions about decoration, by household members, 47–51, 53, 201 n. 6; by patrons of professional decorators, 122, 133; Pl. 64; by professional decorators, 4, 109, 111, 120, 123, 125, 133, 134, 138; by villagers, 121–3, 126, 134, 153, 155, 185; see also Iconoclastic attitudes
Africa, see Negro Africa, North Africa, Chad, Egypt, Ethiopia, Ghana, Nigeria, Sudan; for pre-Islamic Africa, 205 n. 19; kingship in (see also Cosmic kingship), 206 n. 42
Agate, 134
Agremasho (AGRÉE and MÁSHO), two h. recorded as one unit by the government, see *Omodiya* Saras, e.b., sh. Saras-Tahali
Agri (AGIR), h., see *Omodiya* Saras, e.b., sh. Semna
Agriculture, in Nubia, see Farmer, Farming, Food in Nubia; in Khashm el-Girba, 194–5 n. 1
Ahmad Batoul, plasterer and professional decorator (Appendix A, no. 3), 5, 6, 94–116, 122, 127–8, 130–2, 152, 161, 173, 188–93, 203 n. 17; Figs 32–3; 50f,j,l; Pls 38–41, 43–4, 46–8; imitators of, 101–9, 112–14, 179, 190–3; Fig. 34; Pls 42, 45, 49, 77
Ahmad Dviz Jaroun, decorator (?) (Appendix A, no. 2), 178
Ahmad Karafti, artist (Appendix A, no. 29), 84, 86–8, 187; Pls 31–2
Ahmad Osman, decorator (Appendix A, no. 19), 184
Ahmad Suleiman, see Lockmakers
Akasha (AAKÁSHA or 'AKÁSHA), om., sh., h., and site of holy man's tomb, see *Omodiya* Akasha
Aksha, h. and alternate name for sh. Serra W., North, see *Omodiya* Serra, w.b.
Aleppo, 200 n. 35
Al-Hilal, Egyptian pictorial review, 203 n. 22; Figs 45d,e, 46, 11C, 51d
Al-Mussawar, Egyptian illustrated review, 203 n. 22; Figs 46, 11b, 51e
Al-Tira, h., see *Omodiya* Faras W., sh. Faras W.
Alexandria, 60, 108, 204 n. 9
Ali, name of several Sudanese saints, 161; Fig. 48
Ali Hasan Taffoul, builder-decorator (Appendix A, no. 16), 182–3, 201 n. 4; Fig. 48
Ali Ibn Abi Talib, called Ali *karrar*, cousin of Muhammad, 161, 172, 201 n. 14, 204 n. 9
Ali Muhammad Abakr, farmer, carpenter, decorator (Appendix A, no. 12), 181; Fig. 26b
Alifenti, h., see *Omodiya* Saras, e.b., sh. Saras-Tahali
Alphabet boards, 46, 200 n. 40; Fig. 13a
Alwa, Christian kingdom, 30
Amarok, h., see *Omodiya* Abri, e.b., sh. Abri
Amber, 34
Ambikol (AMBU-KÓOL) sh. and island, see *Omodiya* Duweishat
Amka or Amka Sharg (ÁMKA), sh., see *Omodiya* Gemai
Amka Alibek (ALI-BÉEK), h., see *Omodiya* Gemai, sh. Amka
Amtukke (AMTÚKKE), h., see *Omodiya* Saras, e.b., sh. Saras-Tahali
Amulets, 20, 61, 120, 172
Angarib, rope bed, 18, 26; Fig. 5; Col. pls 12, 14; cost of, 181
Angasa (ANGSI), h., see *Omodiya* Duweishat E., sh. Ambikol
Anglo-Egyptian Sudan, see Sudan, Anglo-Egyptian
Angular shapes, Art Deco influence, 134, 149, 151, 203 n. 10; Figs 46, 1b, 111C; 51a–c; Pl. 62; Col. pl. 17
Aniba, Egyptian Nubia, Pl. 9

Animals, see also Birds, Fish, 84, 178; domestic, see Camel, Cat, Cow, Dog, Donkey, Goat, Lamb, Rabbit, Ram, Sheep; wild, see Antelope, Crocodile, Elk, Fox, Hyena, Monitor, Lizard, Scorpion, Snake, Spider; with horns, see Horns; cloth images of, 160; stuffed or dried, 40, 86, 192; Fig. 10a,d

Animal killing, see Killing of animals

Antar, Arab hero, 109, 161

Antelope or gazelle, skulls and stuffed heads of, 40, 192; Fig. 10d; representations of, 36, 60, 140, 160; Figs 10d, 44e

Anthropomorphic shapes; see also Column under knob, Cyclops shape, 46, 108, 123, 154–5; Figs 13, 34a,b, 37b,c, 40; Pls. 53, 57, 82–3; Col. pls 10, 18

Apple trees, 124–5; Col. pl. 12

Apsire (AB-SÍRE), h., see Omodiya Kosha W., sh. Dal

Arab conquest of Egypt, 173; of North Africa, 15

Arab decorators, see Muhammad Suleiman, Sayyid Ahmad Hogla

Arabia (see also Mecca), pre-Islamic, 205 n. 19

Araser (ARASÉR), h., see Omodiya Kosha E., sh. Serkamatto

Archaeological excavations, 79, 178

Archaeology, influence on house decoration, 79, 124–5; superstitions concerning, 160

Arcade, 83; Fig. 30

Arch, rounded, see Dome

Architectural representations, 61, 124; Figs 14, 16b, 23

Architecture in Wadi Halfa district, 195, Introduction n. 1; in Shaiqiyya country, 21; in Nubia (see also House), history of, 15–24; in Khashm el-Girba, 6, 195; Pl. 2; in North Africa and the Middle East, 20, 195; in Western Europe, 91

Argin (ARGÍIN), om., see Omodiya Argin

Are (ARE), h., see Omodiya Ashkeit

Army, Sudanese, 14; representations of, 44, 56; Fig. 19d

Aro, h., see Omodiya Kosha W., sh. Dal

Arrow-motif, 36; as compensation assessment team mark, Pls 28, 38–9, 47, 61–4, 66, 68–9

Art Deco, 134, 140–52, 173, 203 n. 10, n. 22; Figs 45, 46; Pl. 76; Col. pls 16, 17; see Angular shapes, Balloons, Circles, concentric, also Chevron, Light rays, Rainbow arc, Scallops, Stepped pyramid, Vines and flowers enclosed in geometric shapes; Art Deco phase of Hasan Arabi's art

Art schools, in Europe, Bauhaus, 134; in Italy, 59–60

Artificial-limb making, 77, 182

Artinassi (ÀRTI NASSÍ), island, see Omodiya Gemai, sh. Gemai

Artinoka (ARTIN OG or ARTIN OKKA), h., see Omodiya Serra, e.b., sh. Serra E.

Artists, 48–9; boys, 22, 43–4, 48–52, 54, 155, 181; Figs 16, 17g, 20e; Pl. Col. pl. 4; bridegrooms, 48–9, 61, 84; Fig. 15; brides, 48; girls, 48; Figs 11i, 21v; Pl. 25; house-builders, 35, 75–81, 88, 90, 92, 114, 153–8, 201 n. 1; Figs 20q, 25–9, 36(?), 42b, 43–4, 48; Pls. 28, 32, 50–2, 66–7, 69–75, 78–84; Col. pls 1, 19; house-owners, 22, 47–56, 92; Fig. 18; Pls 18, 42; Col. pls 5, 6; men (group unspecified), 49, 51–2, 61, 69; Pls 19, 27; plasterers (kasso) or smoothers, 5, 21, 75–7, 92–9, 114, 131; professional artists, see Professional decorators; relatives of the family, 84–6; Pls 29–30; women, see Women's painting

Arusa (ARÚUSE), h., see Omodiya Saras, e.b., sh. Saras-Tahali

Asheile (ASHÁYLE), h., see Omodiya Gemai, e.b., sh. Amka

Ashkeit (ASHKÉET), om., see Omodiya Ashkeit

Ashtrays, 153

Ashura, festival of, see Festivals, Marks

Asrawarki (ESRAW IRKI), h., see Omodiya Argin

Assistants to professional decorators, 114, 116–17, 127, 188–92, 203 n. 17; to builders, 178, 181–5

Aswan, 9, 11–12, 57, 180, 196 n. 16, 201 n. 1

Aswan Dam floodings, early in twentieth century, 12; in 1964, 3, 6, 9, 25, 54, 160, 175

Atbara, 11, 48, 131, 140, 178–80, 190

Atef crown; see also Crowns, 206 n. 29

Atil acacia wood, see fara, Arabic for same

Atiri (ATTIRI), sh., and h., see Omodiya Saras, e.b.

Attendants to the bridegroom, 32, 34

Automobile headlights, set into mud relief, 4, 40, 78; Figs 10c, 28c

Automobiles, 91; representations of, 49, 56, 59, 91, 138, 140; Figs 15, 19b, 44a, h.; Pls 72, 75

Awwen-Arti (AWWENN ARTI) island, possibly h., see Omodiya Argin, sh. Argin South, Awwen-Arti island and h. Vornarti

Axe, 35, 126

Aztec art, 134

Baash (BAASH), h., see Omodiya Kosha E., sh. Serkamatto

Babikr al-Mansuri, decorator (Appendix B, no. 9), 105, 192

Baksheesh, 75, 180

Ballana, Upper Egypt, 5, 47, 97–8, 182, 189, 192; Pls 49, 77; ancient capital of Nubia, 14–15; treasure found at, 15, 170; Fig. 49a,b

Balloons, Art Deco motif, 151; Col. pl. 17

Balloon-like ovals surmounting columns, possibly representing ostrich eggs, 154; Pls 78–83

Banana leaves, 122, 159, 167, 170; Fig. 50r; Pl. 90

Banana trees, 122, 124; Fig. 50r

Band around three sides of the room, in baskets and mats, 27, Fig. 5; for weddings, in paint or relief, see also Wedding decoration, 67, 69, 71, 83; Figs 21u, 22c,f,k,p,q, 23c,f,t,x; made not for weddings. Fig. 21v; made by women, 53, 67–74, 99; Figs 21–3; Pls 26–37; by men, 53, 84–5, 88, 99, 140, 146–9, 155; Figs 30, 32d,l,s, 34b,g,h, 36b–d, 37a–c, 43g, 44a,b,d,f,h, 45a–c, 46 1a, 1c, 47c,g, 51b; Pls 27, 31, 33–6, 76, 80, 81; variants depending on sex of decorator, 83, 99; Pl. 27

Banu Kanz Arabs, 12

Baraka, see power

Barrel-vault houses, 196 n. 13

Barrenness in women, 160

Basket lids (tabag, tabaqa), 27–8, 30, 34–5, 43, 48, 65, 67; Figs 4, 5, 6n,o, 21a,c,h,i; Pls 7–9; represented on walls, 69, 74, 88, 130, 140, 146, 151, 155; Figs 22c,d,g,h,l,m,p–s, 29a–c, 32m(?), 36a–c, 43d–f, 44a,b,d,f–h, 47g; Pls 26–7, 28(?), 33, 35, 50–2, 59, 61–9, 71–3, 76, 80–1, 90; Col. pls 8, 10(?), 13–15, 18, 19

Basketry bowls, 24, 28, 30, 34–5, 40, 48, 94, 200 n. 36; Figs 5, 20t

Batn al-Hajar (Belly of Rocks or Belly of Stones), 11, 17, 18, 21–2, 42, 52–3, 65, 180

Bauhaus School of Art, see Art schools

Beads (jirtiq), 198 n. 10; see also Bride and Bridegroom, jewellery and objects worn by

Beans, 35

Bed, see angarib

Bedouin Arabs, 30, 153, 182

Beer, 53

Bell, H., 195 n. 11

59; Col. pl. 10; like *ivory bracelets*, 88; Col. pl. 8; *Art Deco balloons*, 151; Fig. 51b; Col. pl. 17; by men, *hollowed into the wall*, Fig. 25d; Pls 18, 58; *marked on the wall*, 3–4, 53, 123, 125, 128, 134, 167, 202 n. 3; Figs 26b, 45a–c, 46 1a, 1c, 47a,c,e,f; Pls 18, 23, 31, 32–3, 45, 58, 67, 71, 73, 77, 79, 80–2; Col. pls 5, 10; method of marking on wall, 3, 145; by compensation assessment teams, Pls 53, 72, 78–84; *between parallel bars*, by women, Fig. 22c,l,m; Pl. 26; as 1930s motif, 149; Fig. 46 11c, 111b; by Hasan Arabi *c.* 1942–6, 149; Figs 42a, 46 1a, 1c, 51b; Pl. 62; Col. pls 14, 16; by Dawud Osman 1942–55, Figs 43d–f, 44g,h; Pls 70–3; by Abdu Batoul 1947, Fig. 47g; *concentric*, in women's art, Fig. 22p–s; in men's art relating to basket forms, 151; Fig. 47g; Pls 35, 76; Col. pls 8, 14; relating to Art Deco concentric circles, 134, 151; Figs 45a–c, 46 1a, 1d, 11d, 111c; Pl. 76; Col. pls 14, 17; by compensation assessment teams, Pls 40, 46, 58–9, 65; *half circles*, see also Domes, Scallops, by Saleh Mirghani (?), 1923, Fig. 36; by Hasan Arabi in his geometric style façades from 1941, Fig. 42a; Pls 62–4; by Dawud Osman as trade-mark from 1940, 137; Fig. 43d–f, Pls 66–7, 69–73; *fitted inside a second half circle*, see also Rainbow arc; in women's art 1939, 23f; in men's art with Art Deco associations, 134, 151; Figs 45c, 46 1a, 1c, 11a, 111c; Pl. 76; Col. pls 16, 17

Circumcision ceremonies, 198 n. 10

Clay, 52

Clothes, see Costume

Cocktail biscuits, 151

Cocktails, illustrated literature about, 151; Fig. 46 111c

Coffee, 176; Pl. 63

Coffee tables, 35, 125; Pl. 11; Col. pl. 12

Collaboration between artists, between professionals and women, see Professional Decorators

Colour, in boys' and women's painting, 52, 98, 114, 155; Col. pls 4, 7; see also Earth colour, Bluing, Chalk, Pigments; used by men, type of colour, see Pigments; use of, 4, 52–4, 56, 78, 83, 88, 99–100, 102, 112, 117, 134–5, 140, 145–6, 149, 151, 153, 180; Figs 15, 18, 26, 29, 33j, 34b,c,g,h, 37a, 39, 43e, 44, 45a–c, 46 1a–1d, 47b; Col. pls 5, 8, 11–12, 14, 16–17, 19; painted on to relief, 4, 112, 134, 140, 154; Figs 34d,e,f, 37a, 43f, 47c; Pls 32, 49, 64, 77–80, 90; Col. pl. 13; colour symbolism, 4, 54

Columns, *free-standing*, under horns, 54; Pl. 18; Col. pl. 6; under ostrich eggs, 32; *painted*, under horns, Pl. 27; *inscribed, singly*, under horns, crescent and star, 100–1; Fig. 32b; marked at each house corner and called *aktaf*, meaning 'shoulders', undecorated, Pls 5, 24, 46; decorated with colour only, Fig. 25d; with relief designs, 4; by Muhammad Osman 1939, Fig. 8e; by Jabir Bab al-Kheir 1944, Pl. 59; by Hasan Arabi 1940–5, Pls 64–5, 68; by Dawud Osman 1942–7, Pls 66, 72; *two inscribed columns*, in Egyptian woodworking, Fig. 35b; flanking doorway, see also Verticals flanking dome; undecorated, Figs 10, 20q, 25; Pl. 84; decorated with simple hollows, additions at top, Figs 10, 20q, 25; Col. pl. 1; with relief patterns, Fig. 28a–c; by Saleh Mirghani (?) 1923, Fig. 36a; by Ahmad Batoul 1928–38, Fig. 32k,q,r; Pls 41, 47; with painted designs by Jabir Bab al-Kheir and Dawud Osman, 1947, 1955, Figs 39, 44g; *four inscribed columns*, two each side of door, first used 1933 by Ahmad Batoul, Pl. 46; by himself and others later, Figs 38, 40, 43f; Pls 28, 32, 40, 44, 46, 50, 52, 59, 78–9; Col. pls 10, 18; *six*, three each side, by Ahmad Batoul 1930–5, 100–1; Fig. 33a,d; Pls 38–9; by Jabir Bab al Kheir 1940s, Pl. 58; see also Doorway surround formula for use by Hasan Arabi and Dawud Osman; *inscribed columns, with concavities on the shank*, peculiar to Batoul brothers, 100–1; Figs 32q,r, 33d,f–h, 47a; *with false windows*, only by Ahmad Batoul, 101; Figs 32q, 33a,d,f–h; Pls 38–41, 44, 46; *with horizontal bars*, other shapes linking them together, see Doorway surround formula;

Surmounted by crescents, see Crescents, *by horns*, 122; Figs 33i, 38, 50r, *by ostrich eggs*, 154, Pls 78–80; *knobs*, 46, 99, 129; Figs 13, 23 0, 32g, 33c, 36a,d, 38, 40–1, 43e,f, 47a, 50l,o; Pls 32, 40, 50, 52, 57–8, 61–4, 67–9, 71–3; see also Knob on a stem

Commercial artists, see Morelli, Sabri

Communication between east and west Nile banks, 9–12, 91

Community gatherings, 4, 14, 176; see also Wedding customs

Compass, makeshift, 145

Compensation assessment teams, marks of, see Arrow-motif; Circle

Compensation money, 6, 54

Competition among artists, see Professional decorators

Composition methods in wall painting, 124–5

Concentric circles, see Circles, concentric

Concrete, 175

Containers, medieval Nubian, see Pottery; modern Nubian Pottery; see also Pot for flowers, Storage pots, Basket lids, Basketry bowls, Wooden bowls, Chinaware, Cups, Plates, Saucers, Ewer, Gourds; put above walls as decoration, 94; put on walls as decoration, see Basket lids, Plates, Saucers; put in cupboards, see Cupboards; hung from the ceiling in nets, see Bowls, hanging, also Nets; represented on walls, Figs 16a, 34b,g,h, 37d, 39, 44b,h, 46 1a, 51b; Pls 29, 36, 74, 76; Col. pls 5, 7, 14, 21; see also Circles, representing basket lids

Contracts made about house decoration, 189–91

Contractor, profiteer from house destruction, 6

Conversion to Christianity, 15, 169, 172

Cooks, Nubian, 11, 101, 150

Coptic, Church, 56, 59, 172–3; language, 14, 15, 172

Copying, from ancient art, 79, 124–5, 202 n. 3; from nature, 49–50, 124–6; from tin boxes, 6, 134, 150–1; towels, 150; Egyptian chests, 108–9; from women's art, 88–9, 98, 142; from other artists, see Professional decorators, design borrowing; see also Magazines, Newspapers

Corners of house, see Columns, inscribed singly at each house corner

Cornice, 79, 153; by Ahmad Batoul 1950, Fig. 33j; by Dawud Osman 1939, 1954–5, Figs 43c, 44g; see also String course; Floating unit at top of doorway design

Corrugated metal, see Metal

Cosmic kingship, 173, 205 n. 19; see also Kingship, Eparch

Costume of Nubians, 52; see Children in Nubia; Men in Nubia; *Jerjar*, Women in Nubia; storage of, 34

Courtyards (*hosh*), 4, 16–22, 52, 125, 154, 182; Figs 3, 20b,c,h,j,m,n,o, 31c, 34d,e,f, 43a,b, 47f; Pls 4, 6, 16, 45, 82–3

Cow, 117, 200 n. 29

Cow-goddess, 167; Pl. 89

Cowrie shells, 34, 198–9 n. 11

Crescent, new moon in wedding ritual, 32; on crown, see Crown with crescent and stem; on tomb of holy man, 162, 205 n. 17; cut from tin, 40; Fig. 43c; Pl. 42; represented in isolation on walls, 49, 53, 83, 134; Figs 21v, 23h, 25b; Pls 35, 37–9, 44; Col. pl. 8; with star, 129, 153; Figs 11h, 22v, 23a, 25b, 32b,e, 36b,c, 40–1, 43c–f, 44c, 47c–f, 50f,h,m, 51; Pls 13, 41, 61–5, 67–73, 76–7, 81, 85–6, 90; Col. pls 14, 15, 18; on flag, Figs 23a,b, 34h, 51a,b; Pl. 76; flag on crescent, 88; Pls 35, 37; Col. pl. 8; on column or pole, 125, 129, 162, 165, 167, 185, 205 n. 17 n. 19; Figs 21w, 36c, 37a,b, 41, 43a–b, 44c, 49a, 50h,m, 51c; Pls 18, 27, 50–2, 61–5, 67–71, 90; Col. pls 6, 15, 18; above dome or peak, 70, 129, 149–50, 159, 205 n. 17, n. 19; Figs 10d, 11f, 23b,h,i,j,k,t,u,v, 25b, 30, 32n, 33e, 34a, 40, 41, 43c,f, 47c,e,f, 51b; Pls 32, 41, 58, 59, 61, 72–3, 77, 79; Col. pls 8, 10, 14, 18, 19; on stem above dome or peak; see also Crown, Eparch's, Tomb of

Halebs, see Gipsies
Half-circles, see Circles
Halfa Degheim, South Wadi Halfa, also om., see *Omodiya* Degheim
Hamakayer, h., see *Omodiya* Debeira, e.b.
Hamid, builder (Appendix A, no. 1), 177–8
Hand, cut out of tin, 40; Fig. 10b
Handprints, in blood, 62, 65; Figs 20c,d,e,f,q; in lime, 43, 62, 65; Fig. 21a–c,i,j,l,m,n; Pl. 25; in mud; Fig. 20s
Hangers for food bowls, see Nets
Haraz, type of Acacia wood, 35, 199 n. 16; see also Acacia
Hasan, son of Ali Ibn Abi Talib, 161, 172
Hasan Arabi, decorator from Argin (Appendix B, no. 6), 6, 95, 112, 114, 127–53, 155, 167, 172–3, 180, 188–92; called Hasan Hawa, 112, 133; Hasan *kedis*, 133; early work, 131–3; Pl. 65; see Doorway surround formula; geometric phase, 134–40, 146; Figs 41–2, 50h,m; Pls 61–4, 68, 90; Col. pls 13–15; Art Deco phase, 134, 140–52; Figs 45–6, 51a,b; Pl. 76; Col. pls 16, 17; late work, 112; collaborators and imitators, 112, 130, 135–46, 150, 153, 203 n. 107
Hasan Beshir, 56, 201 n. 9
Hasan Hawa, see Hasan Arabi
Hasan *kedis*, see Hasan Arabi
Hasan Taffoul of Semna, builder, carpenter, metal-worker, leather-worker, 182; see also Taffoul family
Hasan Zaroug, 204 n. 11
Hassa, sh., see *Omodiya* Debeira
Hassin, house-owner, 84
Hathor, 167, 206 n. 29; Pl. 90
Hawate (HAWWÁTTI), h., see *Omodiya* Duweishat, sh. Melik el-Nasr
Hayya (HAWWI?), h., see *Omodiya* Debeira, e.b., sh. Hassa
Head-dress, ancient Egyptian 169; Figs 49a,b; Pl. 89, medieval, 172; see also Crown
Heads, represented in isolation, Figs 29c, 37d; Pl. 53
Hearts, Fig. 29c
Heretics, Islamic, 161
Hijaz, 197 n. 35
hillet (HILLA), geographical and governmental divisions of a *sheikhship*, 14; see also *Omodiya*
Hills, 9, 176, 203 n. 3; materials obtained from, 52; representations of, Pl. 23
Himad Hasan Taffoul, builder (Appendix A, no. 17), 182–3, 202 n. 4; see also Taffoul family
Hiring artists as house decorators, 53, 60, 84–5, 88–9; see also Payment of professional decorators
Holy men, 44, 161, 172–3, 206 n. 42; Fig. 12, Col. pl. 4; Nubian, 173; see also Mahdi, Tomb; worship in Muslim Africa, 205 n. 18
Holy man's tomb, see Tomb
Hooks at corners of doorway or other decorative unit, 70, 98, 150, 154; Figs 32k,p, 34h; Pls 82–3; see also Horns
Horned creatures, 92, 159–60; Fig. 49a,c; see also Antelope or gazelle, Cow, Deer, Elk, Goat, Sheep; on medieval crowns, 170; Fig. 49c; on medieval pots, 36; in Nubian archaeology, 167–70; Fig. 49a
Horns, deformation, different directions of, 122, 205 n. 25; animals with, see Horned creatures; in archaeological and historical data, 167–71; Fig. 49; in Christian period wall painting, 167; Figs 49c, 50a,t; Pls 85–8; combined with a dome shape or peak, 98, 165, 205 n. 19; Figs 10e, 32g,h, k,p, 33i, 34h; Pls 12, 86–8; on a crown, 169, 170, 205 n. 19; Figs 49a,c, 50c; Pls 85–6; on a pole, 54, 100, 122, 205 n. 19; Figs 32b, 38, 49c, 50r; Pl. 18; Col. pl. 6; on a woman, 116, 125; Pl. 53

Horseshoe, 40; Fig. 10f
Hosh, see Courtyard
House-boys, Nubian, 11, 150
House decoration in Sudanese Nubia, see Design motifs, Objects hung on walls in patterns, Painted decoration, Relief decoration; Dating of wall decoration; see also Distribution; Effort involved in making, 131, 132, 146; on house exteriors, 4, 142, 159, 175, see also Columns, at house corners and flanking doorway; see Cornice, Doorway, Entrance to house, Façade, String-course, Window surrounds; in house interiors, 4, 134, 140, 142, 175, 190; Figs 3c,e,f, 4, 5, 11e–g,m, 13a, 15, 16, 20p, 21a–i, l,o–v, 22b,c,f,k,l,o–s, 23a,c,e,l, 29, 32d–f, 34g, 44a–c,f,h, 50i,k; Pls 8, 9, 26–7, 29–31, 35–7, 60; Col. pls 8, 11, 21; see also Courtyard, *Dehliz*, *Diwan*, *Diwanin hasil*, Men's sitting-room, Store-room, Wedding chambers; for house decorators see Artists, Professional decorators, Payment relation to architecture, 15–24; house decoration in Damer, 198 n. 1; in Dongola, 48, 59–60; in Egyptian Nubia, 5, 27–8, 40, 47, 200 n. 30, 201 n. 1; Pl. 9; in Ghana, 47; in Nigeria, 47; in Khartoum, 47–8; in Omdurman, 47–8
Houses, see also Architecture, Rest house; *builders* of, 5, 20–1, 35, 75–81, 88–90, 92, 94, 114, 177–86, 188–93, 201 n. 1, 202 n. 4; see also Artists, House-builders, see Building, Payment for building; *plans* of, in Sudanese Nubia, 4, 16–24; Fig. 3; outside Sudanese Nubia, 18, 19; earliest known, 16–20, 40–1, 92–4; Figs 3b,c,d, 11a, 50i,k; see also Plasterer; Payment of plasterers; *fittings* for, see Cutwork, Doors, Windows, Locks, also Furniture; payment for fittings, 181; *Owners* of, 56; Pl. 42; Col. pl. 5; representations of owners, Pl. 19; owner's rôle in building, 20–1, 183, 185; in decorating, see Artists, house-owners; in inscribing the house, 1, 54; Pls 1, 78; owner's opinions about decoration, 124; owners or inhabitants who were professional decorators, 60; who decorated their house themselves, 179–80, 182, 184, 192; Fig. 44d; Pl. 42; who allowed others to decorate, 181; who left the house undecorated, 117, 158, 190; *representations* of houses; Fig. 16b; Pl. 23
Huntley and Palmers, biscuits, 134; biscuit tins, 134, 150–1; Figs 45g; 46 11a, 11d; company, 150; company archives, 203 n. 20
Husain Haikal, Nubian villager, 94
Husein, son of Ali Ibn Abi Talib, 161, 173
Huts, 16–20; round, 16–18; Fig. 3d
Hyena, 92, 159–60; Fig. 31c

Ibo, 200 n. 31
Ibrahim Farum, decorator from Abri, 184
Ibrahim Osman Ahmad, builder-decorator (Appendix A, no. 5), 77, 178–9, 181; Figs 25d, 26a
Ibrim, Upper Egypt, 18
Iconoclastic attitudes towards decoration, 56, 126
Id, see Festivals
Iere, h., see *Omodiya* Akasha, sh. Ukma
Illnesses caused by house decoration, 123, 146
L'illustration, Figs 45f, 46 111a,b
Imitators of major artists, see Ahmad Batoul, Hasan Arabi
Income of Nubians, sources of, 11, 20; see also Jobs, Payment
Influence of household members on house decorators, 4–6, 59–60, 77, 88–90, 112, 123; Pl. 64
Inscriptions on walls, 1, 54, 56, 60–1, 84, 88; Figs 13a, 14; Pls 1, 18, 19, 21–2, 31, 36, 62, 74, 78; Col. pl. 20; see Graffiti, Signatures
Interior decoration, see House Decoration, interiors
Insets used in mud relief, see Ashtrays, Automobile headlights, Light bulbs, Plates, Saucers, Shells; Crocodile, skulls of; Antelope or gazelle,

(Appendix A, no. 12), 181; Farajalla Ambar, Fig. 13b; Khalil Saleh, 142; Osman Ahmad Khalil, 77; Sayyid Ahmad Hogla, 178; Yusuf; Fig. 8c

Locks, 35, 45–6, 77–8, 94, 200 n. 38, 202 n. 2; Figs 8c,d, 13b, 23n, 28a,d, 33f,h,j, 34c, 38; Pls 12, 16, 17, 53, 58; Col. pls 1, 7, 10, 15, 18; doubled for strength, Figs 28a, 33d; payment for, 181

Logs, as roof beams, 24, Pls 9, 43, 58; Col. pls 5, 7, 10, 12, 14, 19; hung to suspend clothes, 34; Col. pl. 12

Loin-cloths, 20

Lubatab tribe, 178

Luna deities, 169; see also Isis

Lustreware china, Pl. 39; Col. pl. 14

Magazines as design source, 109, 140, 151, 203 n. 5

Magic, 61–3, 65, 159–60

Magician, 123

Mahai, Mahasi or Marisi, Nubian dialect, see Mahas

Mahallat Saidanawi, Cairo store, 153

Mahas, Nubian ethno-linguistic group, 12, 178–86, 188–90, 192–3; dialect, 14–15, 20, 195 n. 9, n. 11; housing, 20; wall decoration among, 56; Tafulab tribe, 182–4, Uliqi tribe, 192

Mahdi, 173, 205 n. 17

Mahdist forces, 20, 150

Mahmud Muhammad Osman, called Mahmud Itnan, house-builder, decorator (Appendix A, no. 9), 78, 180–1; Figs 8e, 27a

Mahmud Suleiman, builder, 184

Majareb, h., see Omodiya Degheim, e.b., sh. Degheim South

Makuria, Province of medieval Nubia, 9

Mamluk Turks, 20

Manasir, 21, 193; see also Manasiri, Shaiqiyya

Manasiri or Mansuri, Shaiqiyya from Abu Hamed region, 21, 105, 191

Mandara, men's sitting room, 22; Figs 3e,f, 33c; decoration inside, 25, 43–5, 48, 52, 56, 140, 179–80, 182, 186; Figs 18, 19, 26b, 31a, 37d, 44h; Pls 22–3, 29; Col. pl. 4; appearance outside, Figs 25d, 33j, 43c; Pls 5, 40, 46, 66, 72, 84

Manwara, see cupboard

Margarethe of Denmark, Princess, 14

Maris, Coptic name for Upper Egypt and northern kingdom of Nubia, 14, 195 n. 3, 196 n. 18, 205 n. 22

Market, see suq

Marks, on houses, Ashura, 62–5, 201 n. 14; Fig. 20f–t; blood, 62, 65, Fig 20a–f; see also Compensation assessment teams, Trade-marks; on faces, Ashura, 201 n. 14; tribal, 56–7, 59; Pls 14, 22

Marriage in Nubia, 59–60, 98, 117; see also Wedding, Chests

Martyrs, 172

Masongur, h., see Omodiya Kosha E., sh. Farka

Materials, see Building, Paint pigments, Relief decoration

Mats, 24, 26, 27, 34, 43, 48, 63, 69, 74, 198 n. 3, 200 n. 36; Figs 4, 5, 36b; Pls 7, 9; Col. pl. 8; Prayer mats, 54, 161; Figs 15, 21l; Pl. 19

Mbari, goddess shrines among Ibo, 200 n. 11

Mecca, pilgrim route to, 20; pilgrimage to (Hajj), 56, 198 n. 11; art made to celebrate return from pilgrimage, 45, 48, 52–4, 56, 59–61, 140, 201 n. 7; Fig. 14; Pls 19, 20; income of pilgrims, 198–9 n. 11

Medieval Nubia, 9, 12, 15–16, 36, 160, 162–73; see also Dongola, Faras; Sheikh Abd al-Qadir; Pottery; Tombs; houses in, 16; Fig. 3a,b

Mekki, cook and decorator (Appendix B, no. 14), 101, 193

Melik, king, title used in nineteenth-century Nubia, 196 n. 16

Melik el-Nasr, sh., see Omodiya Duweishat E.

Melik Muhammad Hasan, artist (Appendix A, no. 30), 84, 86–8, 187; Pls 33–5; Col. pl. 8

Mementau (MEMENTAWWO), h., see Omodiya Kosha E., sh. Farka

Men, in Islam, 29–30, 37, 61; in Nubia, 11, 176; see Artists, bridegrooms, house-builders, house-owners, men, professionals; costume of, 20, 34; Fig. 7; Pls 6, 11, 16, 42, 45, 46, 54, 72, 76; Col. pls 5, 7, 9, 12–14; quarters in Nubian houseplans, 16, 18, 21–2; see also diwan, mandara

Meroe, ancient site, 15

Meroitic culture, 15, 172, 202 n. 3

Merowe, modern town, Shaiqiyya centre, 20, 204 n. 6

Metal, corrugated, 6; Col. pl. 9; heated to engrave gourds, 35; as cutwork grilles, 77; Figs 25c, 26a; keys, 77–8; tools, 77; trays, 28, 198 n. 4; vessels, 54; worker in, see Smith

Mexico, art from, 134

Microscope, 149; Fig. 45d

Middle East, 194–5 n. 1

Millet, see Dura

Minarets, 61, 124, 201 n. 13; Figs 14, 44c

Mirrors, 35, 40–1; Figs 5, 10b,e, 11b, 34a, 36d, 47e, 50q; Pls 12, 52

Missionaries, Muslims, 197 n. 35

Models for designs, see copying

Money, see Payment, Piastres, Pound

Monitor lizard (warana), 200 n. 28

Monophysite Church, 15, 173

Moon, see Crescent; moon – disc, crown, 169, 206 n. 29; in women's painting, Fig. 21q; moon goddess, 169

Mora Urkuri, Shaiqiyya village, 204, n. 6

Morelli, Italian artist in Cairo; Fig. 45e

Mosques, 61, 201 n. 13; decoration inside, 182–3, representations of, 49, 191; see also Minarets

Mothers of Nubian artists, 133, 188

Motifs used in decoration, see Design motifs, Art Deco

Mountains, source of colour, 181; see also Hills

Mud, 97, 114, 183, 189, 190; building in, see Building in Nubia, Central Sudan, Omdurman; posts from, see Columns, free-standing; see also Relief decoration

Mugraka (MUGRAKKA), sh., see Omodiya Kosha E.

Mugufil (MUGÚFFIL), h., see Omodiya Saras, e.b., sh. Saras-Tahali

Mugufil-narti (MUGÚFFILN ARTI), h., and Nile island, see Omodiya Saras, sh. Atiri (SÁRAS)

Muhammad, Prophet, birthday of, see Festivals; cousin of, see Ali Ibn Abi Talib; tomb of 54; Fig. 14

Muhammad Ali of Egypt, 20, 196 n. 16

Muhammad Ahmad Sayyid, house-owner, 203 n. 14; Pl. 64

Muhammad Beshir, farmer, builder and plasterer (Appendix A, no. 20), 82, 179, 184–6

Muhammad el-Tayib, builder-decorator (Appendix A, no. 6), 179

Muhammad Hamid Hassin, artist, 84; Pl. 29

Muhammad Ibrahim Shoush, 204 n. 5, 6, 11

Muhammad Idris Abdulla, builder, 185

Muhammad Isa, artist-relative of house-owner, 86; Pl. 30

Muhammad Mahmud Abd al-Rahim, builder ?, plasterer (Appendix B, no. 12), 187, 192–3

Muhammad Nur Murran, Nubian elder, 73–4

Muhammad Osman Fadl, house-owner artist, 54, 201 n. 6

Muhammad Saleh from Saras, decorator (Appendix B, no. 11), 187, 192;

Termites (white ant), 22, 24–5, 34, 199 n. 13
Throne, of King Farouk, 149; Fig. 51d
Tin boxes, source of design motifs, 6, 134, 150–1; Figs 45g, 46 IIa, IId
Tin cans, Pl. 16; used to draw around, 145; to contain earth colour, 184; lids of, 35; Fig. 21a; Col. pl. 4
Tin cutters, 77, 179, 181; see also Cutwork designs
Tin sword scabbard, 150
Tino-Tu, h. or sub-division, see Omodiya Gemai, sh. Gemai E., Artinassi Island
Tomb, ancient Egyptian, 125; C-Group, 205 n. 25; Christian period, Fig. 50a(?); Pl. 87(?); of Muslim holy man (qubba), 61, 71, 73, 161–2, 170, 172–3, 204 n. 12, 16, 205 n. 17, 18; Fig. 24; Pl. 24
Tools, 35; used for making mud relief, 3, 92, 117, 123; Col. pl. 9; see also Cutter; Triangles, punch for cutting; for removing relief, 126
Tool making, 77
Torad (TURÁAD), h., see Omodiya Argin
Torrents from Red Sea hills, 97, 203 n. 1
Towels, design source, 150
Town-influenced art, 56, 71, 150–1
Toys, Pl. 69; Col. pl. 14
Trade along Nile, see Nile
Trade-marks, of Dawud Osman, 136–40; Fig. 42b; Pl. 66; see also Chevron, X between parallel bars; of Hasan Arabi, 136–8; Fig. 42a; Col. pl. 15, see Chevron, H-shape, Square with segmented corners, Birds, Flags
Traditions, attempts made to continue, 28, 34, 176
Traditional decoration, 92, 112, 126, 176, see Objects, Women's art, painting; shapes, 71, 122, 125, 173
Training of artists, see Professional decorators, training
Transportation, see Aeroplanes, Automobiles, Boats, Bus, Camel, Donkey, Railway, Roads, Suq lorry; to Mecca, 45; Fig. 14
Trays, 28, 198 n. 4; see also Basket lids
Treasure, guarded by snakes, 160
Trees, see Acacia, Palm; in legend, 161; in house decoration, 124–5; see also Apple, Banana, Palm, Rose; Figs 15, 16; 21v, 44c; Pl. 59; Col. pls 4, 10, 12
Triangles, 35–6, 105, 114, 123, 151, 185–6, 192; as Art Deco motif, see Chevron; punched into mud relief with a cutter, 3–4, 102–8, 132, 153; Figs 32q,r, 33e–h, 34a,b, 37a,b, 40, 47a,c,e; Pls 40–1, 43–8, 50–2(?), 58–9, 61–5, 77; Col. pls 10, 18
Tribal marks, 56–7, 59; added to pin-ups, 44; to Queen Elizabeth, Pl. 22
Tribal structure, 12, 14
Tribes, see Mahas ethno-linguistic group; other groups, see Lubatab, Mansuri, Shaiqiyya
Trowel (muhara), 92
Turmukke (TURMÚKKE), h., see Omodiya Duweishat E., sh. Melik el-Nasr
Twins, superstitions concerning, 133
Tympanum, 125, 165, 167; see also Dome
Types A and B painting, see Women's painting

Ukma (ÚKME), sh., see Omodiya Akasha
Uliqi tribe, see Mahas
Upper Egypt, 5, 9, 173, 188–9, 191–2, 201 n. 7; see also Egyptian Nubia
Uraeus snakes, 202 n. 3; Fig. 49a
Urban planning, of Wadi Halfa and Khashm el-Girba, 176, 194–5 n. 1; Pl. 24
Urwan (URWÁN), h., see Omodiya Saras, sh. Saras-Tahali, e.b.

Vase, 125; Figs 22c, 34g, 37d, 44b; Pls 29, 36; see also Pot with flowers
Verticals flanking dome or peak, in women's art, 98; Figs 23g,o,s,w; in professional's work, 98–9, 114; Figs 11d, 32a,g, 33b, 50j,l,n,q; Pl. 53; relation to inscribed columns flanking doorway, 98–101; see also Columns, Doorway surround formula
Village formula of Gemai, Murshid, 88
Vines and flowers enclosed in geometric shapes, Art Deco influence, 149, 151; Figs 46 Ia, 1c–1d, IId, IIId, 47g, 51a–c; Col. pls 16, 17
Vitamin tablets, Fig. 46 IIb
Vornarti (AWWEN ARTI?), h., see Omodiya Argin, sh. Argin South
Vow, made to holy man, 40

Wadi, dried-up river valley, 202–3, n. 3; affecting place-names, 196 n. 16
Wadi el-Allaqi, Upper Egypt, 189
Wadi el-Arab, Upper Egypt, 5, 189, 201 n. 1
Wadi Halfa town, 125, 175–6, 179; building in, 79, 91, 178, 182–4; communication with neighbouring regions, 11–12, 91; Cults in, 44; decoration in 91, 117; Pls 54–6; Col. pl. 9; history, 20; inhabitants, 101, 193; market, 53
Wadi Halfa district, cults in, 161–2; Decoration in, 5, 12, 28, 35, 52, 61, 71, 75, 77–9, 81, 91–158, 175, 198 n. 3, 201 n. 1; relation to decoration further south, 7, 79–81, 140; houseplans of, 18, 21–2; Fig. 3a,b,e; Kenuzi located in, 12, 198 n. 3; see also Omodiya Debeira, w.b., sh. Hassa, h. Nag el-Kenuz and Omodiya Degheim, w.b., sh. Degheim North, h. Kenuz or Mattukkun Irki; locks of, 46, 77–8, 202 n. 2; superstitions in, 160; see also Urban planning
Wady el Kenous, 196 n. 16
Wady Nouba, with Wady el Kenous, old names for Nubia, 196 n. 6
Wall decoration, see Decoration
Wall-pegs, supporting rolled mats, 27, 198 n. 3; Figs 4, 5; Pl. 9
Wall smoothing, see Plastering, Re-plastering
Walls, construction of, 15–16; Pl. 3
Warana, see Lizard
Water, apparitions connected with, 160; use in building, 183
Water-jar (zeir), centre for decoration, 22; Figs 23b,w, 34f, 43g, 44d, 46 Ib, 47d, 50h,m; Pl. 90; representations of, Fig. 16a; made in Sukkot, 198 n. 6
Water-wheel, 11, 15, 77; representation of, 123, 125; Pl. 59; Col. pl. 10
Wear on house decoration, see Replastering
Weaving, 24, 36; Pl. 10; see also Basket lids, Basketry, Fencing, Mats, Sandals
Wedding, chambers, 4, 21–2, 32, 48, 52, 67; see also diwan, diwanin hasil; customs, 26–8, 32, 34, 60, 69; decoration, 21–2, 25, 43, 159, 162; made by bridegroom or male relatives, 48–9, 84–6; Fig. 15; Pls 29–30; by women, 26–7, 30–4, 48–9, 98; Figs 21u, 22p,q, 23c,f,t,u,x; by professional decorators, 82–3, 113, 126, 191; Figs 30, 36, 44a–c,e; wedding influence on houseplans, 4, 21–2; paraphernalia, 25–8, 30, 32, 34, 198 n. 10; Fig. 7; Pl. 11
Wells, 158
West Africans in the Sudan, 198 n. 11
Whisk-brooms, raffia, 32, 43; Fig. 5
White ant, see Termites
Whitewash (white lime), as painting medium, 62, 65, 83; Figs 21a–d,i,j,l–v, 30; Pls 25, 76, 82–3; Col. pls 8, 13, 14, 16, 17; as ground for painting, 53–4, 56; Figs 14, 15, 18, 34c, 44, 46 Ia–Id; Pls 18–23, 29, 30, 60, 76; Col. pls 5, 11, 12, 19; on surface cut into by relief designs, 3–4, 94, 99–100, 130, 134, 190; Figs 29, 33d–h, 43d–f, 47a; Pls 32, 38–41, 43–4, 46–52,

226